The Pursuit of an Authentic Philosophy

The Pursuit of an Authentic Philosophy

Wittgenstein, Heidegger, and the Everyday

David Egan

OXFORD
UNIVERSITY PRESS

Great Clarendon Street, Oxford, OX2 6DP,
United Kingdom

Oxford University Press is a department of the University of Oxford.
It furthers the University's objective of excellence in research, scholarship,
and education by publishing worldwide. Oxford is a registered trade mark of
Oxford University Press in the UK and in certain other countries

© David Egan 2019

Epigraph to Introduction from GENESIS: Translation and Commentary,
translated by Robert Alter. Copyright © 1996 by Robert Alter.
Used by permission of W. W. Norton & Company, Inc.

The moral rights of the author have been asserted

First Edition published in 2019
Impression: 1

All rights reserved. No part of this publication may be reproduced, stored in
a retrieval system, or transmitted, in any form or by any means, without the
prior permission in writing of Oxford University Press, or as expressly permitted
by law, by licence or under terms agreed with the appropriate reprographics
rights organization. Enquiries concerning reproduction outside the scope of the
above should be sent to the Rights Department, Oxford University Press, at the
address above

You must not circulate this work in any other form
and you must impose this same condition on any acquirer

Published in the United States of America by Oxford University Press
198 Madison Avenue, New York, NY 10016, United States of America

British Library Cataloguing in Publication Data
Data available

Library of Congress Control Number: 2018962645

ISBN 978-0-19-883263-8

Printed and bound in Great Britain by
Clays Ltd, Elcograf S.p.A.

For Granma

Acknowledgements

This book began its life as a doctoral thesis at the University of Oxford. Very little text from that thesis remains in the finished book, but most of the formative thinking took place during my time in Oxford. First in the order of thanks, then, is Stephen Mulhall, whose supervision was insightful, attentive, patient, and inspiring. It often felt as if he knew better than I did what it was that I was trying to say, but he had the restraint to allow me to find my own way toward saying it while also providing the guidance and the criticism that would help me find the sharpest expression for what I was groping toward. In a project that gives a central place to the concept of attunement, I was truly fortunate to have a supervisor who was so deeply attuned to what I was trying to do. The examiners for my thesis, Anita Avramides and Simon Glendinning, subjected the thesis to patient scrutiny and their many insightful criticisms started it on its journey to bookhood.

I enjoyed four years at Oxford free from financial anxiety thanks to the support of the Social Sciences and Humanities Research Council of Canada, the Clarendon Fund, Oriel College, and Oxford's philosophy faculty. These last two were sources not only of financial support, but also of community, intellectual exchange, and friendship. I also cherish the hospitality I received from my aunt and uncle, Pam and Bob Thomas, during my time in Oxford.

The book took its current shape during my four years in the University of Chicago's Society of Fellows. Jim Conant gave generous hours to talking through the big picture and the details with me and I tested out some of the material in Chicago's Wittgenstein Workshop and with my colleagues in the Society of Fellows. My time in the Society broadened my intellectual horizons considerably, and gave me some great friends.

In addition to the people mentioned above, a hopelessly incomplete list of those who have provided feedback on some aspect of this work includes Noah Chafets, Gabriel Citron, P. M. S. Hacker, Edward Harcourt, John Hyman, Dhananjay Jagannathan, Florian Klinger, Denis McManus, Rob Penney, Steve Reynolds, Joseph Schear, Damien Storey, Aaron James Wendland, and Judith Wolfe. My thinking has been enriched and my spirits lifted by other philosophers and friends including Simona Aimar, Amanda Greene, Kevin McCann, Brad Murray, Catherine Offord, Cathal Ó Madagáin, Anne Privett, Robert Schwartzkopff, Robert Simpson, Ronnie de Sousa, and Mark Thakkar. My life is much richer and my German is much better for knowing Aleksandra Prica. This book contains better sentences and fewer sentences thanks to Priya Nelson, who has the wisdom of a first-rate editor and the heart of a first-rate human being. My siblings, Michael and Catherine, have been sources of inspiration and encouragement for literally longer than I can remember. The same applies to my parents, Kieran and Susanna, who have also been careful readers of more than one version of this project, catching everything from typos to bad arguments. Some of them, at least. The faults that remain in this book are mumble mumble of course my own.

This book has been through two rounds of anonymous peer review with Oxford University Press and I regret that I'm unable to thank by name some of the people who have provided the most insightful and constructive criticism. I can happily name and thank Peter Momtchiloff, who was encouraging from the start, patient with the revisions, and generous in his support.

The highlight of my week when I lived in Oxford was my Sunday dinners with my grandmother, Kató Havas. She was an honest and thoughtful sounding board for my ideas, and a reminder of the importance of the life that extends beyond those ideas. Her 98 years were just a few months too few to see this book appear in print. I dedicate it to her with gratitude and love.

Contents

Conventions Used in the Book	xi
Introduction	1

Part One. Average Everydayness

1. Grammar and Ontology	15
1.1. 'One *can* step into the same river twice'	15
1.2. Grammatical and Empirical Investigations	18
1.3. 'Not to present the matter as if there were something one *couldn't* do'	22
1.4. The Sideways Perspective	25
1.5. Heidegger and the Ontological Difference	28
1.6. Wittgenstein, Heidegger, and the Everyday	32
2. Being-in-the-World and Forms of Life	37
2.1. The Analysis of Dasein as Fundamental Ontology	37
2.2. Readiness-to-Hand and Presence-at-Hand	40
2.3. The Question of Priority	46
2.4. Wittgenstein, Cavell, and Criteria	49
2.5. Forms of Life	52
2.6. Words and the World	56
3. Attunement and Being-With	63
3.1. Attunement	63
3.2. Wittgenstein's 'We'	67
3.3. Wittgenstein and Necessity	70
3.4. Being-With and *das Man*	73
3.5. Interpreting Heidegger on *das Man*	77
3.6. *Das Man* and Distantiality	82

Part Two. Authentic Everydayness

4. Anxiety, Scepticism, and Rule Following	89
4.1. Heidegger: Inauthenticity and Falling	90
4.2. Heidegger: Anxiety and Uncanniness	94
4.3. Wittgenstein: Explanations and Rule Following	98
4.4. Wittgensteinian Scepticism and Heideggerian Anxiety	103

5. Authenticity and the Everyday ... 110
  5.1. Kripke's Wittgenstein ... 110
  5.2. An 'Authentic' Alternative ... 112
  5.3. Kripke's Heidegger ... 115
  5.4. Conscience and Resoluteness ... 118
  5.5. Wittgenstein's Bedrock ... 124
  5.6. Authentic Everydayness ... 127
  5.7. 'Therapeutic' and 'Existential' Wittgensteins ... 132

6. Authenticity and Play ... 138
  6.1. Wittgenstein's Language-Game Analogy ... 138
  6.2. The Scene of Instruction ... 141
  6.3. Play and Projection ... 147
  6.4. Improvisation as a Model of Authenticity ... 152
  6.5. Sophistry and Spoilsports ... 155
  6.6. Receptivity and Responsiveness in *Being and Time* ... 160
  6.7. Authentic Philosophy ... 164

Part Three. The Pursuit of An Authentic Philosophy

7. Heidegger's Pursuit of Authenticity in Philosophy ... 169
  7.1. The Problematic of Realism and Idealism ... 169
  7.2. Heidegger and the 'Problem of Reality' ... 172
  7.3. The Problem with Assertions ... 175
  7.4. Formal Indication ... 178
  7.5. Truth and Untruth ... 182
  7.6. Heidegger's Dependency Claim ... 186
  7.7. The Form of Formal Indication ... 189

8. Wittgenstein's Pursuit of Authenticity in Philosophy ... 194
  8.1. Ordinary Language and Terms of Criticism ... 194
  8.2. Hiddenness and the Hermeneutics of Suspicion ... 198
  8.3. Wittgenstein on the Problematic of Realism and Idealism ... 202
  8.4. Pictures and Objects of Comparison ... 208
  8.5. Pictures and Aesthetic Criticism ... 212
  8.6. Truth and Untruth in Wittgenstein's Pictures ... 218
  8.7. Thought Experiments and Questions ... 222
  8.8. The Dialogical Form of Wittgenstein's Investigations ... 227

Conclusion ... 232

Bibliography ... 235
Index ... 247

Conventions Used in the Book

Within quotations, I use *italics* to denote the author's emphases and **bold** to denote my own emphases.

I use the following abbreviations to refer to some of the texts cited in this manuscript:

Works by Wittgenstein

AWL   *Wittgenstein's Lectures, Cambridge 1932–35, from the Notes of Alice Ambrose and Margaret Macdonald.* Alice Ambrose, Ed. Oxford: Blackwell. 1979.

BB   *Preliminary Studies for the 'Philosophical Investigations': Generally known as the Blue and Brown Books* (2nd ed.). Oxford: Blackwell. 1969.

BTS   *Big Typescript: TS 213.* C. Grant Luckhardt & Maximilian A. E. Aue, Eds. & Trans. Oxford: Blackwell. 2005.

CRR   (Wittgenstein and Rush Rhees) Wittgenstein's Philosophical Conversations with Rush Rhees (1939–1950): From the Notes of Rush Rhees. Gabriel Citron, Ed. *Mind*, 124 (493): 1–71. 2015.

CV   *Culture and Value* (2nd ed.). G. H. von Wright, Hekki Nyman, & Alois Pichler, Eds., & Peter Winch, Trans. Oxford: Blackwell. 1998.

LA   Lectures on Aesthetics. In Ludwig Wittgenstein & Cyril Barrett (Ed.), *Lectures and Conversations on Aesthetics, Psychology, and Religious Belief.* Oxford: Blackwell, 1–40. 1966.

LFM   *Wittgenstein's Lectures on the Foundations of Mathematics: Cambridge, 1939.* Cora Diamond, Ed. Chicago, IL: University of Chicago Press. 1976.

LRB   Lectures on Religious Belief. In Ludwig Wittgenstein & Cyril Barrett (Ed.), *Lectures and Conversations on Aesthetics, Psychology, and Religious Belief.* Oxford: Blackwell, 53–72. 1966.

MWL   (G. E. Moore) Wittgenstein's Lectures in 1930–33. *Mind*, 64 (253): 1–27. 1955.

NB   *Notebooks 1914–1916* (2nd ed.). G. H. von Wright & G. E. M. Anscombe, Eds., & G. E. M. Anscombe, Trans. Chicago, IL: University of Chicago Press. 1979.

OC	*On Certainty*. G. E. M. Anscombe & G. H. von Wright, Eds., & G. E. M. Anscombe, G. H. von Wright, & Denis Paul, Trans. Oxford: Blackwell. 1975.
PG	*Philosophical Grammar*. Rush Rhees, Ed., & Anthony Kenny, Trans. Oxford: Blackwell. 1980.
PI	*Philosophical Investigations* (4th ed.). P. M. S. Hacker & Joachim Schulte, Eds., G. E. M. Anscombe, P. M. S. Hacker, & Joachim Schulte, Trans. Oxford: Wiley-Blackwell. 2009.
PPF	Philosophy of Psychology – A Fragment. In Wittgenstein 2009a, 182–243. 2009.
PR	*Philosophical Remarks*. Rush Rhees, Ed., & Raymond Hargreaves & Roger White, Trans. Oxford: Blackwell. 1975.
RFM	*Remarks on the Foundations of Mathematics* (3rd ed.). G. H. von Wright, Rush Rhees, & G. E. M. Anscombe, Eds., & G. E. M. Anscombe, Trans. Oxford: Blackwell. 1978.
RPP I	*Remarks on the Philosophy of Psychology, Volume 1*. G. E. M. Anscombe & G. H. von Wright, Eds., & G. E. M. Anscombe, Trans. Oxford: Blackwell. 1980.
RPP II	*Remarks on the Philosophy of Psychology, Volume 2*. G. H. von Wright & Hekki Nyman, Eds., & C. G. Luckhardt & M. A. E. Aue, Trans. Oxford: Blackwell. 1980.
TLP	*Tractatus Logico-Philosophicus*. D. F. Pears & B. F. McGuinness, Trans. London: Routledge. 1974.
VW	(Wittgenstein and Friedrich Waismann) *The Voices of Wittgenstein: The Vienna Circle*. Gordon Baker, Ed., & Gordon Baker, Michael Mackert, John Connolly, & Vasilis Politis, Trans. London: Routledge. 2003.
WVC	(Friedrich Waismann) *Wittgenstein and the Vienna Circle*. Brian McGuinness, Ed., & Joachim Schulte & Brian McGuinness, Trans. Oxford: Blackwell. 1979.
Z	*Zettel*. G. E. M. Anscombe & G. H. von Wright, Eds., & G. E. M. Anscombe, Trans. Oxford: Blackwell. 1967.

Works by Heidegger

BPP	*Basic Problems of Phenomenology* (Revised ed.). Albert Hofstadter, Trans. Bloomington, IN: Indiana University Press. 1988.
BT	*Being and Time: A Translation of* Sein und Zeit. Joan Stambaugh & Dennis J. Schmidt, Trans. Albany, NY: State University of New York Press. 2010.

FCM *The Fundamental Concepts of Metaphysics: World, Finitude, Solitude.* William McNeill & Nicholas Walker, Trans. Bloomington, IN: Indiana University Press. 1995.

HCT *History of the Concept of Time: Prolegomena.* Theodore Kisiel, Trans. Bloomington, IN: Indiana University Press. 1985.

HS (Heidegger and Eugen Fink) *Heraclitus Seminar.* Charles H. Seibert, Trans. Evanston, IL: Northwestern University Press.

IM *Introduction to Metaphysics.* Gregory Fried & Richard Polt, Trans. New Haven, CT: Yale University Press. 2000.

PIA *Phenomenological Interpretations of Aristotle: Initiation into Phenomenological Research.* Richard Rojcewicz, Trans. Bloomington, IN: Indiana University Press. 2008.

SLT Seminar in Le Thor 1969. In *Four Seminars.* Andrew Mitchell & François Raffoul, Trans. Bloomington, IN: Indiana University Press, 35–63. 2003.

WM What is Metaphysics? In *Basic Writings.* David Farrell Krell (Ed.). New York, NY: HarperCollins, 89–110. 1977.

Introduction

> And all the earth was one language, one set of words. And it happened as they journeyed from the east that they found a valley in the land of Shinar and settled there. And they said to each other, 'Come, let us bake bricks and burn them hard'. And the brick served them as stone, and bitumen served them as mortar. And they said, 'Come, let us build us a city and a tower with its top in the heavens, that we may make us a name, lest we be scattered over all the earth'. And the LORD came down to see the city and the tower that the human creatures had built. And the LORD said, 'As one people with one language for all, if this is what they have begun to do, nothing they plot will elude them. Come, let us go down and baffle their language there so that they will not understand each other's language'. And the LORD scattered them from there over all the earth and they left off building the city. Therefore it is called Babel, for there the LORD made the language of all the earth babble. And from there the LORD scattered them over all the earth.
>
> (Genesis 11:1–9)[1]

The last collective undertaking of all humankind, according to the Book of Genesis, is to build a city and a tower in the land of Shinar, which subsequently comes to be known as Babel. The settlers of Shinar build the tower, we are told, to 'make . . . a name' for themselves. In an earlier story, we learn that God has already bestowed on the first human the authority to name 'each beast of the field and each fowl of the heavens' (Genesis 2:19). In seeking to make a name for themselves, then, they seek

---

[1] Reprinted from *Genesis: Translation and Commentary*, translated by Robert Alter. Copyright © 1996 by Robert Alter. Used by permission of W. W. Norton & Company, Inc: wwnorton.com/books/detail.aspx?ID=6263. This selection may not be reproduced, stored in a retrieval system, or transmitted in any form or by any means without the prior written permission of the publisher.

2 THE PURSUIT OF AN AUTHENTIC PHILOSOPHY

to claim over themselves the sovereignty they already hold over all the animals (cf. Genesis 1:28).[2]

This is no minor adjustment to God's bequest. They are attempting to arrogate to themselves the powers of naming and creation that are proper to their own creator. God's response, then, is a response to the threat of usurpation.[3] He quashes their challenge by bringing about the very thing that the tower is designed to prevent. The goal of creating the tower is to avoid being 'scattered over all the earth'. We have no evidence to suggest that the humans' situation is otherwise precarious, that they have good reason to fear being scattered. Rather, they usher in precisely what they seek to avoid in the act of trying to avoid it.

This story of power and usurpation is prominently concerned with language. It opens with the reminder that, at that time, 'all the earth was one language', and that shared language not only unites the humans in their ambition but is also a condition for their being able to make 'a name' for themselves. God's response to their ambition, in addition to scattering the humans, is to 'baffle their language'.

What is this baffling? It is clear that humans are no longer able to understand one another as they once could, but why not? The story leaves unresolved which 'one language' those primeval humans speak. One possibility, the most intuitive, is that this primeval language is simply destroyed and replaced by the 'babble' of the multitude of languages of the peoples that now inhabit the earth. But no act of creation is described in the Babel story: we are not told that God *created* a multitude of *new* languages, just that he 'baffled' the one we already had. Another possibility, suggested by the many parallels between the story of Babel and the story of Eden, is that, like Eden—which is not destroyed when the first humans are driven out from it, but is rather guarded to prevent our return—this primeval language still exists but is somehow

---

[2] We find a further hint of this ambition for self-sovereignty or self-creation in their baking of bricks, which echoes God's creation of the first human by breathing the breath of life into soil that he fashioned (Genesis 2:7).

[3] Nor is it the first such response. A further echo in the Babel story of the Eden story is God's alarm at the usurping ambition of his human creation. He exiles the first humans from Eden after they eat from the tree of knowledge, saying: 'Now that the human has become like one of us, knowing good and evil, he may reach out and take as well from the tree of life and live forever' (Genesis 3:22).

inaccessible to us.[4] We cannot retrieve it or return to it, perhaps because we are unable to recognize it for what it is. A third possibility, not incompatible with the second, is that we all still speak this primeval language. Although God promises to baffle our language, we are told in the sequel that what he in fact does is scatter us, with no further mention of baffling. Perhaps it is not our language that is baffled but we ourselves who are baffled, still speaking the same tongue but unable to understand one another.[5] Fittingly, the site of this bafflement is named onomatopoeically: the last place where all the earth spoke one language is commemorated with a name that all the earth should still be able to understand.

Both Wittgenstein's and Heidegger's portraits of the human predicament have drawn comparisons with the Biblical story of Eden,[6] but I find in their work even stronger resonances with the story of Babel. Both philosophers see us as subject to the same pattern of baffling in an attempt to 'make a name' for ourselves. In their work, the Babel narrative has salience not as a moment in our mythic past, but as something ongoing: it evokes an enduring characteristic of the kind of being that we are.

In Wittgenstein, the ambition to make a name for ourselves is manifest in our desire to free our words from their seemingly contingent contexts of use and to grasp them in their essence. When philosophers 'try to grasp the *essence*' of the thing denoted by a word, Wittgenstein cautions, 'one must always ask oneself: is the word ever actually used in this way in the language in which it is at home [*in der es seine Heimat hat*]?' (*PI* §116). Words have a home, as Wittgenstein figures it, and this home is a language in which these words have a use—and, as he notes immediately afterward, this use is the 'everyday' and not the 'metaphysical' use of words (*PI* §116). The metaphysical impulse, in this picture, is an impulse to self-exile, an impulse to remove words—and by extension

---

[4] One further intriguing connection between these stories is that the cherubim are 'set up *east* of the garden of Eden' (Genesis 3:24) and the Babel story opens with the unified human family 'journey[ing] **from the east**' (Genesis 11:2)—perhaps hoping to return to the paradise from which they have been expelled.
[5] This third possibility is broached by Daniel Heller-Roazen (2005, 219–31), who offers a rich and suggestive reading of the Babel story.
[6] Most notably in Mulhall (2005a). Stanley Cavell (2005, 196) also finds 'a counter-myth to that of Eden' in Wittgenstein's later philosophy.

the people who use them—from the language in which they are at home in the pursuit of perfect perspicuity.

The self-exile of metaphysics is born of the same self-fulfilling fear as the self-exile of the builders of Babel. We become dissatisfied with the language that people actually use and the standing uncertainty it brings with it whether others will understand us. As an antidote to this dissatisfaction, we become enchanted by the idea of a language that, in its perfection, speaks from nowhere and to everyone neutrally. This fantasy of extricating ourselves from our own skins so that our wording of the world may shed its merely human contingency is a fantasy of taking on a perspective that is in some sense absolute—it is the philosopher's version of a fantasy of apotheosis. As in the case of the settlers of Shinar, the fear that we *might not* make sense to one another brings about conditions in which we actually *do not* make sense to one another.

Wittgenstein exhorts us to give up this fantasy. His story of '[bringing] words back from their metaphysical to their everyday use' (*PI* §116) is, however, more complicated than a straightforward story of exile and return. Such a story would posit two countries, the country of everyday use and the country of metaphysical use, with Wittgenstein trying to bring us from our exile in the metaphysical country back to our home country. Wittgenstein, in contrast, is at pains to show us that this metaphysical country does not exist. It is a utopia in both senses of the word: it is the imagined place where the ills of the everyday world are decisively mended, and it is 'no place'. In fact, Wittgenstein's denial of the country of metaphysical use is even stronger: it is not just nonexistent, but there is not even an 'it' that does not exist. Wittgenstein's 'metaphysical use' is not a different use of *language* but a kind of nonuse, a babbling that we do not realize is babbling. In our aspiration to build a stronghold in which our uses of words are secure against the possibility of misadventure, we bring about the baffling of our language.

If the supposed place of exile is illusory, then the supposed exile is illusory too. The first step in returning us from a non-existent exile, for Wittgenstein, is to make us aware of our bafflement. Before we can find ourselves in our language, we have to acknowledge the manner in which we have become lost.

Heidegger likewise presents a portrait of human beings as lost to themselves in the midst of their lives. We have a constitutional tendency to turn ourselves away from the question of the meaning of being,

Heidegger tells us, and to forget that there is even a question from which we have turned ourselves away. This turning away has a similar Babelic structure to Wittgenstein's account of the realization of our fears precisely in the attempt to escape them. According to Heidegger, we are beings whose nature is fundamentally unsettled and open-ended. The apprehension of our unsettledness induces anxiety, which in turn prompts a race to find comfort in a stable sense of the meaning of our existence. But, in affirming a stability we do not have, we fundamentally misapprehend ourselves, and so thwart the very project of finding meaning in our existence. As a result, we live for the most part in a state of existential babbling.

Heidegger gives our predicament of self-bafflement a name: inauthenticity. *Being and Time* is essentially a project of unbaffling, of revealing the contours of an authentic existence that is the opposite of the apotheosis that the builders at Babel aspire to. Rather than build ourselves up into something we are not, authenticity requires no more—and no less— than that we see clearly what we are and live in that 'clearing' (*BT* 133).

The achievement of authenticity is thus not to come into the truth but to recognize that we were already in the truth to begin with. In this respect, an authentic existence does not transcend or escape from the everyday existence that we inhabit inauthentically. On the contrary, authenticity is the mode in which we inhabit the everyday without denying or rejecting it.

This story of an unbaffling that results in an authentic inhabitation of the everyday finds expression in the work of a figure who exercised a strong influence on both Wittgenstein and Heidegger. Saint Augustine's narrative of his conversion provides a model for the turn to inhabiting the everyday.[7] By the beginning of the crucial eighth book of *Confessions*,

---

[7] Coyne (2016) offers a thorough examination of Augustine's influence on Heidegger. Both Kisiel (1993, especially chap. 4) and van Buren (1994, especially chap. 8) also attest to the influence of Augustine on Heidegger's development. Wittgenstein opens *Philosophical Investigations* by scrutinizing critically the 'picture of the essence of human language' (*PI* §1) he claims to find in Book I of Augustine's *Confessions*, but he was nevertheless deeply impressed by that text. Drury (1984, 90) reports Wittgenstein as saying that Augustine's *Confessions* is possibly 'the most serious book ever written'. Malcolm ([1958] 2001, 59) reports that Wittgenstein revered Augustine and von Wright ([1958] 2001, 19) lists Augustine as a major influence on Wittgenstein, observing that '[t]he philosophical sections of St Augustine's *Confessions* show a striking resemblance to Wittgenstein's own way of doing philosophy'. Burnyeat (1987) also argues that Augustine's views on learning

Augustine is already free of all doubt about the truth of Christianity (*Confessions* 8.1.1) but this confidence is not alone sufficient for conversion. Augustine figures his moment of conversion not as a cognitive, or even a spiritual, achievement—he does not come to believe, know, or otherwise apprehend something new that he had been blind to previously—but as relinquishing something. In particular, he writes of his professional ambition and his sexual desire as driving him to seek a fulfillment that leaves him constantly unsatisfied and anxious. In a moment of anguish, he hears a voice that prompts him to read a passage from Paul's letter to the Romans, and writes that, in a flash, 'it was as if a light of relief from all anxiety flooded into [his] heart' (*Confessions* 8.12.29). At his moment of conversion, he is not bestowed with a new truth, but is rather disencumbered of the burdens that kept him from accepting that he was already living in the light of God's truth.

For both Wittgenstein and Heidegger, the intended outcome of their philosophical work is likewise one of disencumbrance. Wittgenstein presents the challenge not in terms of achieving something new but of seeing clearly where we already are: 'The difficult thing here is not, to dig down to the ground; no, it is to recognize the ground that lies before us as the ground' (*RFM* VI §31). Likewise for Heidegger, Dasein—his term for the distinctive mode of being of human beings—'*is "in the truth"*' (*BT* 221).

In a pivotal passage,[8] Wittgenstein emphasizes that this ground that lies before us, if we are to move across it, requires friction: 'We have got on to slippery ice where there is no friction, and so, in a certain sense, the conditions are ideal; but also, just because of that, we are unable to walk. We want to walk: so we need *friction*. Back to the rough ground!' (*PI* §107). This contrast between slippery ice and rough ground comes at the culmination of a series of reflections in which Wittgenstein characterizes the 'urge to understand the foundations, or essence, of everything empirical' (*PI* §89) as the search for something sublime. Wittgenstein repeatedly

---

language coincide strikingly with Wittgenstein's own—and that Wittgenstein was likely aware of this fact. So whatever Wittgenstein's reasons for choosing to open *Philosophical Investigations* with a quotation from *Confessions*, he did not do so purely in a spirit of criticism. According to Malcolm, Wittgenstein felt the conception of language he subjects to scrutiny '*must* be important if so great a mind held it' (Malcolm [1958] 2001, 60).

[8] Quite literally pivotal: this passage comes directly before Wittgenstein invokes 'the pivot of our real need' around which 'the inquiry must be turned' (*PI* §108). Wittgenstein figures the change he wants to induce in his readers as a conversion.

invokes images of purity and an ideal: he describes the a priori order of the world, which 'must be *utterly simple*' as being 'of the **purest** crystal' (*PI* §97), and describes the language of logic as 'something **pure** and clear-cut' (*PI* §105) and of 'crystalline **purity**' (*PI* §106), while repeatedly invoking the notion of an ideal (*PI* §§98, 100, 101, 103, 105, 107).

Taken at face value, Wittgenstein's parable figures the slippery ice as the metaphysical confusion we bring upon ourselves when we are captivated by a certain image of the ideal and the rough ground as the firm footing we find in the ordinary use of our words. But such figuring recapitulates the story of exile that I questioned earlier: here the slippery ice of metaphysical use, there the rough ground of ordinary use. Such figuring gives us two different places and thereby bestows an autonomous reality on the idea of a 'metaphysical use' of our words. If the notion of a 'metaphysical use' is problematic, we find a resemblance between Wittgenstein's parable and the story of Babel in that the precise nature of the failure is difficult to discern.

One internal reason for mistrusting the face value reading is that it does not take fully seriously Wittgenstein's claim that we find ourselves on an 'ideal' slippery surface where there is '**no** friction'. There is a way to get off any *actual* icy surface—slowly and cautiously—because there *is* friction on an icy surface, just not very much. On a truly frictionless surface, there is no way of getting 'back' to rougher ground because any translational motion at all is impossible. Furthermore, if we cannot move across it, it is unclear how we might have 'got on to' this frictionless surface in the first place.

These internal tensions point to an alternative reading of Wittgenstein's parable, in line with my alternative reading of the story of Babel: we never left the rough ground because there is no other ground to leave to.[9] What keeps us from walking is not the *fact* that we stand on a frictionless surface—something that does not, after all, exist anywhere in nature, but only in the idealizations of physicists—but the *illusion* that we stand on a frictionless surface. The way back to the rough ground is not to move to a different location but 'to recognize the ground that lies

---

[9] James Conant suggested to me this alternative approach to reading the parable of the ice-walkers as well as the intriguing contrast with Kant's parable of the dove, which supposes that it could make even better progress in the absence of the friction of air resistance (Kant [1781] 1997, A5/B8–9).

before us as the ground'. The only thing that keeps us from moving is the self-bafflement that wishes to make of the ground we stand on something other than what it is.

Like Heidegger's authentic mode of being, Wittgenstein's rough ground is the opposite of apotheosis. This is not the place where we free ourselves definitively from our difficulties but rather the place where we apprehend our difficulties as inalienably our own. We need not achieve this apprehension in a spirit of resignation. We are not giving up on anything substantial by abandoning the fantasy of the ideal, but are only dismantling structures of air that had no substance to begin with (*PI* §118).[10] Nor are we even giving up on the aspiration that fed the fantasy of slippery ice in the first place: '[W]e too', says Wittgenstein, 'are trying to understand the essence of language' (*PI* §92).[11] When Wittgenstein says he wants to turn the inquiry around 'on the pivot of our real need' (*PI* §108), then, he retains the 'urge to understand the foundations, or essence, of everything empirical' (*PI* §89) but realigns our sense of what might fulfill that urge. Mulhall (2001, 92) characterizes this pivot as turning us from the vertical axis of penetrating the surface of our ordinary uses of words to the horizontal axis of surveying them. We need to apprehend the world we find ourselves in, not transcend it.

Wittgenstein's method is often characterized in terms of dissolving problems, and we gain a clearer view of his pivot if we take this metaphor of dissolution seriously. One of the few places where Wittgenstein himself invokes the metaphor is *BTS* 310: 'The problems are solved in the literal sense of the word—dissolved like a lump of sugar in water'. When we dissolve a lump of sugar in water, that does not make the sugar go away. All of the sugar remains—it is simply distributed evenly throughout the water where before it was concentrated in a single hard lump. And this is the sense in which Wittgenstein sees himself dissolving philosophical problems. Rather than bore inward to what we think is the heart of a concept, we should broaden our view, and consider how the uses of that

---

[10] My 'structures of air' is a literal rendering of Wittgenstein's *Luftgebäude*, which in both Anscombe's original translation and Hacker's and Schulte's revision is rendered as 'houses of cards'. Their translation carries the unfortunate connotation that *something* substantial is being destroyed, however flimsy and unstable.

[11] I use Anscombe's translation here, which I think remains closer to Wittgenstein's original meaning, although Hacker and Schulte are right to emphasize that the question of whether to translate *Wesen* as 'essence' or 'nature' is a complex and fraught one.

concept are distributed through our lives as a whole. In treating our lives, and the words through which we articulate our understanding of those lives, as a continuous whole, we will not fall victim to the bafflement that results from our overweening ambition to overcome our finite selves.

One consequence that Wittgenstein and Heidegger both perceive in overcoming our fierce determination to reject or deny our everyday existence is that we come to see this existence as our own. Our world, when we apprehend it clearly, is not simply something we find ourselves in, but something whose shape conforms to our own. By taking responsibility for our everyday existence, we find that it is responsive to us.

Wittgenstein in particular figures this responsiveness in terms of play: we articulate our understanding of our lives by playing language-games, and the rules and aims of these games take shape in the way that we engage with one another. This engagement in turn manifests a shared understanding that precedes any deliberate agreement—an attunement between players that enables them to play. As I will argue in the pages that follow, Wittgenstein's rough ground is a play ground.

* * *

Although they worked in different philosophical traditions, and seemed mostly ignorant of one another's work,[12] Wittgenstein and Heidegger have far more in common than just the year of their births. The aim of this book is to trace these philosophers' parallel engagements with the everyday and with authenticity, and their pursuit of an authentic inhabitation of the everyday. In particular, Heidegger's explicit articulation of his conception of authenticity helps me to uncover an implicit conception of authenticity in Wittgenstein's later philosophy. And by tracing the parallels between those two philosophers that far, I am able to

---

[12] I am aware of five instances in which Wittgenstein or Heidegger refers to the other. The best known is Wittgenstein's remark 'On Heidegger' (*LWVC* 68–9), which presumably is a response to 'What Is Metaphysics?' (and not to *Being and Time*, as the editor's footnote suggests), which had also recently exercised Carnap ([1931] 1958), who was a regular interlocutor of Wittgenstein's at the time. We find more extended reflections on the same theme in *Voices of Wittgenstein* (*VW* 69–77), and a brief, disparaging remark in a recently published collection of conversation notes by Rush Rhees (*CRR* 48). The other two are brief remarks by Heidegger, one in which Heidegger makes passing reference to Wittgenstein to illustrate a point about extricating oneself from the hermeneutic circle (*HS* 17), and the other in which he misquotes the *Tractatus* (*SLT* 35). I am grateful to Gabriel Citron for drawing my attention to the second and third of the Wittgenstein references, and, in the case of the Rhees notes, for making them public in the first place.

articulate the two principal ways in which I find Wittgenstein diverging from his unlikely doppelgänger: in the centrality of play in his conception of authenticity and in the methodological innovations by which he resists the will-o'-the-wisp of metaphysical confusion.

Part One treats Wittgenstein's and Heidegger's respective engagements with the everyday, emphasizing three principal parallels. Chapter 1 outlines Wittgenstein's and Heidegger's rejection of the idea that philosophy is a cognitive discipline. Their descriptions of familiar aspects of everyday human existence present an alternative to a philosophical method that seeks to uncover hitherto unknown truths. Wittgenstein sharply distinguishes between grammatical and empirical investigations, and Heidegger distinguishes between ontological and ontic levels of investigation. Both use these distinctions to argue that the philosophical enterprise is radically different in kind from the sciences—and that this distinction is frequently overlooked to the serious detriment of philosophy. Chapter 2 examines the way in which Wittgenstein and Heidegger situate our utterances and activities within a holistic network of human practices. Wittgenstein maintains that 'to imagine a language means to imagine a form of life' (*PI* §19) and Heidegger examines what he calls the 'worldliness' of the human world, in which objects show up as ready-to-hand equipment whose significance is indexed to its role in human life. And Chapter 3 shows how both bring out the shared nature of these practices: Wittgenstein emphasizes our attunement—what he calls our 'agreement... in form of life' (*PI* §241)—and Heidegger claims that human being-in-the-world is essentially a matter of being-with-one-another.

Part Two situates Heidegger's conception of authenticity within his analysis of the everyday and argues that we can find a homologous dynamic of authenticity and inauthenticity in Wittgenstein. Chapter 4 argues that we find in Wittgenstein's treatment of explanation and rule following parallels to Heidegger's articulation of falling (our tendency toward inauthenticity), anxiety (in which we confront the fundamental uncanniness of our existence), and resoluteness (in which we are ready for anxiety). Unfolding these parallels requires distinguishing various interpretive responses to Wittgenstein's treatment of rule following. In particular, the comparison with Heidegger helps us to see that one influential reading—most famously associated with Kripke (1982)—leaves no space for an authentic understanding of our existence.

On the other hand, the comparison with Wittgenstein helps us to see that Heidegger's conception of authenticity is a mode of inhabiting the everyday, and not a way of transcending it. These two interpretive claims—that an 'authentic' Wittgenstein does not embrace Kripke's sceptical problematic and that Heideggerian authenticity is a mode of everydayness—are the central concerns of Chapter 5. Chapter 6 delves more deeply into Wittgenstein's conception of authenticity by exploring the theme of play in his later philosophy. This theme comes to prominence most explicitly in his use of language-games, which, I argue, are based in an appreciation of our capacity for unregulated play. Wittgenstein's deployment of language-games reveals both the active dynamic by which we keep practices 'in play', and the potential fragility of these practices when play breaks down. What emerges is a distinct conception of human agency: people are not so much *agents* as *players*, where our capacity for thought and action rests on our responsiveness to the constantly changing dynamic of our circumstances.

Wittgenstein's and Heidegger's understanding of authenticity cannot be detached from their understanding of what it means to philosophize authentically. Part Three brings to the forefront questions of method that have been a constant background theme in the first two parts. Wittgenstein's and Heidegger's methodological commitment to the everyday means rejecting the idea that philosophy can inform us of anything we did not already know—which raises the pressing question of how it can nevertheless be illuminating. Both Wittgenstein and Heidegger face the challenge of providing words whose efficacy does not rest on being informative, and it is on this question of method that they most diverge. Focusing on Heidegger in Chapter 7 and Wittgenstein in Chapter 8, I consider a number of techniques these two authors deploy—coinages, scare quotes, and formal indication in Heidegger, and objects of comparison and the dialogue form in Wittgenstein—and examine the difference in these authors' chosen terms of criticism. Most notably, where Heidegger uses language of discovering or uncovering (*entdecken*) to talk about a deeper level of ontological disclosure, Wittgenstein uses the same language to talk about exposing nothing more substantial than nonsense. Ultimately, I argue, a greater sense of strain is apparent in Heidegger's work, as if he wants both to tell us something and to tell us that there is no *something* to be told—a struggle more reminiscent of the *Tractatus* than of Wittgenstein's later work. Wittgenstein avoids this strain by using contrasts to jog our preconceptions about the case before us without trying to convey any deeper truths about it. This methodological difference, I argue, manifests the more pronounced performative aspect of Wittgenstein's investigations. Where Heidegger describes the experience of anxiety, for instance, Wittgenstein enacts it in his language-games—and encourages his readers to join him in this enactment.

This comparative project illuminates facets of both philosophers' work that are less evident when we consider them in isolation. Indeed, one aim of this project is to illuminate just *how many* fruitful points of comparison obtain between Wittgenstein and Heidegger. But the most significant achievements of the book, I think, are the ones that are also the least evident: that embedded in Wittgenstein's later philosophy is a strikingly Heideggerian dialectic of authenticity, and that considering the philosophers in tandem allows us to see the depth of the methodological challenge they face—and the range of possible responses to it.

These results are not merely of historical interest. By bringing the theme of authenticity in the work of Wittgenstein and Heidegger into contact with the question of method, this book articulates an understanding of what it means to do philosophy—and why it is so difficult—that remains pertinent in the twenty-first century. Wittgenstein and Heidegger help us to see something that seemed obvious to the ancients but that has faded from view in the modern world: that we cannot *not* be philosophers, and that the manner *in which* we are philosophers is manifest in our manner of living. For Wittgenstein and for Heidegger, the pursuit of an authentic philosophy cannot be detached from the pursuit of an authentic existence.

PART ONE
Average Everydayness

1
Grammar and Ontology

1.1. 'One *can* step into the same river twice'

'The man who said one cannot step into the same river twice was wrong; one *can* step into the same river twice' (*BTS* 304). So runs Wittgenstein's answer to Heraclitus.[1] This reminder of how we ordinarily use words is an expression of Wittgenstein's strategy 'to bring words back from their metaphysical to their everyday use' (*PI* §116):

When philosophers use a word — 'knowledge', 'being', 'object', 'I', 'proposition/ sentence', 'name' — and try to grasp the *essence* of the thing, one must always ask oneself: is the word ever actually used in this way in the language in which it is at home? (*PI* §116)[2]

When we do philosophy, Wittgenstein suggests, we face the peculiar danger of misspeaking, of pressing words into service for which they are unsuited. He conceives his task as calling to mind 'the *kinds of statement* that we make about phenomena' (*PI* §90),[3] reminding us of how our words are used when they are 'at home'. His remark about the claim attributed to Heraclitus seems to fit this model: against the 'metaphysical' claim that one cannot step into the same river twice, Wittgenstein reminds us of how we ordinarily talk about rivers and stepping and the rest: I can go for a swim in the Thames one day, and take another dip in the Thames the next.

---

[1] This is hardly relevant to the present discussion, but the attribution to Heraclitus of the saying that one cannot step into the same river twice is doubtful. Diels and Kranz treat it as apocryphal (see Stern 1991, 579). It first enters the literature, attributed to Heraclitus, in Plato's *Cratylus*, 402b.

[2] A precursor of this remark directly precedes the remark about stepping into the same river twice in *The Big Typescript*.

[3] See also *PI* §§89 and 127.

Wittgenstein's reminder can seem crudely pedantic. Heraclitus—or whoever it was—was hardly unaware that people talk about rivers as the sorts of perdurable entities that one can step into on multiple occasions. The remark's claim to significance comes precisely from its counter-intuitive sound. Although people *ordinarily* talk about stepping into the same river on multiple occasions, the Heraclitean philosopher wants to say, *strictly speaking* they cannot. Responding to this claim by saying that people ordinarily talk about stepping into the same river on multiple occasions appears deaf to the force of the Heraclitean philosopher's claim.

'Metaphysical' pronouncements like the one attributed to Heraclitus have a number of characteristic features. As the metaphysician conceives them, they constitute discoveries of a very particular kind, discoveries that intimate deep truths about the nature of reality, which contradict or are in conflict with our ordinary or commonsense understanding. Asserting them, then, requires saying something at odds with ordinary linguistic usage, and this in turn suggests that ordinary language is inadequate to convey this deeper order of truth about reality, or is even complicit in covering over this deeper order of truth. If Wittgenstein wants to challenge the coherence of such metaphysical 'discoveries', he cannot simply reassert the ordinary expressions that the metaphysician has repudiated. He has to call the repudiation itself into question.

If Wittgenstein simply contradicted the metaphysician's claim to have made a discovery—as indeed he seems to do in responding to Heraclitus—his response would be both pedantic and dogmatic. He would be granting that the metaphysician's words make clear enough sense, but would be asserting that they are false and affirming their negation. Compare my disputing your claim to have discovered a violation of the law of conservation of energy: I know very well what it would mean to discover a violation of the law, but I don't believe you've made such a discovery. Construed in this way, Wittgenstein and Heraclitus would be disputing a factual claim. Where Heraclitus maintains that, as it turns out, one cannot step into the same river twice, Wittgenstein responds that, in point of fact, one can. And if that were the case, Wittgenstein's response would be no less metaphysical than the claim that he disputes.

At best, the 'fact' about how many times one can step into the same river is of a very different kind from the fact about whether the law of

1.1. 'ONE *CAN* STEP INTO THE SAME RIVER TWICE' 17

conservation of energy holds for all isolated systems. In the latter case, we can clearly imagine what a counter-example would look like: we may never encounter a perpetual motion machine but we can specify what something would have to be able to do in order to count as one. In the former case, we are not weighing two different clearly imagined scenarios—the one in which I step into the same river twice and the one in which I cannot—and adjudicating whether the second imagined scenario obtains. Heraclitus and Wittgenstein are imagining the exact same scenario—into the river goes my foot, back out again, back in again—but using different words to construe what has happened. The nature of Heraclitus's alleged discovery is not an empirical one—he has not witnessed a hitherto unwitnessed empirical phenomenon. Its status as a 'metaphysical' 'discovery' is that it allegedly informs us of the nature of *all* empirical phenomena. The nature of all empirical reality is fundamentally one of flux, the Heraclitean philosopher wants to say—change is the only constant—so that nothing that exists at one moment endures into the next such that it can count as 'the same'. (Note that this claim applies not just to the river but also to the 'one' that allegedly cannot step into the same river twice.) It does not *happen* to be the case, or *turn out* to be the case that one cannot step into the same river twice. The Heraclitean philosopher claims to have discovered that there is no such thing as stepping into the same river twice: the words 'step into the same river twice' express a metaphysical impossibility.

The question of whether one can step into the same river twice is not a question about what happens to be the case, but what *must* (or must not) be the case. The difference in kind of such questions from empirical questions of fact gives them the appearance of profound importance. Wittgenstein's criticism challenges precisely the idea of such a higher order of metaphysical questions:

Roughly speaking, according to the old conception—for instance that of the (great) western philosophers—there have been two kinds of intellectual [*wissenschaftlichen*] problems: the essential, great, universal ones, and the non-essential, quasi-accidental problems. We, on the other hand, hold that there is no such thing as a *great*, essential problem in the intellectual sense [*im Sinne der Wissenschaft*]. (BTS 301; cf. CV 20)

The challenge of Wittgenstein's later philosophy, one might say, is to show that there are no 'essential, great, universal' problems for philosophy to resolve but that philosophy as an activity is not thereby made otiose. For Wittgenstein, philosophy still takes an interest in what is essential (e.g. *PI* §89 and §371), what is great (e.g. *PI* §111), perhaps even what is universal,[4] but it does so without discovering truths or resolving problems of an intellectual kind.

The word 'intellectual' translates the German *wissenschaftlich*, that is, concerning knowledge and the systematic production of knowledge. From the very beginning of his philosophical career, Wittgenstein considers the conception of philosophy as a systematic body of knowledge to be a fundamental and pervasive misunderstanding.[5] The trouble with the Heraclitean philosopher's claim, then, is not that it makes a claim to know something about the nature of reality that turns out to be false rather than true. The trouble with the Heraclitean philosopher's claim is that it presents itself as a cognitive achievement at all.[6] Wittgenstein does not want to refute the claim that one cannot step into the same river twice but rather wants to dislodge the idea that this claim amounts to a claim to know something profound about the nature of reality. The point is not that the metaphysician's words express something false or impossible but that the metaphysician's words do not—cannot—mean what the metaphysician supposes they mean.

1.2. Grammatical and Empirical Investigations

Far from the caricature of pedantry, Wittgenstein has great respect for the impulse that prompts the Heraclitean philosopher to speak.[7] He

---

[4] Wittgenstein treats the search for universal or general claims to be symptomatic of the kind of metaphysical philosophy he wishes to overcome. For instance, he chides his earlier self's captivation with the idea of the general form of the proposition (*PI* §§65, 114, 134, 136) and frequently challenges the usefulness of pursuing generality or universality in philosophy (e.g. *PI* §§71, 73, 74, 89, 104). On the other hand, Wittgenstein expresses an interest in 'very general facts of nature' (*PPF* xii §365; cf. also *PI* p. 62), which are often overlooked on account of their generality.

[5] Cf. *NB* 120: 'Logic must turn out to be a *totally* different kind than any other science'. Wittgenstein wrote this in a letter to Russell in 1912, less than a year after he began working in philosophy.

[6] That Heraclitus himself should be read as advancing a metaphysical knowledge claim is far from evident. I suggest an alternative way of reading Heraclitus at the end of section 7.4, where I discuss Heidegger's method of formal indication.

[7] Stern (1991) offers a thorough examination of Wittgenstein's engagement throughout his career with Heraclitean imagery of rivers and flux.

thinks that something has gone wrong in insisting that one cannot step into the same river twice, but that the appropriate response is not outright rejection but careful investigation: 'In a certain sense one cannot take too much care in handling philosophical mistakes, they contain so much truth' (Z §460). The Heraclitean philosopher does not so much manifest a deviation from the sensible thinking of the common person but rather presents openly a tension in our thinking that more often masks itself in prevarication. Wittgenstein is exercised by pronouncements that go counter to ordinary usage because they bring these tensions to the surface. He is less interested in shutting them down than in understanding the impulse to issue them at all.

Characterizing philosophical investigations as conceptual investigations, Wittgenstein adds: 'The essential thing about metaphysics: it obliterates the distinction between factual and conceptual investigations' (Z §458; cf. RPP I §949).[8] Wittgenstein frequently emphasizes the difference between conceptual or grammatical investigations on the one hand and factual or empirical investigations on the other, between the mode of representation and what is represented. At PI §104, for instance, he writes in a diagnostic spirit: 'One predicates of the thing what lies in the mode of representation'.[9] In an adjacent note, he quotes Faraday: 'Water is one individual thing—it never changes'. Faraday says this in the context of claiming that water persists through distillation and other phase changes and takes himself to be making a factual claim about the nature of water (see Faraday [1861] 2011, 30–2). But Wittgenstein wants us to see this as a typical instance of predicating of the thing what lies in the mode of representation. We could imagine an alternative way of talking in which we say that liquid water and water vapour are two different things: a certain quantity of liquid disappears when it evaporates and an equivalent quantity of vapour comes into being, and under condensation the vapour disappears and liquid comes into being. This way of talking could respect all the same empirical observations as our current way of talking. Our way of talking perhaps carries the advantage that it helps us to see the connection between the liquid and the vapour

---

[8] See also BB 18: 'Philosophers constantly see the method of science before their eyes, and are irresistibly tempted to ask and answer questions in the way science does. This tendency is the real source of metaphysics, and leads the philosopher into complete darkness'.

[9] See also PI §114: 'One thinks that one is tracing nature over and over again, and one is merely tracing round the frame through which we look at it'.

more clearly, but nothing in this alternative way of talking provides an insuperable obstacle to talking and thinking clearly about evaporation and condensation. That liquid and vapour are the same 'one individual thing' is not, as Faraday seems to suppose, a fact about water itself. Observation and experiment can show that the liquid and the vapour have the same chemical constituents, but to make the further step of saying that a liquid and a gas with the same chemical constituents are the same 'one individual thing' is not an empirical fact but a mode of representing the facts—a grammatical rule for how to describe the facts and not itself a fact.

Wittgenstein famously coins the expression 'language-game' to talk about segments of natural language, and 'to emphasize the fact that the speaking of language is part of an activity, or of a form of life' (*PI* §23).[10] In one application of this analogy, Wittgenstein distinguishes moves in a language-game from the preparatory work of naming and stating rules that establish what language-game we are playing.[11] The rules governing the language-games we play can make some forms of expression necessary and others forbidden. But their status as necessary or forbidden is a feature of the rules of the language-game and not a feature of some language-independent reality. For example, that sensations are private is not a fact about privacy, but a fact about the language-games we play with the concept of privacy: 'The sentence "Sensations are private" is comparable to "One plays patience by oneself"' (*PI* §248).[12] If we fail to distinguish statements of rules about a game from moves within the game, we fall into the confusion of thinking that the privacy of sensations constitutes an imaginable metaphysical fact, one that we might distinguish from an imaginable alternative way in which reality could be organized, in which sensations are not private.[13] Because the expression of a grammatical rule is similar in form to a statement of fact, such a

---

[10] Wittgenstein introduces three other senses of the expression 'language-game' earlier, at *PI* §7. These other senses, and the multi-faceted nature of Wittgenstein's language-game analogy, receive more detailed attention in section 6.1.

[11] See, e.g., *PI* §31 and §49.

[12] Mulhall (2007a, 60-1) makes the compelling argument that the comparison with patience at *PI* §248 makes better sense if we read it as telling us something about privacy, not about sensations.

[13] Wittgenstein remarks that the problem is not simply that we mistakenly think that grammatical rules stand in contradiction to an alternative way things might be, but that we think the grammatical rules themselves represent a way things are at all: 'But why do I say:

1.2. GRAMMATICAL AND EMPIRICAL INVESTIGATIONS

statement 'produces the illusion of being an empirical proposition, but which is really a grammatical one' (*PI* §251).

The dogmatic reading of Wittgenstein's response to Heraclitus construed him as opposing the alleged discovery that one cannot step into the same river twice with the commonsense fact that one *can* step into the same river twice. But the distinction Wittgenstein draws between grammatical and empirical propositions admits an alternative understanding of those words. 'One *can* step into the same river twice' is not the expression of an empirical fact but rather of a rule—like 'Sensations are private' or 'One plays patience by oneself'. That is, as a matter of grammar, we do talk about the same river—the Thames, the Fraser, the Nile—across time and multiple instances of stepping.

The point of this reminder is not to rule out the Heraclitean claim by grammatical fiat—as if to say that its transgression of our ordinary forms of expression rules it out as nonsensical and that is the end of the matter. To suppose that we could do this would be to suppose that what constitutes our ordinary forms of expression, and what constitutes a violation, is itself clear, so that philosophical criticism becomes the more or less mechanical activity of policing violations of clearly delineated grammatical rules. But a central preoccupation of Wittgenstein's later philosophy is precisely the concern that it is not immediately apparent where and how sharply we can draw a line between sense and nonsense, and that treating philosophical confusion requires careful attention to the circumstances that prompt us to utter it. The dialogical form of the *Investigations* suggests as much: Wittgenstein's procedure is not simply to correct his interlocutors by pronouncing on grammatical rules but to tease out carefully the protean impulses that give rise to confusion. This way of reading Wittgenstein is not obviously the right way—how to understand Wittgenstein's appeal to grammatical rules represents one of the major fault lines in the secondary literature on Wittgenstein's later philosophy—and I will defend it in greater detail later in this book.[14] For the moment, I want simply to propose that

---

"I can't imagine the opposite [of a grammatical rule]"? Why not: "I can't imagine what you say"?' (*PI* §251).

[14] In very broad strokes, the idea that nonsense results from violations of grammatical rules finds its paradigmatic expression in the commentaries of Gordon Baker and P. M. S. Hacker, and the idea that the line between sense and nonsense is subtler than such a reading allows finds its most influential expression in the work of Stanley Cavell and

identifying Wittgenstein's remark that one *can* step into the same river twice as a grammatical rule is the beginning of the matter, not the end of it.

1.3. 'Not to present the matter as if there were something one *couldn't* do'

One upshot to seeing Wittgenstein's response to the Heraclitean claim in a different light—as the expression of a grammatical rule rather than as a statement of empirical fact—is that it allows us to see the Heraclitean claim in a different light as well. If what it opposes is not an empirical commonplace but rather a grammatical rule, then its opposition constitutes not an assertion of metaphysical fact but a proposal for an alternative way of speaking. Wittgenstein entertains such a proposal in connection with the solipsist's insistence that it makes no sense to talk about the pains of others:

If I were to reserve the word 'pain' solely for what I had previously called 'my pain', and others 'L.W.'s pain', I'd do other people no injustice, so long as a notation were provided in which the loss of the word 'pain' in other contexts were somehow made good. Other people would still be pitied, treated by doctors, and so on. (*PI* §403)

Rather than reject outright the solipsist's proposal, Wittgenstein spells it out to show that it does not amount to anything more than a proposal that we speak differently than we do. Wittgenstein could say the same to the Heraclitean philosopher: provided people can still go swimming, ford streams, and the rest, and you are not hindered from talking about these activities, your new way of talking is no worse off. But do not think that you are now able to say anything you could not just as well have said in the old way of talking. You have not made a discovery about the nature of reality but have simply established a new set of linguistic rules.

Cora Diamond, as well as in the late writings of Gordon Baker. I explore Wittgenstein's method—and the importance of the dialogical form of the *Investigations*—in more detail in Chapter 8, and the idea that our grammatical rules are not fixed but constantly 'in play' is essential to an 'authentic' reading of Wittgenstein that I articulate in Part Two, especially Chapter 6.

1.3. 'AS IF THERE WERE SOMETHING ONE *COULDN'T DO*'

The endgame, then, is to reach an understanding of the metaphysician's words where the sense that there was something to say in the first place evaporates. Simply rejecting the metaphysician's words would carry the risk of leaving the impression that there is *something* there to be said, just that this something is, for some reason, ineffable, or at least needs to be expressed differently. We might persuade the Heraclitean philosopher that 'One cannot step into the same river twice' cannot express what she wants to express, but leave her with the impression that there is an insight there—something about the constant changingness of all things—for which she might find other words, or simply reflect upon in a mystical silence.

At an earlier stage in his career, Wittgenstein himself seems attracted to this notion:

What belongs to the essence of the world cannot be expressed by language.

For this reason, it cannot *say* that everything flows. Language can only say those things that we can also imagine otherwise.

That everything flows must be expressed in the application of language, and in fact not in one kind of application as opposed to another but in *the* application. In anything we would ever call the application of language.   (PR 84–5)

Here Wittgenstein seems caught in a double bind. On one hand, he wants to reject the idea that 'everything flows' expresses something definite. 'As opposed to what?', Wittgenstein subsequently asks (PR 85): that *not* everything flows? On the other hand, Wittgenstein seems still to want to maintain that there is an insight there, only one that 'cannot be expressed in language'.

Later, Wittgenstein comes to see this 'cannot' as part of the problem:[15]

The great difficulty here is not to present the matter as if there were something one *couldn't* do. As if there really were an object, from which I extract a description, which I am not in a position to show anyone.   (PI §374)

One danger in challenging philosophical misuses of language is that it might achieve the superficial aim of persuading philosophers not

---

[15] Conant (1992) treats at length the nature of logical necessity and impossibility, and the idea of there being something that one *cannot* do. On Conant's reading, Kant, the early Wittgenstein, and at least some part of Frege anticipate this idea that no definite thoughts are ruled out as a matter of logic.

to use those forms of expression while leaving in place the deeper misunderstanding that those forms of expression, if only they could say what we wanted them to, indicate something deep. Wittgenstein's language-game analogy provides one way of combating the idea that he is telling us that there is *something* that we *cannot* say:

> Do not say 'one cannot', but say instead: 'it doesn't exist in this game'. Not: 'one can't castle in draughts' but — 'there is no castling in draughts'; and instead of 'I can't exhibit my sensation' — 'in the use of the word "sensation", there is no such thing as exhibiting what one has got'; instead of 'one cannot enumerate all the cardinal numbers' — 'there is no such thing here as enumerating all the members'. (Z §134)

By reframing these 'cannots' as laying out the rules of a language-game, Wittgenstein weans us off the supposition that something is forbidden. Castling is not something one *cannot do* in draughts (checkers for the North Americans in the audience) because there is no clear *something* being named and forbidden here. Only within the rules of draughts can a move count as *doing something*, and so a non-move is not *doing* anything, forbidden or allowed.[16] Before we ask whether something is possible, Wittgenstein wants us to consider whether we are imagining a definite something at all. 'Let us ask now, not "Can there be such a thing?" but "What do we imagine?"' (Z §275; cf. also RPP I §826).[17]

The point is not that everything-flows-but-we-cannot-express-it-like-that. The point is to reach an understanding where we no longer feel there is anything to be said about the perdurability of substances, flowing or otherwise. Not because the substance realists are right and things are *not* in a constant flux, but because things simply are as they are—in a 'non-essential, quasi-accidental' way, they are sometimes changing, sometimes not—and there is not a further 'essential, great, universal' sense in which they are either in flux or not. The liberation Wittgenstein seeks for the metaphysically-inclined philosopher comes not in refuting her claims but in liberating her from the feeling that there are claims to be disputed.

---

[16] At Z §356, Wittgenstein distinguishes between two similes: of a road that is physically impassable and of the non-existence of a road.

[17] In a similar spirit, Wittgenstein questions the sense of asserting that a rose has no teeth at PPF xi §314.

1.4. The Sideways Perspective

The Heraclitean philosopher's words respond to the feeling of having been struck by something important. But she missteps in thinking that what she has been struck by is a fact about reality whose expression requires repudiating our ordinary forms of expression. These two ideas—that what she has been struck by is a fact about reality and that expressing this fact requires repudiating our ordinary forms of expression—are interestingly twinned. The Heraclitean philosopher's self-understanding as expressing a claim about the nature of reality brings with it the corollary idea that our ordinary forms of expression encode claims about the nature of reality. The fact that I can talk about the Thames today, yesterday, and tomorrow suggests to the Heraclitean philosopher that encoded in ordinary language is a metaphysics of perdurable objects. Without even noticing it, the Heraclitean philosopher wants to say, we assume that things like rivers endure across time, and this assumption is deeply problematic. Reforming our metaphysics requires reforming ordinary language.

Articulating the idea that ordinary language encodes a metaphysics of perdurable objects requires an Escherian feat of philosophical contortionism. In effect, the complaint here is that ordinary language smuggles in what we might call a theory of rivers—that our concept of rivers articulates certain metaphysical conjectures about rivers that warrant critical scrutiny rather than blind acceptance. But to attribute covert theorizing to our concepts presumes that we can get some distance between our thought and the concepts with which we think. As if we can somehow think *about* rivers (say) independent of our concept of rivers. Asking if we have the *right* concept of rivers, metaphysically speaking, requires that we make a comparison: we need to set our concept of rivers alongside something else—rivers-as-such—and assess whether our concept fits the thing it is the concept of. But to make this comparison we need to be able to hold two things in mind: 'our' concept of rivers and the concept of rivers-as-such. To suppose that we can apprehend a concept of rivers-as-such that may or may not coincide with 'our' concept of rivers is to suppose that we can think about rivers without thinking about (with 'our' concept of) rivers.

John McDowell famously describes this supposition as the idea that we can contemplate our thought and language 'not only from the midst of our ... practices, but also, so to speak, from sideways on.... As if, by a special emphasis, one could somehow manage to speak otherwise than out of one's own mouth' (McDowell 1981, 150). The critic of ordinary language needs a point of view from outside of our thought and language from which to contemplate that thought and language and to evaluate its fittingness. To repeat, the problem here is not that the critic of ordinary language wants to occupy a point of view that, due to the constraints of thought and language, she *cannot* occupy—the problem is not an epistemological one that we can never *know* whether our concepts are the correct ones. The problem is that the idea of such a point of view is itself a fantasy—and so the question of correctness and incorrectness has no place.

We can, of course, imagine different language-games we could play with the word 'river'. We could imagine a language-game in which 'I swam in that river yesterday and again today' is as nonsensical as 'that moment occurred yesterday and today' is in ours. The consequences of changing our language-game in this way would likely ramify broadly and it would take careful investigation to work through these ramifications—and, indeed, it would be an open question whether we should say that we are talking about 'the same thing' when we use the word 'river' in the two different language-games, or whether we are operating with two entirely different concepts that just happen to be homonymous. But no standards determine which language-game is the correct one because standards of correctness are determined *within* language-games. Within our language-game, talking about swimming in the same river yesterday and today is an acceptable move, and within the other language-game such talk is forbidden, but neither can be deemed right or wrong independent of any language-game. The moves that are permissible for the king in chess are different from the moves that are permissible in draughts/checkers, but there is not some further standard according to which there are permissible or impermissible moves for a king independent of the game we are playing, such that chess or draughts might conform to this standard better or worse.

In a different context, Wittgenstein examines our concept of seeing and notes that, in addition to being able to see the eyes of others, we can also talk about seeing the glance that those eyes cast. This, he claims, is not a physiological claim, and he has 'not *made any admissions* by using that manner of speaking.... For "naïve language", that is to say our naïve, normal way of expressing ourselves, does not contain any theory of seeing—does not show you a *theory* but only a *concept* of seeing' (*Z* §223; cf. *RPP* I §1101). A theory of seeing can be correct or incorrect, but such theoretical investigations are scientific and not philosophical. The investigations Wittgenstein pursues are conceptual because they aim to gain clarity with regard to the contours of the concepts we use in making theoretical claims, rather than to make theoretical claims themselves.

Where theoretical investigations seek to explain, conceptual investigations simply describe (*PI* §109). Wittgenstein repeatedly emphasizes that he does not want to tell us anything new (*PI* §89), but just to remind us of what we already know (*PI* §127). Wittgenstein intends his own remarks to have this character of simply describing and saying nothing controversial:

On all questions we discuss I have no opinion; and if I had, and it disagreed with one of your opinions, I would at once give it up for the sake of argument because it would be of no importance for our discussion. We constantly move in a realm where we all have the same opinions. (*AWL* 97)[18]

We can have differing opinions over matters of fact, as well as matters of taste or judgment. For Wittgenstein, philosophy involves none of these things. Instead, philosophy consists of disentangling the sorts of confusions that might prevent us from expressing coherent opinions in the first place. In such an activity, disagreement is itself a sign of confusion, a sign that people are talking past one another. So much philosophy consists of drawing battle lines, of staking out a position that one can contrast with other, rival positions. But for Wittgenstein, the very notion of a philosophical position that contrasts with another one is a sign of confusion. Wittgenstein pushes on these alleged positions in appropriate ways—presenting descriptions, reminders, illuminating objects of comparison—until we realize that we cannot coherently articulate them as opposed to one another.[19]

Whatever the Heraclitean philosopher thinks she has discovered, it cannot contravene ordinary language because ordinary language does not assert anything that might need to be contravened. Our forms of expression do not assert anything—they determine what counts as an

---

[18] See also *LFM* 22 and 103, and Rhees 1970a, 43.
[19] I discuss Wittgenstein's use of objects of comparison in more detail in Chapter 8.

assertion and what form assertions take, but they themselves assert nothing—which means that our forms of expression also do not themselves deny anything. Reforming—or affirming—ordinary language is not going to get us anywhere, metaphysically speaking. The very idea of 'ordinary language' as a philosophical category is a manifestation of this bogus idea that our forms of expression can be a productive site of philosophical contestation: on one hand, the language of the metaphysician, on the other hand, ordinary language. But Wittgenstein's point is precisely that the metaphysically inclined philosopher has failed to express anything that puts her at odds with the rest of us. Ordinary language is all the language there is.[20]

If we abandon the idea that reforming our language might place us in better stead metaphysically, we must also abandon the idea that ordinary language has any kind of metaphysical authority. Wittgenstein warns us against supposing 'that certain concepts are absolutely the correct ones' (*PPF* xii §366). Although I have focused on the example of a Heraclitean philosopher feeling the compulsion to reform our ordinary forms of expression because they are out of line with the metaphysical facts, we must also ward off the supposition that our ordinary forms of expression reveal anything about the metaphysical facts. What Wittgenstein resists as 'metaphysical' is not simply the repudiation of our ordinary ways of speaking but also what that repudiation wants to repudiate.

1.5. Heidegger and the Ontological Difference

Much of what I said in characterizing 'metaphysical' pronouncements like that of the Heraclitean philosopher would seem to apply to the project of Heidegger's *Being and Time*. Heidegger presents himself as

---

[20] This point dovetails with the argument, made by Baker (2004a) and Kuusela (2008, 275f.), that the 'everyday use' of language mentioned in contrast with a 'metaphysical' one in *PI* §116 is not meant to provide any kind of philosophical traction against the metaphysician. Both argue that Wittgenstein does not have a demarcated conception of 'everyday use' that serves to rule out metaphysical misuses as aberrant. 'Everyday use', they argue, is not defined by a set of identifiable features but is simply what we are left with when we have cleared up our confusion. However, if nothing is expressed in 'metaphysical' language, Baker cannot be right to say that the term 'metaphysical' 'wears the trousers' in the everyday/metaphysical pairing (Baker 2004a, 100). I am grateful to James Conant for pointing out this infelicity in Baker's exposition.

uncovering the 'ontological significance' of our everyday practices, a significance which is 'constantly overlooked' in our ordinary ways of talking about them (*BT* 43). His self-consciously difficult prose is meant to get into view something our everyday ways of talking cover over. In this regard, Heidegger seems to epitomize the philosopher who repudiates our ordinary forms of expression in a misguided attempt to formulate metaphysical discoveries. Indeed Carnap ([1931] 1959), drawing inspiration from Wittgenstein's *Tractatus*, takes Heidegger's 'What Is Metaphysics?' as a signal case of metaphysical nonsense. In a contorted sentence like 'The nothing itself nihilates' [*Das Nichts selbst nichtet*] (*WM* 103), Carnap alleges, Heidegger first treats 'nothing' as the name of an object and compounds the confusion by inventing the verb 'to nihilate' (*nichten*) without stipulating the criteria for the correct application of this word.

Carnap's criticism differs from the approach taken in Wittgenstein's later philosophy. As we have seen, Wittgenstein's criticism works from the inside, as it were: he works to inhabit the point of view that makes a given utterance seem natural, meaningful, or important, and to explore what makes this form of words seem compelling. By contrast, Carnap approaches his targets from the outside, applying criteria for meaningfulness that are meant to be universally applicable. The burden of proof is on Heidegger in Carnap's criticism: either he must show how his sentences accord with Carnap's criteria for meaningfulness or he must accept that his work consists in large part of pseudo-statements, sentences that have the appearance of meaningful propositions but that are in fact meaningless. On Carnap's approach, we have no reason to try to inhabit the metaphysician's point of view until he can persuade us that we should take him seriously.

Carnap can criticize his targets from the outside because he has clear criteria for distinguishing sense from nonsense: either a sentence is empirically verifiable or it is not, and we can test it for empirical verifiability by reducing it to basic protocol sentences. Wittgenstein's later emphasis on how sentences are *used* means that the sense of a sentence cannot be verified according to external criteria in this way. Before we can reach any verdict about a sentence, we first need to understand what that sentence is trying to *do*, and, as Wittgenstein emphasizes at *PI* §23, we might want to do indefinitely many different things with a sentence besides asserting empirically verifiable truths.

Even by Carnap's own standards, though, his criticism of Heidegger seems misdirected. Carnap motivates his choice of 'What Is Metaphysics?' as a target for criticism on account of Heidegger's contemporary influence, but adds: 'We could just as well have selected passages from any other of the numerous metaphysicians of the present or of the past; yet the selected passages seem to us to illustrate our thesis especially well' (Carnap [1931] 1959, 69n). As other instances of metaphysical nonsense, Carnap adverts to expressions of the form 'x is the principle of y' and logically muddled references to God (Carnap [1931] 1959, 65–6). The trouble with these sorts of sentences is that they try to say something true about ultimate reality without adequately stipulating their truth-conditions: it remains unclear what exactly would have to be the case to make these sentences true and what might prove them false.

Far from replicating this muddle, Heidegger comes surprisingly close to sharing Carnap's standards for criticism, and in a way that places him even closer to Wittgenstein. The contorted phrasing on 'What Is Metaphysics?' is not part of an effort on Heidegger's part to put forward metaphysically obscure truth-claims but precisely to find a way of understanding the role of metaphysics as he understands it as lying outside the domain of empirically verifiable truth-claims. Heidegger's treatment of 'the nothing' [*das Nichts*] begins with a play on words: he happily accepts that the sciences are complete in their investigation of beings [*das Seiende*]—and leave *nothing* out (*WM* 95). Heidegger seems to share with Carnap the view that any truth-claims we might meaningfully make about beings are proper to the sciences: there are no extra-scientific truths about beings.

But then he slyly asks: 'What about this nothing?' (*WM* 95). What if there is a kind of investigation that precisely does not concern itself with beings and hence is not in the business of advancing empirically verifiable truth-claims? A fuller discussion of how nullity and 'the nothing' feature in these investigations will have to wait until Part Two, but it is part of Heidegger's project to 'work out the question of the meaning of "*being*"' (*BT* 1). This question is not a scientific question but the central question of what he calls 'fundamental ontology'. And one of Heidegger's central methodological concerns is that philosophers have not been sufficiently rigorous in distinguishing this kind of ontological investigation from the kinds of factual investigations that characterize the sciences. In this respect, he agrees with Carnap's contention that attempts

1.5. HEIDEGGER AND THE ONTOLOGICAL DIFFERENCE

to formulate factual claims about fundamental issues are bound to misfire. And closer to the interests of this book, he shares Wittgenstein's concern that we should not confuse factual and conceptual investigations. Heidegger at least sometimes seems to accept 'metaphysics' as an adequate name for the latter kind of investigation, but he thinks the word needs to be rescued from contemporary abuses: '[T]he question of the meaning of being [is] not only unresolved, not only inadequately formulated, but despite all interest in "metaphysics" has even been forgotten' (*BT* 21).

For Heidegger, the central challenge is not so much to *answer* the question of the meaning of being but simply to retrieve it and make it visible to philosophy. 'This question has today been forgotten' (*BT* 2), he tells us at the opening of *Being and Time*, and subsequently notes that 'not only is the *answer* to the question of being lacking, but even the question itself is obscure and without direction' (*BT* 4). The first impediment to addressing this question is that we do not know what such an inquiry would look like. In particular, Heidegger draws a sharp distinction between fundamental ontology and the ontic sciences—'ontic science' being Heidegger's term for the knowledge-generating disciplines in the German sense of *Wissenschaften*. The ontic sciences generate knowledge about various kinds of beings, distinguishing them into 'particular domains' in which knowledge is 'exposed and delimited' (*BT* 9): biology, physics, linguistics, and so on. These domains are shaped by their distinctive 'fundamental concepts' (*BT* 9)—for instance, research in physics is shaped by fundamental concepts such as matter, time, space, and force. Any ontic science can experience 'a crisis in its basic concepts' (*BT* 9)—as, for instance, physics was in Heidegger's time with the advent of relativity and quantum mechanics—in which the basic constitution of these concepts is called into question. This sort of regional ontological inquiry is familiar enough, but also shares with the ontic sciences a basic orientation toward particular beings: it 'amounts to nothing else than interpreting these beings in terms of the basic constitution of their being' (*BT* 10). By contrast, fundamental ontology is concerned not with beings of any sort, but with being itself, which is 'the condition of the possibility of the [regional] ontologies which precede the ontic sciences and found them' (*BT* 11). Fundamental ontology does not provide a new, deeper level of knowledge—it is not an extra set of truths couched within a novel theoretical framework that the Heideggerian phenomenologist discovers—but rather investigates how beings show up for us such that they can be objects of knowledge. Heidegger is clear, however, that he is not offering us a theory of knowledge (*BT* 10–11) but something more like the logic by which beings are intelligible to us.[21]

The difference between ontic science and fundamental ontology is, according to Heidegger, the difference between beings [*das Seiende*] and being [*das Sein*]—a difference that he dubs 'the ontological difference' (*BPP* 17). He marks the difference—and signals the difficulty in respecting it—by famously announcing: 'The being of being "is" itself not a being' [*Das Sein des Seienden »ist« nicht selbst ein Seiendes*] (*BT* 6). The scare-quoted 'is' suggests the difficulty in keeping this difference in view. We use the copula to predicate properties of an object—in other words, an expression of the form '*x* is *y*' treats the item in the *x* position as a kind of object—and Heidegger's point is precisely to emphasize that being is *not* a kind of object.[22] Our language and thought are primarily oriented toward ontic investigations of beings of various kinds such that we face considerable obstacles in even apprehending what fundamental ontology might look like. This sort of inquiry does not concern itself with beings and it does not generate knowledge. And, Heidegger tells us, it is only by respecting this fundamental difference between ontic and ontological investigations that 'we first enter the field of philosophical research' (*BPP* 17).

1.6. Wittgenstein, Heidegger, and the Everyday

Heidegger's emphasis on the sharp distinction between his own ontological investigations and the ontic investigations of scientific inquiry is strikingly similar to Wittgenstein's emphasis on the distinction between what he calls at turns grammatical or conceptual investigations on the one hand and factual or empirical investigations on the other.[23] Both philosophers register a fundamental difference between their own

---

[21] Rhees (1970a, 37) makes a similar point regarding Wittgenstein: 'Wittgenstein wanted the two books [the *Tractatus* and the *Philosophical Investigations*] read together. But this has not helped people to see that the *Investigations* is a book on the philosophy of logic; it has led many... to read the *Tractatus* as a theory of knowledge'.

[22] The issue at play here has striking resonances to the 'concept horse' problem in Frege's 'Concept and Object' (Frege [1892] 1997). Priest (2002, 240) also remarks on this resonance.

[23] This point also receives emphasis in Mulhall (2013).

1.6. WITTGENSTEIN, HEIDEGGER, AND THE EVERYDAY

investigation and the kind of investigation that produces knowledge—and both warn of the danger of misconstruing philosophical investigation as a scientific endeavour.[24] For both of them, the danger of such misconstrual bespeaks a particular difficulty for their own method: if they are not to be understood as communicating truths in propositional form that have the form of knowledge, what *are* they doing?

As it happens, Wittgenstein and Heidegger give strikingly similar answers to this question: rather than providing *explanations* of phenomena, they aim simply to *describe*. 'All *explanation* must disappear, and description alone must take its place', says Wittgenstein (*PI* §109), and in characterizing his method as phenomenological, Heidegger says that the phrase 'descriptive phenomenology' is a 'basically tautological expression' (*BT* 35). Although their descriptive methods differ in a number of important respects, both offer these descriptions as alternatives to the cognitive discoveries announced by the sciences. Both Wittgenstein and Heidegger style themselves as furnishing *reminders* of things we already know but have somehow lost sight of. Wittgenstein presents himself as 'marshalling recollections for a particular purpose' (*PI* §127) and Heidegger emphasizes our tendency to become 'lost' or to 'forget' ourselves, and conceives his own project as bringing us back to ourselves.

Because they style themselves as not telling us anything new, as only furnishing descriptions and reminders, both Wittgenstein and Heidegger occasionally encourage the view that they are not—and that philosophy more generally should not be—advancing theses of any kind. At *PI* §128, Wittgenstein famously writes: 'If someone were to advance *theses* in philosophy, it would never be possible to debate them, because everyone would agree to them'. In a similar spirit, Heidegger writes: 'Rightly conceived, phenomenology is the concept of a method. It is therefore precluded from the start that phenomenology should pronounce any theses about being which have specific content, thus adopting a so-called standpoint' (*BPP* 20). How we should interpret such 'no thesis' claims—are they not themselves theses of a kind?—is a matter of considerable

---

[24] Section 1.2 offered representative claims from Wittgenstein at *Z* §458 and *BTS* 301. For Heidegger, consider *BT* 94: '[T]he expression *substantia* functions sometimes in an ontological, sometimes in an ontic meaning, but mostly in a meaning which shifts about in a hazy mixture between the two. But behind this slight difference of meaning lies hidden the failure to master the fundamental problem of being'.

controversy, especially in the secondary literature on Wittgenstein. What I think they mean—and what sorts of constraints it places on each philosopher's method—will become a central concern in Part Three of this book. But at this early stage, we can at least register that they are marking a deep difference in method from most of the philosophical tradition that precedes them and that this deep difference stems from wanting to mark rigorously the difference between empirical/ontic and grammatical/ontological investigations.

In the previous two paragraphs, I have adduced three methodological consequences of Wittgenstein's and Heidegger's similar concerns for respecting what Heidegger calls the ontological difference: they aim to describe rather than to explain, they want to remind us of things we already know but have somehow lost sight of, and they will not pronounce theses. These three methodological commitments lead them to a similar starting point: their reminders are primarily reminders of our everyday activities, and, especially with Heidegger, their descriptions are descriptions of everyday activities as well.[25] The attention they give to the everyday follows from a further shared methodological commitment: not to try to adopt a sideways perspective.[26] We cannot as it were step outside of ourselves and assess our practices and forms of expression from an objective remove but must rather ameliorate our self-understanding from within. Their project is not so much to *reform* our everyday practices and forms of expression but rather to come to a clearer understanding of what exactly they amount to.

However, Heidegger does not share Wittgenstein's confidence that our everyday practices and forms of expression are metaphysically innocent.

---

[25] With Wittgenstein the situation is a bit more complicated, as many of the language-games he describes are not descriptions of *our* practices but of unexpected or unusual behaviour, often by imagined tribes quite different from us. The purpose of these descriptions is to present points of contrast by which our own practices become visible in a way we might not otherwise notice, which is why these descriptions of extraordinary practices can nevertheless serve as reminders of our ordinary practices. I explore these features of Wittgenstein's method in more detail in Chapter 8.

[26] Glendinning (2007, 14–20) outlines five 'theses' (a term he uses with appropriate caution) of phenomenology, while noting that the approach he identifies as 'phenomenological' applies equally to the later philosophy of Wittgenstein as well as to a number of other figures who are canonical 'analytic' philosophers, such as J. L. Austin and Gilbert Ryle (Glendinning 2007, 6). Among the five 'theses' are the rejection of philosophical theses, the focus on description over explanation, and the rejection of the idea of a sideways perspective.

1.6. WITTGENSTEIN, HEIDEGGER, AND THE EVERYDAY

Those forms give expression to an 'average everyday' understanding of ourselves and our world, and this understanding manifests a deep and pervasive *mis*understanding of the distinctive way of being of human beings. We are complicit, as Heidegger sees it, in a motivated form of self-blindness that he calls 'inauthenticity'. This self-blindness is in turn a part of what keeps us from even seeing that there is a question of the meaning of being to be recovered and addressed.

In this respect, then, and in spite of the similarities I noted above, Wittgenstein and Heidegger seem to be on a collision course. The Heidegger who calls us to attend to the question of the meaning of being seems much more like the Wittgenstein of the *Tractatus*, who, in the book's preface, announces that he has 'found, on all essential points, the final solution of the problems [of philosophy]' (*TLP*, preface). Wittgenstein does not here indicate, as Heidegger does, that there is one central question to philosophy, but he does think that the method of the *Tractatus* has provided a 'final solution' 'on all essential points' to the problems of philosophy, which indicates a similar confidence that philosophical problems lend themselves to a unified treatment.[27] By contrast, the Wittgenstein of *Philosophical Investigations* writes: 'Problems are solved (difficulties eliminated), not a *single* problem' (*PI* §133). In a note immediately following that remark, he adds: 'There is not a single philosophical method, though there are different methods, different therapies, as it were'. That word 'therapy' has been asked to shoulder a considerable burden in the secondary literature. My interest here is less on the word itself than the fact that it, with 'method', occurs in the plural. The idea of a central, unifying question that allows us to come to grips with the problems of philosophy wholesale is a characteristic of Wittgenstein's early philosophy that he deliberately moves away from in his later work.[28]

---

[27] We find an even stronger statement of this unifying impulse in Wittgenstein's pre-*Tractatus* notebooks: 'Don't get involved in partial problems, but always take flight to where there is a free view over the whole *single* great problem, even if this view is still not a clear one' (*NB* 23).

[28] Conant (2011) dates this change to 1937 and argues that it marks one of the most significant shifts in Wittgenstein's thinking. The comparison between Wittgenstein and Heidegger on the question of a fundamental question in philosophy is developed in more detail in Kuusela (2018).

Heidegger's effort to tease out the question of the meaning of being indicates that he thinks that there is *something*—one central, all-important question—that we have missed and that our everyday existence is marked by a motivated ignorance of this question. Getting this question into view, then, means ultimately moving beyond the 'average everyday' understanding of our existence that he analyses in Division I of *Being and Time* to a non-average, 'authentic' self-understanding.

It might seem, then, that the fissure between Wittgenstein and Heidegger concerns these issues of authenticity and the everyday. In fact, I think Heidegger's aspiration for an authentic self-understanding is very much manifest in Wittgenstein's later philosophy as well and that the real fissure between them concerns method: what it means to philosophize in an authentic manner. But before I can spell out their similar stances with regard to authenticity (in Part Two) or their differences regarding method (in Part Three), I need to spell out in more detail the parallels in their engagement with the everyday. In the next chapter I look at their treatment of the world of our everyday activities and in Chapter 3 I consider the importance to each of them that this world is essentially shared with others.

2
Being-in-the-World and Forms of Life

2.1. The Analysis of Dasein as Fundamental Ontology

In the previous chapter, we saw that Heidegger wants to raise the question of the meaning of being, and the initial impediment to such a project is that it is unclear how to pursue it. In particular, Heidegger wants to keep his project of fundamental ontology sharply distinct from the ontic sciences, which produce new knowledge about beings. We have a clear picture of what is involved in an investigation of beings; not so with an investigation of being itself.

Heidegger's solution is to take as his starting point not an investigation of being itself but an investigation of the being of a particular kind of being—namely, the being that has an understanding of being—which he calls 'Dasein'. This most famous of all Heidegger's coinages is not in fact a neologism. It is also one of the most likely to go untranslated in discussions of Heidegger. Literally rendered as 'being there', it is most commonly translated in non-Heideggerian contexts as 'existence', although here it differs from *Existenz* in referring not so much to the bare fact of being, but rather to the mode or quality in which someone exists. I might assert the *Existenz* of a paternal aunt, but then talk about the misery of her *Dasein* and how I might alleviate it. Tellingly, we can use *Existenz* to talk about the existence of plants and animals, but would rarely use *Dasein* to refer to the existence of any beings besides humans.[1]

'Dasein', then, is not simply an alternative name for human beings, but indicates the particular way in which our existence is distinctive.

---
[1] I owe this last point to Aleksandra Prica.

Heidegger introduces the term, saying that he will use it to describe '[t]his being, which we ourselves in each case are and which includes inquiry among the possibilities of its being' (BT 7). Dasein is different from other beings in that its being is an issue for it: rocks simply are what they are, whereas *what* Dasein is gets articulated in the living out of its life. We find an eloquent expression of this point in Seamus Heaney's 'Elegy':[2]

> The way we are living,
> timorous or bold,
> will have been our life.

What my life will turn out to have been will be nothing more, and nothing less, than the way in which I live it. The present progressive of the first line is hardened into the future perfect of the third: each fleeting moment is a brushstroke in my evolving self-portrait. In this respect, Dasein's essence is open-ended and open to change, and this openness means that, at every moment, the meaning of our being is in question.

Dasein is distinct from all other beings precisely by virtue of this fact that it relates to itself as a question. Dasein is the being that raises the question about the meaning of being: 'The ontic distinction of Dasein lies in the fact that it *is* ontological' (BT 12).[3] Heidegger's point is not that we *can* interpret our own being but that we *cannot not* interpret our own being. That we relate to ourselves as a question is an 'existential' in Heidegger's terminology: a necessary feature of what it means to be Dasein. We may not pursue Heidegger's project of fundamental ontology thematically, but our existence necessarily exhibits what Heidegger calls a 'pre-ontological understanding of being' (BT 13). How I relate to my own existence is manifest in that existence: how I behave, what projects I pursue, what I prioritize—all these contain an implicit answer to the question of my understanding of the meaning of my own being. Before giving any explicit answer as to how it understands being, Dasein already gives an implicit answer in its practical engagement with the world.

---

[2] I owe my knowledge of this passage, and of its pertinence to Heidegger, to a talk by Denis McManus.

[3] '*Die ontische Auszeichnung des Daseins liegt darin, daß es ontologisch* ist'. A footnote in the Macquarrie and Robinson translation remarks that there is a revealing ambiguity in the German: Heidegger can equally be read as saying that Dasein '*is* **ontologically**'. So we could read this ontological/ontologically as either a property or an activity: 'being ontological' is a characteristic feature of Dasein's way of being and Dasein is such that its existence is something that Dasein lives out 'ontologically', that is, in relation not just to beings but to being.

2.1. THE ANALYSIS OF DASEIN AS FUNDAMENTAL ONTOLOGY

We may not be able to launch a frontal assault on being itself but Heidegger thinks we can approach the question of the meaning of being obliquely through an existential analysis of Dasein's way of being. Dasein is different from other beings by virtue of relating to itself and its world in a questioning manner—and, as we will see shortly, Heidegger defines Dasein as being-in-the-world so that relating to ourselves and relating to the world are really two sides of the same coin. That means that it is not only our *own* being toward which we relate as a question but also toward the being of other beings. Dasein '*is* ontological' in that it relates to the world in a mode of questioning, interpreting, and understanding. We are not simply *there* along with other beings but are constantly engaged in making sense of ourselves and our world. Heidegger calls Dasein a 'clearing' (*BT* 133) because it is only within the space opened up by Dasein that beings are interpreted in their being. This interpretive capacity crucially depends on Dasein's self-understanding: we make sense of how being has meaning for Dasein by grasping how Dasein's world is meaningful to Dasein. 'Thus', Heidegger tells us, '*fundamental ontology*, from which alone all other ontologies can originate, must be sought in the *existential analysis of Dasein*' (*BT* 13).[4]

Because the understanding of being that interests Heidegger is always with us, whether we acknowledge it or not, he takes as his starting point not the thematic self-understanding of human existence that we find in the work of philosophers, but the pre-theoretical understanding with which Dasein engages in the world initially and for the most part.[5]

---

[4] Hubert Dreyfus (1991, 28) cites three reasons that Heidegger gives for taking Dasein as a starting point—that Dasein relates to its being as a question, that Dasein understands itself in terms of its average understanding, and that Dasein's understanding of its being implies an understanding of all modes of being—and argues that none is fully convincing. I am not sure they are meant to be, or could be. Heidegger conceives of his project as a hermeneutic circle: no matter where we start, we will have to take some things provisionally for granted and then circle back to question those assumptions and reconfigure our project in light of this further questioning. If there were rock-solid reasons for taking just this starting point, there would be no reason to circle back and reinterpret it. And indeed, Division II of *Being and Time* can be read as just such a reinterpretation.

[5] This frequent Heideggerism is Stambaugh's translation of *zunächst und zumeinst*. Macquarrie and Robinson have it as 'proximally and for the most part'. *Zunächst* can mean either 'initially' or 'proximally', depending on context, and both translations are appropriate: Heidegger emphasizes that we tend to encounter equipment as ready-to-hand *before* we contemplate it in a disengaged manner (in a hermeneutic sense—see the discussion of priority below), and we encounter it in this way because it is ontically *near* to us (*das ontisch Nächste* (*BT* 43)).

Heidegger's attempt to retrieve the question of being begins by investigating Dasein as being-in-the-world: he begins, that is, by considering Dasein as embedded in and engaged with its world rather than considering it from a position of detached contemplation. Heidegger describes this analysis of practically-engaged Dasein as an analysis of Dasein 'in its average *everydayness*' (*BT* 16). As I observed at the end of the previous chapter, Heidegger begins with the ordinary.

2.2. Readiness-to-Hand and Presence-at-Hand

Heidegger's phenomenology, much like Wittgenstein's later philosophy, draws our attention to things we have passed over because they are already so familiar. For Heidegger, the most familiar beings are the ones whose significance is the most difficult to assess: 'What is ontically nearest and familiar is ontologically the farthest, unrecognized and constantly overlooked in its ontological significance' (*BT* 43). When we consider the nature of an object, bring it to explicit awareness, we abstract it from its surroundings and our own uses for it. This abstraction distorts our pre-ontological understanding of it and makes it difficult to assess its ontological significance.

One basic and easily overlooked aspect of the world is that it shows up to Dasein as meaningful. Dasein's environment is familiar—so familiar that its familiarity rarely even registers. I am sitting in a chair, typing on a laptop that sits on a table in front of me. To my left is a window through which I can see a road with cars, a bridge, electrical wires overhead, and numerous other buildings. The sky is blue and partly cloudy, and the late afternoon sun casts long shadows over the streets while illuminating the trees with a warm, gentle light. All of these observations exhibit a basic understanding of the world I inhabit. The assemblage of wood, leather, and cushioning I am sitting on shows up as a *chair* because my world is one in which chairs have a familiar place and use.

My understanding of the chair is exhibited not in the fact that I can tell you what it is and what it is for (as we will see in section 2.6, giving a definition of 'chair' is a surprisingly tricky business) but in the way that I relate myself to it. This understanding is evident not just in how I relate myself toward the chair on its own—by sitting on it—but how this relationship engages the chair in a broader set of activities. I have pulled the chair up to a table whose height is just right so that, sitting in the chair, I can bend my elbows at a little more than right angles and type comfortably at my laptop. The chair, table, and laptop all have their place in a familiar world in which they are suited to one another and to the task I am engaged in. They also presuppose a natural environment with trees and metals and other materials from which they are assembled.

When we consider what this typing is *for*, a whole new set of connections opens up. Just as the chair shows up as a chair because of the way I relate myself to it, these finger movements count as *typing* because of the way they pertain to a world not just with chairs and tables and laptops but also with books and universities and colleagues. I use chairs because they enable me to pursue a range of other activities—from writing an academic book to eating breakfast—that presuppose certain ends—from engaging in a philosophical conversation to satiating my hunger. These ends are all related to one another—I need calories to philosophize, and the philosophizing pays for the groceries—and also necessarily involve others—ranging from the fact that I write this book in the hopes that others will read it to the fact that I can write on a laptop while sitting at a table because others have given their time and skills to manufacturing these things.

These ends are not just related to one another but also have a definite shape. Taken as a whole, my activities manifest a distinctive understanding of the meaning of my being. I pursue *these* goals, set *these* priorities, arrange my circumstances like *this*, for the sake of realizing particular possibilities of my being. Heidegger calls the broader self-understanding we realize through our activities Dasein's 'for-the-sake-of-which' (*Worumwillen*; *BT* 84). That each person's existence has a definite shape does not mean that we are entirely consistent in our choices. Nor, as any procrastinator can attest, do our actual choices always line up with what we explicitly say our priorities are. But whether we explicitly endorse it or not, our lives have a definite shape and that shape manifests the self-understanding that we actually live out.

The chairness of the chair, then, brings with it a whole world of objects, material, activities, and social relations. Chairs are part of a *world*, the word Heidegger uses for the meaningful environment in which Dasein exists (this is the sense in which Dasein is being-in-the-*world*). Chairs, tables, laptops, and the like show up in this world as what Heidegger calls equipment (*Zeug*) that is ready-to-hand (*zuhanden*) (*BT* 71).[6] Its status as equipment necessarily involves it in a complex system of relations to other equipment and Dasein: 'Strictly speaking, there "is" no such thing as *an* equipment. There always belongs to the being of any equipment a totality of equipment in which this equipment can be what it is' (*BT* 68; translation modified). And this system of relations is ultimately a manifestation of Dasein's self-understanding.

We should be careful not to overstate the extent to which Heidegger is presenting us with a pragmatic picture of Dasein as a tool-using *Homo oeconomicus*, whose primary relation to beings is as resources to be leveraged to Dasein's practical advantage. Heidegger occasionally encourages this line of thought—as when he writes that '[t]he forest is a forest of timber, the mountain a quarry of rock, the river is water power, the wind is wind "in the sails"' (*BT* 70)—but his category of tools (*Werkzeug*) is a subset of the broader category of equipment (*Zeug*). The sun may be a tool for extracting solar power, but it also shows up as ready-to-hand in its non-tool place within the equipmental totality of Dasein's world: '[T]he sun whose light and warmth we make use of every day has its circumspectly discovered, eminent places in terms of the changing usability of what it gives us: sunrise, noon, sunset, midnight' (*BT* 103). Indeed, the German *Zeug* lacks the specificity of the English 'equipment': the word tends to denote an undifferentiated stuff, which gains specificity by being compounded with another word that denotes the kind of stuff it is: *Werkzeug* for tools, *Spielzeug* for toys, etc. Showing up as equipment does not yet entail a tool ready to be manipulated by a practically-oriented Dasein. Heidegger's category of readiness-to-hand

---

[6] On the whole, I find Stambaugh's translation to be more accurate than Macquarrie and Robinson's, but many of her translations of particular items of Heideggerian terminology are inferior to Macquarrie and Robinson's, which have the added advantage of being more familiar in the secondary literature. For instance, Stambaugh's 'useful thing' for *Zeug* is an awkward mouthful, and 'equipment' has the added advantage that, like *Zeug*, it is a mass noun, which is suggestive of its involvement in a totality: we cannot speak of 'an' equipment (cf. *BT* 68, cited below). I also prefer Macquarrie and Robinson's translation of *zuhanden* and *vorhanden* as 'ready-to-hand' and 'present-at-hand' respectively, as they capture the implied contrast between the two terms more neatly than Stambaugh's 'handiness' and 'objective presence'.

illuminates the more general point that Dasein is engaged in a world of beings that show up as familiar.[7]

Our engagement with ready-to-hand equipment is holistic and transparent. This ready-to-hand engagement is holistic in the sense, discussed above, that every item of equipment is essentially connected to a broader network of equipment and activities. Our engagement is transparent in that we see through the equipment we use to the activities we are engaged in. To use a hammer I have to keep my eye on the nail and my mind on the task at hand. My practical engagement with the hammer and nail refers to a holistic context of house-building and shelter and the meaningful existence of which these things are a part, but to the extent that I want to hammer the nail and not my thumb, I had better not give too much of my attention to this broader referential totality.

Because it is transparent, there is a sense in which we do not 'see' equipment when we engage with it. We do not look *at* equipment but rather look *through* it to the task at hand. The philosophical tradition strongly favours this looking at (the Greek word for it is *theorein*, whence we get our word 'theory') but Heidegger emphasizes that our practical engagement with equipment involves its own distinctive form of seeing: in contrast to sight (*Sicht*), Heidegger calls it circumspection (*Umsicht*; BT 69). And circumspection is a manifestation not of our knowledge-seeking gaze but of what Heidegger calls concern (*Besorge*). We 'see' equipment in the sense of circumspection because, in our practical engagement with it, this equipment is of concern to us.

But if the referential totality of our circumspective concern is invisible to theoretical contemplation, how does Heidegger, in a theoretical text, get circumspection into view? In a move that we will see echoed later on in his treatment of anxiety, Heidegger argues that we come to see this referential totality most clearly when things break down. In §16 of *Being and Time*, Heidegger explores various ways our ordinary dealings with equipment can be disrupted—from a tool being damaged in a way that makes it awkward to use to our activity coming to a halt entirely because an essential tool is missing—and claims that these disruptions suddenly

---

[7] Polt (1999, 49–50) emphasizes this point, noting that Heidegger himself subsequently disavowed a strongly pragmatic reading of *Being and Time*: 'It never occurred to me . . . to try and claim or prove . . . that the essence of man consists in the fact that he knows how to handle knives and forks or use the tram' (*FCM* 177).

bring this formerly transparent referential totality into view. If my keyboard were to stop working, I would stop seeing through it to the work I am engaged in, and my attention would be trained more directly on the keyboard itself as a (unhandy) tool. This disruption has a ripple effect: in noticing my keyboard as something that stands in the way of my ordinary activity of typing, I become more aware of what I was trying to do by typing, of the day's plans that will now have to be rethought, and so on. Just as a tool in use slots into a referential totality, so a tool in disuse disrupts the referential totality as a whole. This disruption brings into view what Heidegger calls the 'worldliness' of the world (*BT* 65): the way in which the totality of equipment and Dasein are all linked together as part of a coherent whole.

Such disruptions are one opening to a different kind of encounter with beings: rather than encountering them as ready-to-hand equipment that is entwined in a referential totality constituting a world, we can encounter beings detached from this totality as present-at-hand (*vorhanden*) when we are withdrawn from our ordinary dealings with them. Heidegger talks about a scare-quoted 'world' of present-at-hand beings. In contrast to the holistic world to which Dasein and ready-to-hand equipment belong essentially, this 'world' is a container contingently furnished with present-at-hand beings. Things, on this atomistic view, are what they are independent of how they stand in relation to other things, and independent of how Dasein relates to them.

This 'world' is the world presented to us by the ontic sciences and by traditional ontology.[8] Heidegger's phenomenological description of our everyday world as encountering beings initially and for the most part as ready-to-hand equipment offers a kind of inversion of this traditional ontology. Where a scientific reductionist picture begins with an ontology of elementary particles and forces and builds from there up through chemical reactions to biological organisms to the human social world with its proprieties of behaviour and tool use, Heidegger begins with the Dasein as being-in-the-world among whose possibilities of being is the formulation of a scientific reductionist picture of its world. Rather than treat the norms and values of our concernful dealings with the world as

---

[8] McManus (2012, 62–8) has an illuminating discussion of the question whether the scientist's self-understanding accurately reflects the way in which beings are disclosed through scientific practice.

something added on to a 'world' of bare facts, Heidegger argues that, initially and for the most part, the world is disclosed to a Dasein that is concernfully embedded in it, and that Dasein arrives at a 'world' suitable for scientific contemplation only by withdrawing this concern. 'Sciences and disciplines are ways of being of Dasein in which Dasein also relates to beings that it need not itself be', Heidegger tells us. 'But being in a world belongs essentially to Dasein' (*BT* 13).

A further reason for taking ready-to-hand equipment as his starting point is that Heidegger believes he can account for how we retreat from engagement with equipment to the detached contemplation of the ontic sciences, but an ontology that takes all beings as primarily present-at-hand cannot account for readiness-to-hand. This claim is at least contestable: scientific research has hardly found itself at a loss in terms of explaining our practical engagement with the world, much as we might question its success. More fundamentally, however, Heidegger claims that an ontology of present-at-hand objects cannot escape from the sceptical problematic, which cannot even arise within the terms he lays out. I return to this point when I engage with Heidegger's discussion of realism and idealism in Chapter 7.

The tradition has passed over this world of Dasein concernfully engaged with ready-to-hand equipment precisely because this engagement is transparent. The contemplative mood in which we pursue ontological investigations detaches us from our everyday dealings with things, and in this state of detachment, we encounter things as present-at-hand. We turn from the *Umsicht* of circumspection to the *Sicht* of theoretical contemplation. The irony of turning our philosophical attention to ready-to-hand equipment is that, Medusa-like, we turn it into a collection of inert present-at-hand objects in doing so.[9] As a result, we tend to characterize beings, and the world we find them in, as present-at-hand, since that is how they appear to us when we contemplate their nature and seek to characterize it.

---

[9] The weight of this 'turn it into' is controversial. When we see a being as ready-to-hand at one moment and then as present-at-hand at the next, are we seeing the *same* thing under two different aspects or two metaphysically distinct things? The former seems to be the majority view in the secondary literature, but McDaniel (2013) provides a compelling argument for the latter view.

Heidegger's investigation of the worldliness of the world invites a conceptual inversion similar to the inversion experienced in seeing the two different aspects of the Necker cube. The Necker cube is a simple line drawing of a cube with no depth cues to indicate which face is in the foreground and which is in the background. Whichever face we see as foregrounded, we are still in some sense looking at the 'same' picture, but our entire orientation toward the picture shifts with the shift in aspect. Similarly, Heidegger is not trying to press on us new information in his account of a world of interrelated ready-to-hand equipment but is rather asking us to invert the aspect under which we see this world—namely, to see this holistic world of ready-to-hand equipment of our circumspect concern as prior and the atomistic 'world' of present-at-hand objects of theoretical knowledge as derivative. And although we do not thereby 'see' anything we could not see before, our apprehension of the whole is transformed through the shift in aspect.

2.3. The Question of Priority

That Heidegger wants to afford some sort of priority of readiness-to-hand over presence-at-hand seems fairly clear. But clarifying the nature of that priority reveals that matters are far less straightforward than we might initially suppose. To begin with, what sorts of categories are readiness-to-hand and presence-at-hand and what sort of priority is the former supposed to have over the latter? One of the aims of Heidegger's phenomenological-ontological project is to reveal the inadequacy of traditional philosophical categories, so reading him as drawing an epistemological or metaphysical distinction, or inverting an epistemological or metaphysical priority, would seem not to go deep enough. Heidegger's prioritization of readiness-to-hand over presence-at-hand is not the epistemological claim that we must do something akin to Heideggerian phenomenology before we can do ontic science. Nor is it a metaphysical claim: Heidegger is not telling us that the objects we thought of as present-at-hand are in fact ready-to-hand instead. His purpose is not simply to invert the metaphysical categories we have become accustomed to but rather to call those categories themselves into question.[10]

---

[10] Heidegger discusses the traditional use of *res*—and its limitations—at *BT* 68. Mulhall (2005b, 42) argues that we should not read the ready-to-hand/present-at-hand distinction

We find firmer footing with the claim that readiness-to-hand has priority over presence-at-hand in terms of the ontological project of grasping the meaning of being that I discussed above. The ontic sciences give us rich and detailed knowledge of various beings, but they cannot reveal why these beings are intelligible to these particular sciences in the way that they are. The ontic sciences provide various kinds of understanding, but Heideggerian phenomenology is interested in the conditions for the possibility of such understanding. We must already be in a world animated with ready-to-hand equipment if we want to understand these beings in the ways that the various ontic sciences make available to us. This priority is not a chronological priority, in the sense that readiness-to-hand is disclosed to Dasein first in temporal sequence.[11] The priority is rather a hermeneutical one: the disclosure of a worldly world of ready-to-hand equipment is a condition for the possibility of the disclosure of a 'world' furnished with present-at-hand objects.

This hermeneutical priority of readiness-to-hand over presence-at-hand can be misunderstood in two ways. First, we should not take this priority to show that, whereas it is essential to Dasein's world that it encounters ready-to-hand equipment, the disclosure of presence-at-hand things is inessential and accidental. Brandom criticizes what he calls a '"layer cake" model, according to which there could be Dasein and *Zuhandensein* [being-ready-to-hand] without *Vorhandensein* [being-present-at-hand], which arises from them only if Dasein adopts certain optional practices and practical attitudes' (Brandom 2002, 328).[12] Brandom argues instead that presence-at-hand is just as essential to Dasein's having a world as readiness-to-hand: Dasein's existence essentially involves language, which in turn essentially involves the assertions that disclose beings as present-at-hand. Brandom shares roughly the picture sketched above of the priority of readiness-to-hand

---

as metaphysical. On the other hand, McDaniel (2013) provides an intriguing argument for understanding presence-at-hand and readiness-to-hand as metaphysical categories after all, and argues that Heidegger sees the ready-to-hand as metaphysically dependent on the present-at-hand.

[11] Both Carman (2003, 196) and McManus (2012, 69) emphasize this point.

[12] Above I cited a passage that might seem to contradict Brandom here: 'Sciences and disciplines are ways of being of Dasein in which Dasein also relates to beings that it need not itself be. But being in a world belongs essentially to Dasein' (*BT* 13). But I do not think Heidegger's point here contravenes Brandom's. Ontic science is surely an 'optional practice' for Dasein, even if *some* sort of encounter with beings as objects of assertion is not.

over presence-at-hand—he calls it an 'explanatory priority' (Brandom 2002, 332)—but reminds us that the explanatory posteriority of presence-at-hand does not make the disclosure of presence-at-hand any less essential to Dasein's existence.

Second, we should bear in mind that this hermeneutical priority of readiness-to-hand over presence-at-hand is part of Heidegger's analysis of *average everyday* Dasein. Beings are disclosed to us as ready-to-hand *initially and for the most part*, which does not necessarily mean that these beings are primordially or fundamentally ready-to-hand.[13] Joseph Fell (1992) notes in particular that the disclosure of beings in anxiety—which will enter my discussion in more detail in Chapter 4—reverses the priority of average everyday disclosure, and notes that Heidegger uses 'presence-at-hand' in at least three distinct senses, whose priority with respect to readiness-to-hand is relative to different forms of disclosure.

The different senses of presence-at-hand that Fell disentangles raise a further issue, which is that it is far from clear exactly what it means to encounter a being as present-at-hand. McManus (2012, 53–6) distinguishes thirty-six different accounts of presence-at-hand from Heidegger and his interpreters, ranging from what is unintelligible (*HCT* 217–18) to what is revealed by interpretation (*BT* 61–2). Rouse (1985) and Blattner (1995) both argue that scientific investigation is itself an engaged way of dealing with the world, so that the beings disclosed by ontic science should count as every bit as much ready-to-hand as the beings disclosed through our everyday dealings. On this view, the category of readiness-to-hand expands so as to swallow entirely the category of presence-at-hand, leaving this latter as an empty and confused notion that Heidegger could have done without. This last point shows that, as our sense of the contours of the present-at-hand shift, so, accordingly, does our sense of the contours of the ready-to-hand.

Part of the difficulty we encounter with the ready-to-hand/present-at-hand distinction, I think, is that readiness-to-hand is what Austin (1962, 70–1) calls a 'trouser word'. In the pairing of these two expressions, 'readiness-to-hand' is the one that 'wears the trousers'. That is, Heidegger gives primary attention to the ready-to-hand as an overlooked form of

---

[13] Cf. Fell (1992, 66): 'Heidegger has more than one notion of primacy, and clearly the interpreter of *Being and Time* must not conflate what is "first [initially] and for the most part" with what is "fundamental" or "primordial" (*ursprünglich*)'.

disclosure, and then consigns a range of different ways beings might be disclosed as *not* ready-to-hand—as damaged tools, as objects of scientific investigation, as bare things stripped of their ordinary familiarity by our anxious apprehension—as disclosing beings as present-at-hand. Given its use as a term of contrast, we should not be surprised if we cannot find any tight unity to Heidegger's conception of presence-at-hand.

2.4. Wittgenstein, Cavell, and Criteria

At the end of section 2.2 I noted that getting into view the holistic world of ready-to-hand equipment demands a conceptual inversion similar to seeing the different aspects of the Necker cube illusion. Rather than approach human existence as an object of scientific investigation under the lens of anthropology, psychology, or biology, Heidegger invites us to consider scientific investigation as itself a manifestation of one aspect of Dasein's being (*BT* §10). Wittgenstein's investigations involve a similar shift. He encourages us to see our concepts as interconnected and structured by an understanding of our lives and our world. And, like Heidegger, he thinks that we need not new information but a Necker-like conceptual aspect shift in order to see these things.[14]

In section 1.4, I argued that standards of correctness apply *within* language-games but that we have no standard independent of our language-games by which to judge whether the language-games themselves are correct or incorrect. This idea of language-games as giving us standards for correctness finds rich articulation and complication in Cavell's discussion of criteria, which he views as central to Wittgenstein's conception of ordinary language: '[W]hat philosophically constitutes the everyday *is* "our criteria" (and the possibility of repudiating them)' (Cavell 1989, 51).[15]

To say that criteria articulate the standards for the correct use of words is not to say that the use of words is everywhere governed by rules that can be given explicitly and without exception. Cavell imagines a tribe

---

[14] Braver (2012, chap. 3) develops the connections between Wittgenstein and Heidegger with regard to their shared holistic orientation toward our engaged practical activity. And Guignon (1990, 657–8) also argues that Wittgenstein and Heidegger are alike in inverting the traditional order of philosophical explanation.

[15] See also Cavell 1990, 68: '"[O]ur criteria"... articulate the ordinary'.

that uses a strange plank with handles that leaves us uncertain as to whether we should call it a chair (Cavell 1979, 71) and Wittgenstein imagines a chair that vanishes and reappears seemingly at random (*PI* §80). Our criteria for using a word are no more precise or exhaustive than the contexts in which we learn the word and apply it in future cases—and so we cannot exhaustively specify the criteria for misusing a word, and hence for speaking nonsense, either. Criteria are not a set of fixed rules that dictate how we must go on in every conceivable case and Wittgenstein's conceptual investigations are as much concerned with where our confidence in our criteria breaks down as with where it holds together.

Cavell develops his conception of criteria over the course of Part One of *The Claim of Reason*, and explains the distinctive role of criteria in Wittgenstein's later philosophy in contrast with the role of criteria in common discourse, and with the role it finds in the philosophy of J. L. Austin.

Criteria ordinarily determine the standards by which a group evaluates an object of assessment. For instance, the size of the splash as the diver enters the water is a criterion for judging a dive, but the colour of the diver's swimsuit is not. Criteria in diving competitions facilitate evaluative judgments. We know what a dive is, and we have a rough sense of what a beautiful dive is, so the criteria codify evaluations we are already somewhat competent in making.

Austinian and Wittgensteinian criteria apply to words: criteria specify the circumstances in which words or phrases are used, when they are called for, when they are appropriate, what it makes sense to want to say with them, and so on. For instance, Austin warns us not to assume that any action whatsoever can be described either in terms of one adverb ('voluntarily') or its opposite ('involuntarily'), reminding us that both adverbs have particular, and not exactly complementary, criteria for their use (Austin 1979c, 191–3).[16] Unlike the ordinary conception of criteria, Austinian and Wittgensteinian criteria do not help us judge how well a word was used (how well a dive was performed) but rather give us the conditions under which a word is used *simpliciter*.

The difference between Austinian and Wittgensteinian criteria hinges on a distinction Cavell draws between specific and generic objects.

---

[16] I examine Austin's method in more detail in section 2 of Egan (2018).

A specific object—like a goldfinch or an elm or a Louis XV *chaise*—is a species of a more general type. Differentia pick out the specific object from other objects of its genus, and we can know what genus an object belongs to without knowing the criteria that distinguish it from other objects of its genus. I know that goldfinches are birds, for instance, and although I can distinguish a goldfinch from an ostrich or a crow, I lack the specialized knowledge that would distinguish a goldfinch from, say, a linnet. Austin's criteria tend to apply to such specific objects—the goldfinch example, for instance, finds extensive application in Austin's paper 'Other Minds'.

Wittgensteinian criteria, by contrast, apply to generic objects—like birds or trees or chairs—where no question of specialized knowledge arises. Understanding these criteria is a prerequisite for saying or understanding anything with the word at all. Wittgensteinian criteria cover the fact that birds are animals, that they have wings and feathers and lay eggs, that, as animals, they are the sorts of things that are alive and can die but cannot be rebooted or asserted, that they can look at us but cannot smoulder with jealousy as they do so. Where Austinian criteria help us identify things, Wittgensteinian criteria make things available to us *as* things in the first place:

If you do not know the (non-grammatical) criteria of an Austinian object (can't identify it, name it) then you lack a piece of information, a bit of knowledge, and you can be told its name, told what it is, told what it is (officially) called. But if you do not know the grammatical criteria of Wittgensteinian objects, then you lack, as it were, not only a piece of information or knowledge, but the possibility of acquiring any information about such objects *überhaupt*; you cannot be told the name of that object, because there is as yet no *object* of that kind for you to attach a forthcoming name to: the possibility of finding out what it is officially called is not yet open to you. (Cavell 1979, 77)

One consequence of this emphasis on generic objects is that it draws attention to the ways in which concepts are interconnected. With specific objects, we face a problem of identification: I already know what a bird is and I know that a goldfinch is a bird but I need to know which specific concepts attach to goldfinches in order to identify them from amongst other similar birds. Knowing how to talk about birds, however, is not so much a matter of having specific knowledge but of knowing how that concept fits into our larger web of concepts. According to Cavell, Wittgensteinian criteria do not relate a name to an object, but, we might say, various concepts to the concept of that object. Here the test of your possession of a concept... would be your ability to use the concept in conjunction with other concepts, your knowledge of which concepts are relevant to the one in question and which are not; your knowledge of how various relevant concepts, used in conjunction with the concepts of different kinds of objects, require different kinds of contexts for their competent employment.   (Cavell 1979, 73)

Wittgenstein's grammatical investigations examine the complex ways in which concepts intersect with one another—and how quickly our use of a given concept is thrown into confusion when we imagine alterations to the circumstances in which it is at home. For example, starting at *PI* §138, Wittgenstein launches an investigation of the concept of understanding. Over the sections that follow, he considers how the concept of understanding intersects with a number of others—of fitting, pictures, mistakes, rules, mental states, mechanisms, knowledge, ability, and so on. The discussion flows into an extended discussion of reading, and subsequently into an even more extended discussion of rule following. Wittgenstein's investigations flow in this way—as he puts it in the Preface to the *Investigations*, they 'travel criss-cross in every direction over a wide field of thought' (*PI*, p. 3)—because he does not treat concepts piecemeal but rather considers the ways in which they are connected.[17]

2.5. Forms of Life

Wittgenstein often uses the metaphor of a mechanism to show how our words and concepts are interconnected:[18] we understand a part of a larger whole by considering how it connects to other parts, and what these parts accomplish in moving together. For instance, at *PI* §6, Wittgenstein notes that a brake requires not just a connection between rod and lever, but also integration into a larger mechanism upon which it acts as a brake: 'Only in conjunction with that is it a brake-lever, and

---

[17] Cf. *Z* §465/*RPP* II §311: 'The treatment of all these phenomena of mental life is not of importance to me because I am keen on completeness. Rather because each one casts light on the correct treatment of *all*'. See also Diamond (2004) for a more detailed treatment of Wittgenstein's 'criss-cross philosophy'.

[18] E.g. *PI* §§6, 12, 193–4, 270–1, 559. We have to be careful in reading Wittgenstein's use of the machine metaphor, though, as he also frequently uses it to exemplify a kind of automatism in our thinking that he wishes to overcome.

separated from its support it is not even a lever; it may be anything, or nothing' (*PI* §6). This analogy with a mechanism, like the analogy with games, invites us to think of our concepts in connection with how they are put to use.

Wittgenstein wants us to consider our concepts from the perspective of the activities in which they are used and, conversely, he sees philosophical confusion arising when we detach a concept from the activities where it has a use. For instance, at *PI* §88, Wittgenstein puts forward 'Stay roughly here' as an explanation that could 'work perfectly' under some circumstances—if it serves its purpose, what more can we ask of it? His interlocutor finds this an 'inexact explanation' and pushes for something more exact. Wittgenstein asks in what way such an explanation is inexact and how it might be rendered more exact. He considers the possibility of drawing a boundary line in chalk to delineate the region he means by 'here'. But even so, the chalk line has a thickness, and so the region could be more exactly defined. And there remains the question of what constitutes overstepping the region—how much of the foot must cross this line, how that should be measured, and so on. 'But has this exactness still got a function here', Wittgenstein asks, and invokes the metaphor of a mechanism. '[I]sn't it running idle?'

This image of a mechanism idling belongs to a family of Wittgensteinian terms of criticism. We also find images of a mechanism idling at *PI* §132 and §507. In all three cases, the German is *leerlaufen* or *leerliefen*, literally 'running emptily', *leer* being the German word for 'empty'. So these moments of idling connect to the criticism that the expressions we use are in some way empty (e.g. *PI* §§107, 131, and 414), a notion that echoes the remark that 'philosophical problems arise when language *goes on holiday*' (*PI* §38), and in the repeated concern that the expressions we want to use seem to have lost the significance we wanted them to have.[19] The concern is that, under a certain kind of philosophical pressure, the expressions we want to use no longer do the work they are expected to do. And we can see that something has gone off the rails when we consider the work a given concept is meant to do.

In the context of offering explanations, exactness has a function because explanations can be misunderstood, and exactness is one way

---

[19] See, e.g., *PI* §§57, 63, 142, 345, 385, 398, 449, 493.

of preventing or removing misunderstandings. 'Stay roughly here', with a vague hand gesture, may be enough to be understood—or it may not, in which case some supplemental explanation that is more exact might be called for. We can even imagine circumstances where an exactingly precise chalk outline is called for: suppose I am testing out my new teleportation device, which is exquisitely sensitive to the location of the teleportee. Planting the feet by even a millimetre from the intended spot could have catastrophic consequences. But now my chalk outline has a use. If, by contrast, I just want to indicate to a friend in an airport lounge where I will look for her when I return from the toilet, the chalk outline has no use: it makes no difference to the ease with which I find my friend. Untethered from any actual purpose, the demand for exactness spins free. And just as a gear that comes detached from a mechanism starts spinning wildly, so the demand for exactness spins into a demand for infinite, 'ideal exactness' (*PI* §88) when that demand is no longer doing any work: '[A] wheel that can be turned though nothing else moves with it is not part of the mechanism' (*PI* §271).

Acknowledging that a concept like explanation has a use means acknowledging that explanation is a *practice*. In thinking about explanation, it helps to remember that we use this concept, that there is an activity—namely the activity of explaining things—that has a role in our lives. Creatures that never explained things and never sought explanations from others would have very different lives from the ones we have. To get clear on what an explanation is, it helps to consider what else must be in place for explanations to have a use—to consider how explanation connects to other parts of the mechanism. For example, we would not need to explain things if people never risked misunderstanding things, or one another, and we would not try to explain things unless our explanations were at least sometimes—fairly often, in fact—successful in resolving misunderstandings. Explanation has a role in the lives of creatures that sometimes misunderstand things, and whose misunderstandings are sometimes resolved.

Wittgenstein's conceptual investigations do not just situate concepts in their relations to other concepts and in their contexts of use but also in what he calls the 'forms of life' in which they have a use.[20] It is this last

---

[20] See *PI* §§19, 23, 241, *PPF* i §1, *PPF* xi §345, *RFM* VII §47, *OC* §358.

2.5. FORMS OF LIFE

point that is missed in the view—less influential now than it once was—that Wittgenstein's later philosophy provides an account of meaning in terms of assertion conditions, in contrast to a truth-conditional theory allegedly found in the *Tractatus*.[21] Diamond criticizes this account precisely because it neglects the place of our assertions within our life as a whole. To treat the meanings of expressions in terms of their assertion conditions, Diamond says, assumes that these conditions are 'explicable independently of what the life is like within which the asserting goes on' (Diamond 1989, 14). To list the conditions under which we are entitled to use the word 'fear', for instance, does not explain 'how the commerce with the word "fear" is interwoven with the rest of the lives of the people who use the word' (Diamond 1989, 15):[22]

> To give an account of meaning in terms of assertion-conditions is to remain with our eyes fixed in the wrong direction. A sound that people came out with when certain conditions were fulfilled would not be a word meaning fear; it is also most unclear why it might be thought that this was a word at all, or that what these people were doing was asserting. (Diamond 1989, 15)

Diamond is concerned that Dummett and others leave out something crucial about our traffic in language. They focus on the circumstances in which utterances are made without considering the life in which those circumstances have significance. As a result, they have nothing to say about *why* we have the language we have, why, for instance, our language might mark subtle distinctions between fear, terror, horror, and dread: what sorts of creatures feel the need to draw just *these* kinds of distinctions? Accounting for this question requires giving something more like what Wittgenstein calls 'remarks on the natural history of human beings' (*PI* §415).[23]

This emphasis on the forms of life in which words have a use echoes Heidegger's conception of a totality of equipment that is structured by

---

[21] This view originates with Dummett (1959, 358), and finds influential expression in Kripke (1982, 73). See also Wright (1980, chaps. 12 and 13).

[22] Wittgenstein makes a similar point with regard to pain at *Z* §§532–4.

[23] We find other references to natural history at *PI* §25, *BB* 98, *Z* §469, *RPP* I §78, 950, 1109, *RPP* II §§15, 18, *RFM* I §§63, 142, *RFM* II §40, *RFM* IV §§11, 13, *RFM* VI §49, *RFM* VII §17, and *PPF* xii §365. This last passage complicates the idea that the facts of natural history are what matters to Wittgenstein, 'since we can also invent fictitious natural history for our purposes'. That Wittgenstein brings clarity to our forms of life by deploying fictitious 'objects of comparison' (*PI* §130) receives extended treatment in Chapter 8.

the relevance and significance of Dasein's world. As I noted earlier, a chair shows up to me as a *chair* because it has a role in my life in coordination with other equipment. And the variety of roles it has points to a broader 'for-the-sake-of-which' that is a distinctive possibility of my being. Chairs show up as chairs, in other words, in the context of a life that has a distinctive shape and significance.

Similarly, language-games involving chairs, fear, or what have you are part of a life that has a distinctive form. Wittgenstein's emphasis on our use of words is no more crudely pragmatic than Heidegger's emphasis on our use of tools. The answer to the question of what a given word or tool is useful *for* ultimately points back to a more general question of the significance of the life in which the word or tool is used. One way of putting this point is to say that our criteria are not simply *given to* us but are *expressive of* us. Diamond takes as a launching point for the discussion I cited above Rhees's (1970a, 45) remark that Wittgenstein wants to '[s]how how rules of grammar are rules of the lives in which there is language'. A grammatical investigation in this respect is essentially an investigation of what Heidegger calls Dasein's being-in-the-world.

2.6. Words and the World

I have been arguing that Wittgenstein's treatment of language-games, criteria, and forms of life has the same holistic character as Heidegger's analysis of the worldliness of the world, and that the character of equipment for Heidegger and the character of our concepts for Wittgenstein ultimately manifest a broader understanding of the meaning of our being. Despite these similarities, one important difference seems to stand out: Heidegger talks about equipment and Wittgenstein talks about language. Or, to put it another way, Heidegger is oriented toward the *world* whereas Wittgenstein is oriented toward *words*.

But the idea that Wittgenstein's project is essentially concerned with the philosophy of language is related to the misapprehension that his criteria essentially give us the assertion conditions for expressions. Wittgenstein is not concerned with the meanings of words *rather than* with the world those words are about. This misreading would portray him as simply changing the subject on the metaphysician: where the metaphysician wants to investigate the essence of things, Wittgenstein redirects our attention toward the uses of words. But Wittgenstein does not disown the metaphysician's project 'to understand the foundations, or essence, of everything empirical' (*PI* §89), but rather refigures it. For instance, he writes of the imagination:

> One ought to ask, not what images are or what goes on when one imagines something, but how the word 'imagination' is used. But that does not mean that I want to talk only about words. For the question of what imagination essentially is, is as much about the word 'imagination' as my question. (*PI* §370)

Immediately following this remark, he famously writes: '*Essence* is expressed in grammar' (*PI* §371). For Wittgenstein, a grammatical investigation of a word simply *is* an investigation of the essence of the world.

We risk misreading this remark if we characterize Wittgenstein's grammatical investigations too straightforwardly as a substitute for what metaphysical investigations were supposed to offer us. Where metaphysics sought the essence of the world in a realm of metaphysical facts, this reading goes, Wittgenstein seeks the essence of the world in a realm of grammatical rules. For instance, Hacker glosses 'Grammar tells what kind of object anything is' (*PI* §373) as: 'The nature or essence of anything is given by rules of grammar which determine the application of an expression, for they fix the concept in question' (Hacker 1990, 441). The role of grammatical rules, on this reading, is that they are the source of our criteria. This reading brings Wittgenstein uncomfortably close to offering against the metaphysician an alternative thesis about the source of necessity, which contravenes the claim in *PI* §128 that such disputes over theses can get no purchase in philosophy. But perhaps more worrisome for the present discussion, it draws the rules of grammar apart from the lives in which they find expression, proposing for grammar something close to Dummett's assertion conditions. To suggest that our concepts are 'fixed' by rules of grammar presents these rules as distinct from the concepts we use, dictating their application as it were from without, and leaves little room for these concepts to be given shape by the shifting needs of the people who use them.

It helps to bear in mind the question that is always central to Wittgenstein's investigations: how a word is used. If we learn what essence is by investigating the way that the word 'essence' is used, we should read *PI* §371 to be telling us something about the use of that word. Not: 'Essence [as such] is expressed [not in the fundamental structure of the world, but rather] in grammar', but rather: '[In your attempts to pick out what we describe as] Essence[, you will find that nothing gets an explanatory hold beyond a description of what] is expressed in grammar'.[24] This reading has Wittgenstein identifying the kind of investigation that will help us think productively about essences—namely, a grammatical one—without giving the concept of grammar itself any explanatory heft.[25]

In his discussion of criteria, Cavell emphasizes that, for both Austin and Wittgenstein, looking at how we use words does not mean looking at words *rather than* looking at the world.[26] Criteria articulate words and world together. But in Cavell's own philosophical evolution—from the early influence of Austin to an approach that takes its bearings primarily from Wittgenstein—we see the distinctive inflection this thought acquires in Wittgenstein's focus on generic objects. In an early paper, Cavell invites us to consider what we learn when we look up 'umiak' in a dictionary: do we learn what 'umiak' means or do we learn what an umiak is (Cavell 1976a, 19)? Cavell's answer to this question is 'either':

> If this [finding out about the world by looking in a dictionary] seems surprising, perhaps it is because we forget that we learn language and learn the world *together*, that they become elaborated and distorted together, and in the same places.... When we turned to the dictionary for 'umiak' we already knew everything about the word, as it were, but its combination: we knew what a noun is and how to name an object and how to look up a word and what boats are and what an Eskimo is. We were all prepared for that umiak. What seemed like finding the world in a dictionary was really a case of bringing the world to the dictionary.... [T]he learning is a question of aligning language with the world. What you need to learn will depend on what specifically it is you want to know; and how you can find out will depend specifically on what you already command.
> (Cavell 1976a, 19–20)

---

[24] Baker (2004b, 246–7) draws attention to the italics in '*Essence* is expressed in grammar', taking these italics to mean that Wittgenstein is self-consciously avoiding making a dogmatic claim about essence as such.

[25] Cf. Kuusela (2008, 212): 'The concept of grammar does not explain what makes something essential or necessary, but questions about essences and necessities can be clarified by way of grammatical observations'. Kuusela (2008, chap. 5) offers an extended discussion of Wittgenstein's views on essence and necessity that engages critically with Hacker's reading. I return to the question of how to understand Wittgenstein on necessity in section 3.2.

[26] We have seen Wittgenstein make this point at *PI* §370. Austin makes similar claims at Austin (1979a, 58), (1979b, 83n2), and (1979c, 182).

In this early essay (he first presented a shorter version of it in 1957), Cavell is very much under Austin's influence, and he illustrates his point with the example of a specific object. His answer to the question of what we learn when we learn a word—what a thing is or what a thing is called—is 'either'. In *The Claim of Reason*, Cavell recognizes that the answer could just as well be 'neither' (Cavell 1979, 170): a dictionary helps us to identify a specific object like an umiak, but if we lack the concept for a generic object, a dictionary might not help. Cavell considers the example of a chair:

> There are technical handbooks which give us the features of various types and periods of furniture... but none which teach us what a chair is and what sitting on a chair is. None, we might say, which illustrate the essence of the matter.... [W]e are to recollect those very general facts of nature or culture which we all, all who can talk and act together, do (must) in fact be using as criteria; facts we only need to recollect, for we cannot fail to know them in the sense of having never acquired them. If someone does not have them, that is not because his studies have been neglected, but because he is for some reason incapable of (or has been given up on as a candidate for) maturing into, or initiation into, full membership in the culture. (Cavell 1979, 72-3)

Compare the definitions the *Oxford English Dictionary* provides for 'umiak'—'A large Eskimo boat, consisting of a wooden frame with skins drawn over it, and propelled by paddles'—and 'chair'—'A seat for one person (always implying more or less of comfort and ease); now the common name for the movable four-legged seat with a rest for the back, which constitutes, in many forms of rudeness or elegance, an ordinary article of household furniture, and is also used in gardens or wherever it is usual to sit'. The definition of 'umiak' is clear, to the point, and tells us what we need to know. With the definition of 'chair', we feel the lexicographer floundering, offering a definition that uses a near synonym ('seat': if you don't know what a chair is, are you likely to know what a seat is?), draws on inessential features (not all chairs have four legs), and is more than twice as long as the definition of the less familiar word. If you don't already know what a chair is, we can feel the lexicographer shrugging, looking it up in the dictionary isn't going to help you.

Perhaps rather than 'neither' or 'either', we could answer the question of what we learn when we learn a word—what a thing is or what a thing is called—with 'both'. Looking in a dictionary will not help us if we do not already know what a chair is, but a child who learns the word 'chair' does not learn *either* what the word 'chair' means *or* what a chair is, but rather learns both of these things together. We find this point in Cavell as well:

> In 'learning language' you learn not merely what the names of things are, but what a name is; not merely what the form of expression is for expressing a wish, but what expressing a wish is; not merely what the word for 'father' is, but what a father is; not merely what the word for 'love' is, but what love is. In learning language, you do not merely learn the pronunciation of sounds, and their grammatical orders, but the 'forms of life' which make those sounds the words they are, do what they do—e.g., name, call, point, express a wish or affection, indicate a choice or an aversion, etc. (Cavell 1979, 177–8)

To know what a chair is means knowing, among other things, what a chair is *for*, and that means being acquainted with the forms of life in which chairs are used. One common use of chairs is that we sit on them at a dining table. Understanding that use of chairs is tied up with understanding the dining habits of a particular group, which in turn bring with them distinctive notions of fellowship, sharing, inclusion and exclusion, servitude and hierarchy, and so on. In saying this, I am not setting an impossibly high bar for claiming to know what a chair is—as if you cannot properly be said to know what a chair is if you have just arrived in a Western dining room from a culture in which one eats cross-legged on the ground—but rather to show that the word 'chair' has a use because chairs have uses, and we learn these uses together.

This argument—that we learn words and the world together—is ultimately one consequence of acknowledging the unavailability of a sideways perspective on our practices, which I discussed in section 1.4. I argued there that there is no coherent question as to whether 'our' concept of rivers accurately represents rivers-as-such. To suppose that we could ask such a question would be to suppose that we can think about rivers-as-such without thinking about (with 'our' concept) of rivers. One upshot of the exercise is that the scare-quoted 'our' drops out of the picture: in thinking about rivers, we are not 'only' thinking about 'our' concept of rivers, since there is no non-perspectival alternative. Granted, we could devise different grammatical rules for talking about rivers—say the Heraclitean rule according to which 'I stepped into the same river yesterday and again today' is incoherent—but there is no extra-conceptual perspective from which we could compare different ways of talking about rivers and adjudicate which one more accurately represents the thing—a river—itself. When it comes to talking about essences, then—to talking about what a river, say, *really* is—there is no further metaphysical fact beyond the grammatical facts of how we talk about rivers. In investigating how we use the word 'river', we are also investigating *what rivers are*.

The comparison with Heidegger helps us see that a grammatical investigation of the concept of rivers points in two directions. On one hand it gives rivers a place in our discourse and on the other it reveals something about us. We have the concepts we have because those concepts are used and those uses are aspects of a life that has a certain coherence and significance. It is not *simply* arbitrary that our grammar allows us to talk about the 'same' river across time. This way of talking has a certain usefulness to people whose lives with rivers—fetching water, navigating, fording, swimming—involve a certain regularity. If people never fetched water from the same river more than once, say, we would have one less reason to find it convenient to talk about 'the same river' that we stepped into yesterday.

In a number of places, Wittgenstein writes about our grammatical rules as arbitrary, although he also hedges this claim.[27] The rules of language are arbitrary in the sense that they cannot be more or less 'true to the facts'. Comparing the rules of language to the rules of cookery, Wittgenstein remarks:

You cook badly if you are guided in your cooking by rules other than the right ones; but if you follow other rules than those of chess you are *playing another game*; and if you follow grammatical rules other than such-and-such ones, that does not mean you say something wrong, no, you are speaking of something else.

(Z §320)

We cannot be 'wrong' in our grammar but our rules are not entirely arbitrary in the sense alluded to in the previous paragraph. That we follow *these* rules, observe *these* regularities, register *these* similarities reveals the distinctive patterns of interest and senses of significance that give our lives their distinctive shapes. In questioning whether our rules of grammar are entirely arbitrary, Wittgenstein remarks:

It is not every sentence-like formation that we know how to do something with, not every technique that has a use in our life; and when we are tempted in

---

[27] For statements of the arbitrariness of grammar, see, for example, *PI* §§372, 497, 508 or *Z* §320 and §331. Wittgenstein resists a full-throated endorsement of the arbitrariness of grammar at *PI* §520 and *Z* §358.

philosophy to count something quite useless as a proposition, that is often because we have not reflected sufficiently on its application. (*PI* §520)

In proclaiming the arbitrariness of grammar, Wittgenstein wants us to see that our grammar is not beholden to some realm of fact external to our language. But grammar is non-arbitrary in that it *is* beholden to the people who use it.

Cavell (1979, 186–8) interprets the claim from *PI* §371—that essence is expressed in grammar—as 'retrieving' the concept of essence from the impulse to detach it from our lives. Heidegger's analysis of the worldliness of Dasein's world enacts a similar retrieval. Chairs, rivers, and so on have the ready-to-hand character that they have by virtue of being integrated parts of an equipmental totality, and this totality is structured by its significance to Dasein's possibilities of being. In that respect, *what* a chair is—namely, a ready-to-hand item of equipment with relations to tables, meals, and work, among other things—is reflected in what Dasein is—namely, a being that relates to itself and its world in a questioning manner.

These sorts of claims risk sounding like a form of transcendental or linguistic idealism. Is Heidegger, and by extension Wittgenstein, saying that the being of beings is dependent on the being of Dasein? I will respond to a transcendental idealist reading of Wittgenstein in the next chapter but I can only fully address this worry once I have said a great deal more about both authors' methodological commitments in Part Three. My next step is to consider another feature of the everyday world that both Wittgenstein and Heidegger examine: that we share it with others. Our concepts and equipment are not simply *used* but are used similarly across a community. How to give weight to this point is the source of considerable disagreement in the secondary literature on Wittgenstein and bringing Wittgenstein into contact with Heidegger adds yet a further wrinkle: for Heidegger, an unreflective absorption in shared practices is a mark of inauthenticity. In the next chapter, I provide an account of Wittgenstein's treatment of our shared practices that follows from the interpretation I have presented so far and I explore the echoes in Heidegger's treatment of being-with. And then in Part Two I turn to the question of authenticity and inauthenticity and articulate and defend an interpretation of an 'authentic' Wittgenstein.

3
Attunement and Being-With

In the previous chapter, we saw that Wittgenstein and Heidegger picture the human world as having a distinctively human shape: the ways in which our concepts and equipment are related to one another reflect the uses that we have for them, and these uses in turn manifest a more general understanding of the significance of our lives. Both of them also maintain that we articulate the significance of concepts and equipment, and of our lives more generally, in concert with others. The precise nature of this shared world is a fraught issue for both philosophers and will ultimately bring to the forefront the theme of authenticity, which will be the central concern of the remainder of this book. I begin by examining Wittgenstein's treatment of our shared world and then turn to the tensions and puzzles raised by Heidegger's.

3.1. Attunement

Wittgenstein remarks on the agreement that structures our forms of life, and distinguishes this agreement from agreement in opinions: 'What is true or false is what human beings *say*; and it is in their *language* that human beings agree. This is agreement not in opinions, but rather in form of life' (*PI* §241). The German word translated as 'agreement' here is *Übereinstimmung*, and the difference between the agreement in form of life and the agreement in opinions that Wittgenstein mentions here can be understood in terms of a distinction between two German expressions that can be translated as 'agree': *übereinstimmen* and *einverstanden sein*. This latter is the kind of agreement Wittgenstein mentions at *PI* §128: 'If someone were to advance *theses* in philosophy, it would never be possible to debate them, because everyone would agree [*einverstanden wären*] to them'. *Einverstanden sein* is the kind of explicit agreement that people reach particularly with regard to propositions: you assert that *p* and in my agreement I express my assent to the truth of *p*. *Einverstanden sein* is an agreement between people but *übereinstimmen* need not be. This is the kind of agreement we might describe when a mark conforms to a larger pattern: an accord between two items rather than an explicit agreement between two people. The word is sometimes translated in the *Investigations* as 'accord' as well as 'agree' and Wittgenstein uses it synonymously with 'harmony' at *PI* §429.[1]

Wittgenstein encourages us to see not just the agreements but also the disagreements between people—the agreements and disagreements of *einverstanden sein*—as manifesting a deeper agreement—in the sense of *übereinstimmen*—in form of life. We can also express this point by rephrasing *PI* §241 in terms of language-games: it is *within* language-games that people say things that count as true or false, and they agree (in the sense of *übereinstimmen*) in the language-games that they play. Explicit agreement and disagreement (in the sense of *einverstanden sein*) are moves within a language-game, and we only speak to one another in agreement or disagreement when we are playing the same language-games. That we play the same language-games is not something we arrive at through explicit agreement because explicit agreement occurs only when we are already playing the same language-game.

This agreement in language-games is part of a pervasive agreement in form of life: we share enough common ground that our lives are intelligible to one another. That we can exchange opinions at all, whether to agree or disagree, means we recognize each other's opinions as opinions, and share a sense of what it means to have an opinion, to form one, to shift one, and so on. Much of the common ground we share is so basic that we scarcely notice it.

Cavell (1979, 32) calls this agreement in form of life 'attunement': what I say not only reaches you, but resonates in you. In an oft-cited passage, he elaborates on this attunement as

a matter of our sharing routes of interest and feeling, modes of response, senses of humour and of significance and of fulfilment, of what is outrageous, of what is similar to what else, what a rebuke, what forgiveness, of when an utterance is an

---

[1] *Übereinstimmung/übereinstimmen* is translated as 'accord' or one of its derivatives at *PI* §§186, 201, 224, 271, 352, 465, 607 and as 'agree' or one of its derivatives at *PI* §§134, 139, 234, 241, 242, 386, 416, 429, 442, 538, 594. '*In Übereinstimmung*' is translated as 'consistently' at *PI* §492.

assertion, when an appeal, when an explanation—all the whirl of organism Wittgenstein calls 'forms of life'. (Cavell 1976b, 52)

A practice like explanation—to return to an example I discussed in section 2.5—is a part of the life we share with one another: we share a sense of what circumstances call for explanation, what kinds of explanation are called for, are required, are adequate. In drawing our attention to our attunement with one another, Wittgenstein reminds us that language has a place—and has a point—within the broader weave of human life. Appeals to 'ordinary' language, or to how expressions are 'ordinarily' used, then, invite us not simply to consider the standard usage of a given expression, but to reflect upon the role that expression has in our lives, and how in turn the contours of our lives come into view when we consider that we are the kinds of creatures that have a use for such an expression.

Cavell introduces the passage above by pointing out that nothing ensures this attunement, and follows it by remarking that '[h]uman speech and activity, sanity and community, rest upon nothing more, but nothing less, than this. It is a vision as simple as it is difficult, and as difficult as it is (and because it is) terrifying' (Cavell 1976b, 52). This vision is terrifying because our attunement is not itself the kind of thing that can be justified in a way that would assure us that it has a stable foundation or grounding.[2] On the contrary, the practice of justification is a manifestation of our attunement: among other things, we are the sorts of creatures that justify things to one another, and share a sense of when justifications are called for, what sorts of justifications are acceptable and what are not, and so on. The practice of justification is one aspect of the lives we share with one another, and there is no position outside of that life—no sideways perspective on that life—from which we can ask whether these forms of life are themselves justified.[3] Justifying attunement would be as circular as justifying the practice of justification itself. This vision is difficult because it demands a shift of aspect in our thinking, much like the aspect shift we experience when looking at the Necker cube illusion, where background becomes foreground and vice

---

[2] In Part Two, I connect this 'terrifying' aspect of Wittgenstein's vision with Heidegger's account of anxiety.

[3] Cf. *PI* §486: 'Was I justified in drawing these consequences? What is *called* a justification here? — How is the word "justification" used? Describe language-games! From these you will also be able to see the importance of being justified'.

versa. This shift of aspect reverses the expected order of investigation, seeing the practice of justification as a manifestation of attunement rather than treating attunement as something we need to account for through the practice of justification.[4]

Wittgenstein gives voice to this difficulty early in *Philosophical Investigations*: 'Explanations come to an end somewhere' (*PI* §1). Philosophy traditionally has been in the business of providing rock-bottom explanations, giving the final word on why things are the way that they are. In pushing us to see explanation itself as a practice, as a manifestation of our attunement, and this attunement as itself not subject to explanation, Wittgenstein's investigations seem to fall short of the difficult questions. Why do we find ourselves in agreement? What grounds this agreement? What grounds our language-games? How do these language-games accord with reality? But for Wittgenstein, the real philosophical difficulty is to stop without this feeling of having stopped short:

> Here we come up against a remarkable and characteristic phenomenon in philosophical investigation: the difficulty—I might say—is not that of finding the solution but rather that of recognizing as the solution something that looks as if it were only a preliminary to it. 'We have already said everything. — Not anything that follows from this, no, *this* itself is the solution!'
>
> This is connected, I believe, with our wrongly expecting an explanation, whereas the solution of the difficulty is a description, if we give it the right place in our considerations. If we dwell upon it, and do not try to get beyond it.
>
> The difficulty here is: to stop. (*Z* §314)[5]

We can describe the language-games that we play—we can say '*this is the language-game that is being played*' (*PI* §654)—but the urge to *explain* our language-games leads us astray. We saw this pursuit of an explanation where no explanation is needed with the case of the Heraclitean philosopher in Chapter 1, who took her dissatisfaction with ordinary language to be a disagreement over facts. The idea that one way of talking about rivers or another might be justified by appeal to the way things *really* are is an attempt to justify our language-games. Metaphysical

---

[4] I discuss the Necker cube as an illustration of Heidegger's analysis of Dasein's world at the end of section 2.2 and connect it to Wittgenstein at the beginning of section 2.4. Wittgenstein talks about 'putting the cart before the horse' [*falsch aufgezäumt*] in a similar connection (*Z* §542 and *RPP* I §917).

[5] See also *PI* §§654–5 and *RPP* I §723.

explanations are what we proffer when we succumb to the temptation to explain where Wittgenstein wants us to stop.

3.2. Wittgenstein's 'We'

Wittgenstein's exhortation to stop short of the kind of explanation we feel we need can feel as dogmatic as his insistence against the Heraclitean philosopher—which I discussed in Chapter 1—that one *can* step into the same river twice. To begin with, we should note that Wittgenstein himself recognizes that stopping with descriptions rather than explanations is difficult. And it seems especially difficult when considering the community of language users who are attuned in their forms of life. The first person plural appears frequently in *Philosophical Investigations*—for instance, Wittgenstein wants to draw our attention to 'the *kinds of statements* that **we** make about phenomena' (*PI* §90). Wittgenstein is interested not in empirical research, but in discovering 'what is possible *before* all new discoveries and inventions' (*PI* §126), so his 'we' is not an empirical 'we'—not an anthropological entity that could be captured through surveys or field studies. But then who is this 'we', and what role does it play in Wittgenstein's investigations?

Wittgenstein's 'we' relates to the concept of necessity. Wittgenstein often invokes the first person plural to draw attention to features of grammar: not contingent matters of fact, but the form by which we represent matters of fact. For instance, at *PI* §199 Wittgenstein asks of 'what **we** call "following a rule"' whether it is something 'it would be possible for only *one* person, only *once* in a lifetime, to do?' Wittgenstein answers no: following a rule is a custom, and we only make sense of the concept of a rule or of following it because rule following is a common practice in our lives. To regard the impossibility of one person obeying one rule only once as a *factual* impossibility would be to suppose that there is a clearly imaginable activity—imagine a person following a rule, now suppose that this is the first and only time anyone has ever followed that rule—that Wittgenstein declares could *never* happen. But the point of seeing it as a *grammatical* impossibility is to say that no imaginable activity could correctly be described as 'a person obeying one rule only once'. (The aim of many of Wittgenstein's investigations is to take an expression that we *think* describes an imaginable scenario and to push us to the point of recognizing that no imaginable scenario corresponds to that expression.)

The 'we' at *PI* §199 retrieves the concept of necessity from the supposition that necessity is grounded in a domain of metaphysical facts. In reflecting on what 'we' say or do, Wittgenstein's grammatical investigations describe the ways in which our concepts are interrelated. Remove the concept of a rule from its connections with concepts like regularity and correctness, and we lose our grip on the concept.

But then this 'we' might be seen as simply locating an alternative ground for necessity: necessities are to be found not in our stars but in ourselves. Near the end of section 2.5, I touched on what might be called a conventionalist reading of Wittgenstein that we find in diverse forms in Dummett, Wright, and Kripke. Dummett's Wittgenstein embraces a 'full-blooded conventionalism', whereby 'the logical necessity of any statement is always the *direct* expression of linguistic convention' (Dummett 1959, 329). What we take to be logically necessary, on this view, is due to individual conventions and nothing more. Wright also emphasizes the importance of communal agreement, claiming that our concept of correctness is relative to a community: 'None of us unilaterally can make sense of the idea of correct employment of language save by reference to the authority of securable communal assent on the matter; and for the community itself there is no authority, so no standard to meet' (Wright 1980, 220). Kripke's Wittgenstein, as we have seen, proposes that we think of meaning instead in terms of assertion conditions or justification conditions (Kripke 1982, 74): rather than ask whether a rule is followed *correctly*, we should ask under what conditions we are licensed to follow a rule in a particular way; and the answer, it turns out, is that it depends on the agreement of a community.

The account of necessity that these authors give in terms of communal convention treats our attunement as a matter of empirical fact and takes that fact to be the basis for other facts. Four is the sum of two and two, no object can be coloured red and green in the same place at the same time, rivers are perdurable across time, and so on *because* we happen to share linguistic conventions that constitute things so. This interpretation misreads Wittgenstein in two crucial respects. The first is that it 'obliterates', as Wittgenstein puts it, 'the distinction between factual and conceptual investigations' (*Z* §458). The community of language users and rule followers that the conventionalist envisages is an empirical entity: it so happens that there exist in the world these communities that agree in these ways. Presumably, different communities could be differently constituted, and working through these matters would be a matter for empirical linguists and anthropologists, not philosophers.

The second problem with the conventionalist reading is that it treats our attunement as some *thing* that exists as a kind of condition for the possibility of our various practices, as if we are able to agree and disagree, explain and justify, play, quarrel, love, build cities, and do philosophy *because* we share this separate thing called attunement that binds all these activities together. But our attunement is not distinct from these activities. Our attunement does not *ground* our shared activities, but rather these shared activities *manifest* attunement.[6] Our engagement in shared activities that manifest attunement simply is what it means to share forms of life. In that sense, we cannot appeal to our attunement to *account for* our statements of necessity any more than we can appeal to lightning to account for the flash of light we see in the sky: the flash simply *is* the lightning.[7]

An alternative reading of Wittgenstein as a transcendental idealist— advocated by Bernard Williams (1981) and Jonathan Lear (1982, 1984)— criticizes the conventionalist reading on the first point, but shares with it the second problem.[8] Lear thinks our attunement should be understood not as an empirical fact about an actual community but as an expression of what he calls our 'mindedness': we share 'perceptions of salience, routes of interest, feelings of naturalness' (Lear 1982, 385). Lear takes Wittgenstein's discovery of our mindedness as 'a transcendental insight' (Lear 1982, 387): not an empirical fact, but a discovery of a different order. This reading, then, also treats our attunement as a kind of ground for our shared practices, a transcendental fact by which we can account for our agreement in criteria and forms of life.[9]

---

[6] Warren Goldfarb distinguishes his reading of Wittgenstein on rules from that of Kripke along similar lines: 'Agreement is exhibited in rule following, but does not ground it' (Goldfarb 1985, 485).

[7] The example comes from Nietzsche ([1887] 1998, 25).

[8] A. W. Moore (1985) also explores this transcendental reading, although he shows greater scepticism about finding transcendental idealism in the later Wittgenstein. Moore (2007) later claims Wittgenstein rejects transcendental idealism, but struggles against the powerful temptation to adopt it.

[9] Mulhall (2008) offers a detailed critique of the transcendental reading that focuses on Williams. He arrives at two conclusions that I endorse in this book: first, as I will argue

3.3. Wittgenstein and Necessity

Both conventionalist and transcendental readings of Wittgenstein place him in disagreement with the metaphysician. Like the metaphysician, the conventionalist and transcendental readings of Wittgenstein treat statements of necessity as statements of fact, but account for them differently: they state facts about communal convention or transcendental 'mindedness' rather than metaphysical truth. Contrary to the reading I offered in Chapter 1, these readings take ordinary language to commit us to the perdurability of rivers across time, only they construe this commitment as a commitment enshrined in linguistic convention or shared 'mindedness' rather than as a matter of metaphysical discovery. It is because these readings treat statements of necessity as statements of fact that there seems to be something here to be explained: what makes these facts obtain?

But, as I emphasized in Chapter 1, Wittgenstein's aim is not to prove the metaphysician wrong but to reach an understanding of the metaphysician's words such that no disagreement remains. His grammatical investigations aspire to reach this understanding. I will not here conduct a thorough investigation of the concept of necessity, but I will attempt to sketch an outline of the way in which we might see beyond the disagreement between the conventionalist and the metaphysician.[10] If we understand our concept of necessity not as something to be accounted for, but as a manifestation of an attunement that is not subject to explanations, the space for disagreement dissolves.

Let me describe how we use statements of necessity. The concept of necessity works in connection not just with other modal concepts, but also with a broader set of ideas about justification and agreement. Propositions that we consider to be necessarily true admit of no empirical confirmation or disconfirmation, we treat their truth as independent of our will, and so on. We take necessary truths to hold across time and

---

shortly, the position that Williams attributes to Wittgenstein cannot so much as find coherent expression; and second, Wittgenstein's use of 'we' is far less uniform and confident than Williams supposes.

[10] Kuusela (2008, chap. 5) examines the concept of necessity in greater detail and also argues that Wittgenstein does not want to ground necessity in conventional, transcendental, or grammatical facts. His primary target is a conventionalism that he associates with Hacker.

cultures: different political practices may suit different people differently but there is no room for preference or opinion in arithmetic. To the extent that we can justify them, we justify them by appeal to other propositions we take to be necessarily true. And with the most basic propositions of this kind, justification seems to bottom out in self-evidence. We have little more to say to the wayward pupil of *PI* §185—who follows the rule 'Add 2' after 1000 with 1004, 1008, ... —than 'Look what you're doing!' and 'But can't you see . . . ?' I cannot give *reasons* why bachelors are unmarried: if you do not already know this, then you do not know what a bachelor is (what 'bachelor' means).

These descriptions bring out the forms of life in which the concept of necessity is used: they describe what we are like such that the concept of necessity is salient to us. Neither the conventionalist nor the metaphysician would dissent from these descriptions. Nor would they disagree that we use the word 'necessary' to describe propositions of this sort. They would further agree that propositions describing what sorts of practices are natural to us, what customs we observe, how we use words, and so on are not propositions of this sort: we consider our forms of life to be contingent because we can—and often do—imagine them otherwise. And this, Wittgenstein wants to tell us, is all the story there is to tell.

An account of the necessity of mathematical truths amounts to a description of our mathematical practices, and the inexorability with which we insist that mathematics leaves no room for deviation or debate. In taking the laws of logic to be inexorable, 'it is *we* that are inexorable in applying these laws' (*RFM* I §118).[11] The conventionalist might want to seize on this description and insist that mathematical truth is therefore relative to the practices in which the concept of mathematical truth finds application, and is therefore conventional. But such insistence misfires, since the description tells us just the contrary: what we call necessary is precisely *not* relative to our practices, and if we regarded so-called necessary propositions as relative to our practices, we would not describe them as inexorable. To try to extract a conventionalist message from this description is to try to regard this description from sideways on, to invoke once again McDowell's turn of phrase: it supposes that we can

---

[11] See also *Z* §299.

regard our concepts from a perspective to which those descriptions do not apply. But these descriptions are descriptions of the life in which our concepts are used. A description of how we use the concept of necessity is a description of what necessity *is*. If we abandon that description in trying to talk about necessity, it is no longer necessity that we are talking about.

The metaphysician might want to seize on the same description as evidence that Wittgenstein does not appreciate that the truth of necessary propositions is independent of what we say or do, but such a claim misfires as well. The description does say necessary propositions are independent of what we say or do. However, Wittgenstein is also no metaphysician: he describes how we use certain concepts, but does not say anything about what these concepts *really* correspond to, since there is no 'really' to grope toward beyond these descriptions.

Cavell (1979, 118) describes Wittgenstein's as 'an anthropological, or even anthropomorphic, view of necessity', and acknowledges the disappointment such a view may engender:

> ... as if it is not really *necessity* which he has given an anthropological view of. As though if the a priori has a history it cannot really be the a priori in question.—'But something can *be* necessary whatever *we* happen to take as, or believe to be, necessary'.—But that only says that we have a (the) concept of necessity—for it is part of the meaning of that concept that the thing called necessary is *beyond our control*. (Cavell 1979, 119)[12]

The sense of disappointment, and the disagreement between the conventionalist and the metaphysician, arises from the confused notion that our concepts have a reality independent of the forms of life in which we use them. To speak about an independent reality, we would have to step outside our forms of life, and hence step outside ourselves, and such ecstasies are not for the sober philosopher.

In resisting the idea that our attunement can or needs to be accounted for, I have been resisting the temptation to treat our attunement as a matter of fact, as something over and above our shared practices that serves to ground them. But there is another problem with trying to account

---

[12] As Kuusela (2008, 332n50) points out, there is nothing particularly special about the concept of necessity in this regard. It is not that the concept of necessity belongs to a certain class of concepts—namely the anthropomorphic ones, or the ones that have a history—but rather that what Cavell says about necessity here is true of *all* concepts.

for our attunement. Any such account would act as a kind of guarantee: we find ourselves in agreement *because* such-and-such. But, along with his reminder that we find ourselves in agreement, Wittgenstein wants to remind us that such agreement is not guaranteed. I will endeavour to give this point its appropriate weight in Part Two. But to understand its importance, I now turn to Heidegger's treatment of our communal agreement. Heidegger's analysis of being-with and *das Man* raises the prospect of authentic and inauthentic modes of existence and, I will propose, authentic and inauthentic modes of philosophizing. Which of these two modes is manifest in Wittgenstein's philosophy depends crucially on how we read his understanding of our attunement.

3.4. Being-With and *das Man*

Division I of *Being and Time* offers an analysis of what Heidegger calls Dasein's 'average everyday' existence. Both words in the phrase 'average everydayness' carry their own crucial inflections. 'Everydayness' draws our attention to those features of Dasein's existence that we pass over because their familiarity makes them inconspicuous. In the previous chapter, we saw that Heidegger gives hermeneutical priority to a 'worldly' world in which we encounter beings as a holistic totality of ready-to-hand equipment that is responsive to the uses that Dasein has for it. This world is 'visible' to the circumspection (*Umsicht*) of our practical concern (*Besorge*) but for precisely this reason it becomes invisible to the disengaged theoretical gaze of the philosopher. We circumspectly 'see' the everyday world by engaging with it and we withdraw our engagement when we step back from it to theorize about it.

To understand how this everydayness can be 'average'—and to consider the possibility of a non-average everydayness—we must come to grips with another crucial feature of Heidegger's analytic of Dasein: the fact that we are not Dasein alone, but exist essentially in this world *with* other beings that have Dasein's mode of existence. Just as we encounter equipment initially and for the most part *as* equipment, and not as present-at-hand objects whose significance we must subsequently infer, we encounter other people initially and for the most part as Dasein, and not as the sealed-off enigmas that the problematic of scepticism about other minds presents to us. I do not encounter other individuals and then infer that they are people rather than automata; instead, I encounter other people as other people and only subsequently can I even entertain the possibility that they might be automata rather than people.

Heidegger tells a story about our encounter with other Dasein that parallels the story he tells about equipment. The philosophical tradition has a tendency to treat all beings as having the same kind of being—presence-at-hand—but that is because the philosophical tradition looks at all beings with the same detached, theoretical gaze. But that theoretical looking (*Sicht*) is a privative mode of seeing that becomes available only when we step back from our everyday engagement with the world. The practical 'looking' of circumspection (*Umsicht*) discloses equipment as ready-to-hand and similarly we 'see' other Dasein initially and for the most part not through theoretical contemplation but through considerateness (*Rücksicht*) and tolerance (*Nachsicht*) (*BT* 123).[13] And just as the readiness-to-hand of equipment is 'visible' to circumspection because we have a particular way of relating to equipment that Heidegger calls 'concern' (*Besorge*), other Dasein are 'visible' to considerateness and tolerance because we have a distinctive way of relating to others, which Heidegger calls 'solicitude' (*Fürsorge*) (*BT* 122).[14] In our everyday dealings, we not only do not treat other Dasein as bare things, we also do not treat them as equipment to be manipulated.

The traditional conception of the self as an isolated consciousness is inadequate on Heidegger's view because Dasein comes into its Daseinhood as being-with-one-another: the 'who' of everyday Dasein is not the isolated individual, but the individual constituted by its social existence. Being-with is an essential feature of Dasein's existence—an 'existential' in Heidegger's jargon—because it is a condition for the possibility of the kind of articulated, intelligible world that is characteristic of Dasein. Each of us makes sense of the world in our own way, but the very notion of making sense of the world in the first place, as well as the concepts with which we make sense of the world, are things we articulate together.

If being-with is constitutive of Dasein's existence, then Dasein's existence is largely constituted by features that are not uniquely its own. One

---

[13] Subsequently, Heidegger talks about considerateness without mentioning tolerance. We should not place much weight on the specific connotations of either word. Heidegger's interest in these words is less a matter of their specific connotations and more with finding parallel -*sicht* constructions to pair with the *Umsicht* of circumspection.

[14] I am using Macquarrie and Robinson's translation here. *Fürsorge* is 'concern' in Stambaugh's translation.

feature of equipment's readiness-to-hand is that it is ready-to-hand for others as well. A shoe is only a shoe if—*pace* Cinderella—anyone with the same sized foot can wear it. My shoes are available to me *as* shoes only insofar as they are available as shoes to others as well. This promiscuous availability is part of what makes a shoe a shoe: it is available to many people indiscriminately because there is a way that *one wears shoes* that applies the same to everyone.

Brandom notes that, unlike present-at-hand objects, ready-to-hand equipment essentially comes with norms for correct use: there are *right* and *wrong* ways to wear a shoe, hammer a nail, and so on. 'Whereas what is *vorhanden* has *properties*', Brandom writes, 'what is *zuhanden* has *proprieties*' (Brandom 2002, 76). If we think about Brandom's proprieties as anything that is subject to evaluative assessment, the categories of correct/incorrect are probably unduly limiting. It is not simply that we can hammer a nail correctly or incorrectly but also gracefully or awkwardly, efficiently or inefficiently, and so on. As Austin (1979c) observes, the range of evaluative adverbs that we can apply to actions is large, and the subtle distinctions between them are sometimes very important.

Heidegger observes that these various dimensions of assessment share an often unvoiced presupposition of what *one* does with a given item of equipment—the averageness of the average everyday. Heidegger gives the name of *das Man* to this 'one' that seems to tell us what 'one' does.[15] *Das Man* is not an individual, nor a group, nor even a particular mode of existence—a point I will argue below—but, as Carman has it, 'the impersonal normative authority underwriting the social practices that make things intelligible on a mundane level' (Carman 2003, 138). *Das Man* does not simply articulate the norms according to which one wears shoes, but renders shoes intelligible as shoes in the first place: only because there are proprieties for how 'one' wears shoes do shoes show

---

[15] Both Stambaugh and Macquarrie and Robinson translate this term as 'the "they"', which renders unsatisfactorily a term for which there is no good English equivalent. *Man* is the German impersonal third person singular, the same as 'one' in English, but translating *das Man* literally as 'the one', as Dreyfus (1991) and Carman (2003) do, carries confusingly Messianic connotations. However, as Dreyfus (1991, 152) points out, 'we' or 'anyone' fail to 'capture the normative character of the expression. *We* or *Anyone* might try to cheat the Internal Revenue Service, but still, *one* pays *one's* taxes'. I leave *das Man* untranslated, but bring out the implications of Heidegger's usage by using verbs with either the impersonal third person singular or the passive voice: *das Man* speaks to what 'one does' or what 'is done'.

up as equipment rather than as arbitrary assemblages of leather, canvas, and rubber. *Das Man* is not an individual, nor a group, but it 'articulates the referential context of significance' (*BT* 129). By highlighting the existential role of being-with and *das Man*, Heidegger emphasizes that the intelligibility of Dasein's world involves sharing and shaping this intelligibility in concert with others. This claim is stronger than simply saying that I am inevitably a creature of my times. I am not simply *of* my times, but in an important sense, I *am* my times: the social norms of my milieu are a constitutive feature of who I am, even if I react against them. The idea of the sovereign individual is not so much false as incoherent on this picture: part of what it means to be Dasein is to be a socially constituted being, so a being *not* constituted by *das Man* would *not* be Dasein. We could say that Heidegger has an externalist conception of the self.[16]

What I have said here about being-with and *das Man* has some clear affinities to the idea of attunement I articulated at the beginning of this chapter.[17] And indeed, the emphasis that Wittgenstein and Heidegger both place on the social aspect of human language, thought, and activity is the commonality that has probably received the greatest emphasis in the secondary literature that compares the two.[18] Because this work for the most part uses Wittgenstein to clarify an aspect of Heidegger's thought, it does not often consider a challenge that arises when we read in the opposite direction—namely, that Heidegger's unflattering remarks about Dasein's 'lostness' in *das Man* might apply equally to Wittgenstein's socially-constituted subject. To this point, I have presented *das Man* in fairly neutral terms—and indeed, Heidegger repeatedly insists that his ontological descriptions do not convey value judgments.[19] But I will now argue that we have reason to suspect that Heidegger finds something deeply problematic about *das Man*, in a way that poses a challenge to Wittgenstein as well.

---

[16] Carman (1994 and 2003) describes Heidegger as a 'social externalist'.
[17] 'Attunement' is also commonly given as a translation for Heidegger's term *Befindlichkeit*. This sense of 'attunement' is different from the kind I emphasize in this book—and which I have borrowed from Cavell—and the two senses should not be confused.
[18] See, e.g. Brandom (1994 and 2002), Rorty (1979 and 1993), Schatzki (1993 and 2013) and Taylor (1985 and 1995). Dreyfus (1991) makes frequent reference to Wittgenstein in developing his account of everyday social practices in Heidegger, and we find a similar strategy in Carman (2003), Guignon (1983), and Haugeland (1982).
[19] See e.g. *BT* 43, 50, 138, 152, and 175.

3.5. Interpreting Heidegger on *das Man*

Given the affinities between Heidegger's account of *das Man* as a set of impersonal norms that make our shared world intelligible and Wittgenstein's emphasis on our attunement in shared forms of life, we should find it worrying that Heidegger sees in *das Man* a problematic tendency toward inauthenticity.[20] When we talk about what *one does*, we talk about something that is done not because one has decided to do things this way, but because this is how things *are done*. The passive voice is revealing: we identify with *das Man* passively rather than actively choosing our own course. In our average everydayness, Heidegger suggests, we allow our actions and opinions to be dictated to us by what 'one' does or thinks, such that we become 'lost in the publicness of *das Man*' (*BT* 175). Heidegger characterizes this lostness in terms of 'a *flight* of Dasein from itself as an authentic potentiality for being itself' (*BT* 184): he contrasts the '*authentic self*' with the '*one-self*',[21] characterizing the former as 'the self which has explicitly grasped itself' and the latter as both '[t]he self of everyday Dasein' and '*dispersed* in *das Man*' (*BT* 129). In identifying with the one-self, we fail to grasp our lives as our own— *Eigentlichkeit*, the German word translated as 'authenticity' has at its root *eigen*, or 'own'—and so not as something for which we are ultimately responsible. In according ourselves with what 'one does', we do not simply choose not to find our own way of doing things, but we avoid acknowledging that there is even a choice there to be made.

Heidegger's discussion of *das Man* is notoriously confusing and inconsistent. It is one thing to say that shoes are available to many others indiscriminately, and another thing altogether to say that we subsume our actions and opinions to groupthink. Hubert Dreyfus (1991, 154) argues that Heidegger's discussion of *das Man* fails to distinguish between conformity and conformism. Talking about the 'dictatorship' of *das Man*, Heidegger describes the conformism it induces: 'We enjoy ourselves and have fun the way *one* enjoys oneself. We read, see, and judge literature and art the way *one* sees and judges' (*BT* 126–7). The sorts of judgments that involve conforming with popular views on

---

[20] This section and the next adapt, in compressed and modified form, ideas first published in Egan (2012).
[21] Here and elsewhere, I modify the translation to render *man* as 'one' instead of 'they'.

literature and art are a far cry from the sorts of agreement that are constitutive of our social existence. The latter kinds of agreement are what make discourse possible at all; the former are the sorts of matters over which we can debate, agree, and disagree because of the fundamental agreements of the latter kind. The basic conformity that is constitutive of our social existence opens up a space for engaging in the kinds of inquiry that are characteristic of Dasein; conformism with popular opinions closes that space down. This contrast between conformity and conformism echoes the distinction we saw at the beginning of this chapter between the agreement of *einverstanden sein* and the agreement of *übereinstimmen*. Dreyfus raises the question whether Heidegger has confused these two forms of agreement.

This tension is present in Heidegger's text as well. On one hand, he presents being-with and *das Man* as existentials, essential constituents of Dasein's existence, to which no valuation, positive or negative, can be attached.[22] But on the other hand, Heidegger's avowed neutrality with regard to what he calls 'deficient' modes of existence is very difficult to square with the language that he uses. As if 'deficient' and 'inauthentic' were not themselves laden with negative value judgment, he also refers to inauthentic Dasein as 'lost' and 'fallen', among other things, in language that ranges in its associations from psychoanalytic notions of repression and self-denial to theological notions of sin. The initial discussion of *das Man* in §27 of *Being and Time* uses particularly strong language. Heidegger refers to the 'averageness' of *das Man*, saying it

watches over every exception which thrusts itself to the fore. Every priority is noiselessly squashed. Overnight, everything that is primordial is flattened down

---

[22] Actually, even on this point Heidegger is unclear. Certainly, in §27 of *Being and Time*, where Heidegger introduces *das Man*, he speaks of it as an existential: 'das Man *is an existential and belongs as a primordial phenomenon to the positive constitution of Dasein*' (*BT* 129). Later, Heidegger makes the priority of *das Man* over authentic Dasein even more explicit: 'Authentic being-a-self shows itself to be an existentiell modification of *das Man*, which is to be defined existentially' (*BT* 267). Puzzlingly, Heidegger later still seems to say the reverse: 'The one-self is an existentiell modification of the authentic self' (*BT* 317). This later point is bolstered by a passage that seems to reject the earlier discussion as provisional: '*The existential analytic of Dasein up to now cannot lay claim to primordiality*. Its forehaving never included more than the *inauthentic* being of Dasein, of Dasein as *less than whole*' (BT 233). I am grateful to Aaron James Wendland for drawing my attention to some of these passages.

as something long since known. Everything won through struggle becomes something to be manipulated. Every mystery loses its power. The care of averageness reveals, in turn, an essential tendency of Dasein, which we call the *leveling down* of all possibilities of being. (*BT* 127; translation modified)

If Heidegger truly wants to present the notion of *das Man* free from any condemnatory language, he does a spectacularly bad job of it.

One way to focus our attention on the various forms of conformity and conformism that Heidegger seems to characterize as manifestations of *das Man* is to consider the range of activities that have the normative structure that Brandom characterizes as 'proprieties'. If *das Man* comprises those activities that we can assess as being done in some way rightly or wrongly, an exhaustive catalogue would include features that constitute a mere conformity to the most basic structures of intelligibility as well as features that constitute the most craven conformism. I offer below a classification of the sorts of norms and forms of behaviour comprised by *das Man*, more in order to provide a sense of the diversity such norms and forms of behaviour than to provide a comprehensive taxonomy:

(a) *Agreement in definitions*: That we agree for the most part in the uses of words, and can correct misuses of words, is constitutive of language. Without such agreement, there is no language.

(b) *Agreement in basic judgments*: The sorts of propositions that interested G. E. Moore and the Wittgenstein of *On Certainty*: that the earth has existed for more than five minutes, that I have hands, and so on. That is, the sorts of propositions about which agreement is necessary before rational debate can even begin.

(c) *Use of equipment*: Equipment is ready-to-hand for any Dasein indiscriminately, and there are particular ways in which one uses hammers, wears shoes, turns doorknobs, etc.

(d) *Social and historical situatedness*: One's particular cultural and historical situation opens up certain possibilities, makes certain options live, and closes off other possibilities that might be open to other people at other places and times. I can coherently pursue a career as a plumber or a statistician but not as a samurai or a warp drive engineer.

(e) *Coordination principles*: What side of the road one drives on is largely arbitrary, but it is important that everyone in a given country drive on the same side of the road to avoid collisions. A great deal of our social life depends on such simple conventions.[23]

(f) *Social rules*: Some conventions are imposed by authority. Social rules range from laws and other official rules to norms like 'Don't address your teacher by his or her first name'.

(g) *Moral norms*: Between the ages of five and eight, children learn to distinguish social conventions from moral norms, the former drawing on authority, and the latter holding independent of any authority (one characteristic of psychopathy is the failure to recognize the difference). While one only pays one's taxes because the government requires it, one is expected not to need the imposition of authority in order to keep one's promises.

(h) *Relations to kin and non-kin*: One of the central areas of interest to anthropologists is the kinship structures within a society: who counts as family and what sorts of relations are appropriate between different members of one's family. We can include here also one's relations to those outside one's family structure: how one relates to strangers, and what levels of intimacy are appropriate in what circumstances.

(i) *Etiquette*: In the West, one greets with a handshake or a kiss on the cheek; in Japan, one greets with a bow. Principles of etiquette are somewhat weaker than moral norms, but still shape and ease a great deal of social interaction.

(j) *Ceremonies*: From religious rituals to birthday parties, we have various ceremonial means of expressing and affirming our solidarity, and there are more or less strict guidelines for how one participates in such ceremonies.

(k) *Common wisdom and proverbs*: No centralized authority dictates that a stitch in time saves nine or that a rolling stone gathers no moss, but these sorts of proverbs encode a shared sense of appropriate or prudent conduct.

(l) *Behaviour appropriate to specific roles*: Particular occupations have their own particular norms and principles: that one turn out the lights and lock up if one is the last to leave the office, that

---

[23] Lewis (1969) is the *locus classicus* for discussions of such coordination games.

one leave the driver's area tidy for the next bus driver, and so on. The same can be said for the various non-professional social roles that people take on, whether it be behaviour appropriate to one's class, gender, age, and so on.

(m) *Common modes of thought, behaviour, and feeling*: A very broad class, which can include everything from what one thinks of a film to what one feels on hearing the news that a friend's parent has died to one's gait when walking down the street.

(n) *Common modes of expression for thought, behaviour, and feeling*: What one thinks of a film is one thing; how one talks about it is another. What one feels upon hearing bad news is one thing; how one expresses that feeling is another. Also, while the fact that one wears clothes is covered by (c) above, what kinds of clothes are fashionable fall under this category.

Heidegger's seeming inconsistency as to whether *das Man* represents conformity or conformism reflects the broad spectrum that *das Man* covers. Some items toward the top of this list are necessary for any kind of social existence at all—one could not renounce one's general linguistic agreement with others without renouncing language itself[24]—but they seem to be in the minority. Heidegger speaks disparagingly about the Dasein who shares popular tastes in art and literature because Dasein can lead a coherent and socially acceptable life without giving in to such conformism, but he could not as easily disparage Dasein's agreement with others that the earth has existed for more than five minutes. But where do we draw the line between conformity and conformism? Are we bowing to conformism in paying our taxes? What about driving on the agreed-upon side of the road? Conformity and conformism are more like two ends of a spectrum than two distinct forms of accordance. Some kinds of conforming are more coercive than others, but no sharp line distinguishes the sorts of conformity that make social life possible from the conformism of certain social habits.

---

[24] Although even with agreement in the use of words, the line between conformity and conformism is blurry. Disputes do not normally break out over the use of words like 'dog' or 'table', but the appropriate use of words like 'terror' or 'torture', or of gender pronouns, give rise to heated moral and political disagreement. That the search for definitions is a central occupation for philosophers should make us wary of taking our agreement in definitions too much for granted.

3.6. *Das Man* and Distantiality

Much of the commentary on *das Man*—and indeed, in Heidegger's own writing on the subject—characterizes *das Man* as having the same existential status as Dasein. Heidegger defines *das Man* as the 'who' of everyday Dasein (*BT* 126), and Dreyfus (1991, 158) characterizes *das Man* as a '[s]ubstitute Dasein'. Whether couched in the language of conformity or conformism, *das Man* is portrayed as a way that Dasein could or must *be*. However, we should be careful not to describe the being of *das Man* on too close an analogy with the being of Dasein. Noting the differences will help to dissipate the tension between the various forms of conformity and conformism I identified in the previous section. I will focus on two differences: that *das Man* lacks particularity and that it lacks unity.

The most straightforward difference between Dasein's way of being and *das Man*'s is that the language we use to talk about what 'one' does differs in some crucial respects from how we speak about what 'I' or 'you' or 'he' or 'she' does. We can talk about impersonal norms in the first person singular or the impersonal third person singular with equal ease: 'I look people in the eyes when toasting' versus 'One looks people in the eyes when toasting'. However, references to what 'one' does by their nature lack particularity: I can say that *I* want the Vancouver Canucks to win the Stanley Cup or that *she* wants the Montréal Canadiens to win the Stanley Cup, but the most that one can say for *das Man* is that *one* wants one's favourite (or perhaps home) team to win the championship.

A second difference between *das Man* and Dasein is that *das Man* lacks unity. *Being and Time* itself, and much of the secondary literature, often speak of *das Man* as a unified set of norms that we identify with to greater or lesser extents, as if there were one particular way in which 'one' behaves. But social norms are rarely so univocal. One does not take tea with salt or maple syrup, but one might take it with milk and/or sugar, or even with honey or a twist of lemon. If there were a single way in which 'one' takes tea, there would be no need to ask 'milk or sugar?' when serving it. Proverbs, the quintessential repository of common wisdom, are notoriously contradictory. Should one look before one leaps, or remember that he who hesitates is lost? Do many hands make light work, or do too many cooks spoil the broth? Even if we wanted to subsume all our decisions to the dictates of the impersonal authority of social norms, we could not live on autopilot: these norms point in many different directions at once. *Das Man* is not a uniform cloth, but one with many wrinkles and holes through which the individual emerges.

One troubling feature of Heidegger's discussion of *das Man* is that he treats it as an existential—a constitutive feature of Dasein's existence (*BT* 129)—while also talking about it in terms of conformism. But the differences I have registered between the kind of being of *das Man* and the kind of being of Dasein diminish this worry somewhat by showing that regularities in human behaviour can be pervasive without being suffocatingly restrictive. Following the latest fashions is hardly a necessary or constitutive feature of Dasein's intelligibility, but we could plausibly argue that one condition of public life is that there *be* fashions of some sort. Whether any particular Dasein conforms in a given way or not, the fact of its social existence means that it lives in a society that has norms about how one dresses, how one expresses opinions, what kinds of opinions are acceptable, and so on. The stringency of the normative demands placed upon us is not sharply defined: at what point an innovation becomes a trend and a trend a cliché is open to debate. That there are social norms, however, is undeniable, and these norms are an inescapable aspect of Dasein's being-with. Even deviation from social norms is understood as deviation only in its relation to these norms.

Even conformism can be part of Dasein's existential structure because *das Man*'s way of being is not existence. Because *das Man* lacks the particularity and unity of Dasein, Dasein cannot simply adopt the way of being of *das Man*. One consequence of these differences is that *das Man* cannot be *the* source of the intelligibility of the world, as Dreyfus (1991, 154f.) claims. *Das Man* provides a normative structure that is an essential feature of Dasein's existence, but this structure does not provide the whole story on intelligibility.[25] We do better, I propose, to consider *das Man* as one—but only one—aspect of Dasein's existential structure. Equally important, though mostly unnoticed, is distantiality.

---

[25] Keller and Weberman (1998) provide a cogent critique of the notion that *das Man*, or any other existential, can be *the* source of intelligibility.

Heidegger's discussion of *das Man* is prefaced by a discussion of *Abständigkeit*, a term both Macquarrie and Robinson and Stambaugh render as 'distantiality':[26]

> In taking care of the things which one has taken hold of, for, and against others, there is constant care as to the way one differs from them, whether this difference is to be equalized, whether one's own Dasein has lagged behind others and wants to catch up in relation to them, whether Dasein in its priority over others is intent on suppressing them. Being-with-one-another is, unknown to itself, disquieted by the care about this distance. Existentially expressed, being-with-one-another has the character of *distantiality*. (BT 126)

Heidegger defines distantiality, like *das Man*, as an existential: it is not a feature that Dasein may or may not have at any given moment, but is an essential feature of Dasein's constitution. Thus it cannot be 'a kind of diffidence, an inhibition of personal rapport, a kind of social skittishness', as Carman (1994, 219) has it, but something more abiding. What kind of 'something more', however, is unclear, and Heidegger gives us very little to go on.

According to Dreyfus (1995, 427–8), distantiality is 'our essential tendency to minimize the distance between ourselves and others by subtle coercion or co-option, especially when we are not aware of doing so' and 'denotes an essential structure of all *Dasein's* activity that inconspicuously reduces difference and so performs the ontological function of establishing norms and thus opening up a shared human world'. This account conflates two separate aspects of Dasein's constitution. Dreyfus tells us that (a) we have an awareness of our difference from others, and (b) this awareness of difference prompts a tendency to minimize this difference. Heidegger's talk about 'constant care' lends some plausibility to the conflation, but I believe we do better to understand distantiality as consisting only of (a) and not also of (b).

Three textual reasons incline me toward this reading. First, Heidegger's neologism *Abständigkeit* derives from the German *Abstand*, which means a gap or a distance between things. The term connotes the fact of our distance from one another and not our response to that fact. Second,

---

[26] Carman translates this term as 'standoffishness', which I think is inappropriate. In his translation of *The History of the Concept of Time*, Theodore Kisiel renders it felicitously as 'apartness'. I will stay with 'distantiality' for the ease of familiarity that this term will have with readers of *Being and Time*, and because, unlike 'the "they"', I do not think the term is misleading.

Heidegger talks about the care we have for our distance from one another, but he introduces distantiality as a feature of being-with-one-another *simpliciter*, not as a feature of a particular kind of being-with-one-another.[27] And third, Heidegger does discuss our tendency to reduce our difference from others as an existential elsewhere—he calls it 'falling' (*Verfallen*). I discuss falling in the next chapter, but for now I simply note that it would be odd for Heidegger to give two different labels—'distantiality' and 'falling'—to essentially the same phenomenon. Reading distantiality as just an awareness of distance from others not only keeps it distinct from falling, but it also makes for a cleaner reading of some of the interpretive issues surrounding *das Man*. On this reading, *das Man* and distantiality are a contrasting pair, and the contrast diminishes some of the worries that might arise from treating *das Man* as an existential.

The normative authority of *das Man* can be ubiquitously in effect without ubiquitously controlling our behaviour. *Das Man* steals the limelight in the secondary literature, but we risk exaggerating its restrictiveness if we do not see it in contrast with another existential that Heidegger introduces in §27 of *Being and Time*, namely distantiality. I maintain that *das Man* and distantiality are best understood as complements to one another, together revealing Dasein as suspended between two poles, never entirely itself alone and yet never entirely given over to socially constituted norms. On one hand, Dasein is inescapably constituted by *das Man*, but on the other hand, every Dasein is equally inescapably unique: an ineradicable distance separates Dasein from others. Despite Heidegger's dire talk of being lost in *das Man*, we can no more erase all traces of individuality than we can exist entirely free of norms.

This account of *das Man* as paired with distantiality does not diminish Heidegger's sense that Dasein exists under the shadow of inauthenticity: its existential status as being-with means it is constitutionally susceptible to lostness in the one-self. And, as I have noted before, the parallels between Wittgenstein and Heidegger that I have traced over the previous three chapters raise the question of whether we can identify a dynamic of authenticity and inauthenticity in Wittgenstein's later philosophy. In altered form, I believe we can, and the burden of the remainder of this book is to explore that dynamic.

---

[27] Macquarrie and Robinson's translation is misleading on this point. Stambaugh's rendering, given above, is more accurate.

PART TWO

Authentic Everydayness

PART TWO

4

Anxiety, Scepticism, and Rule Following

At this point, a potential challenge to Wittgenstein should be clear. I have argued that Heidegger's analysis of Dasein's everyday existence shares many of the features of Wittgenstein's later philosophy. In Chapter 2, I connected Heidegger's treatment of readiness-to-hand to Wittgenstein's treatment of language-games as descriptions of language use embedded in activities and forms of life. And in Chapter 3, I argued that these two philosophers share a conception of our language and practices as socially constituted. However, as we began to see in my discussion of *das Man* in the previous chapter, Heidegger thinks our average everyday social existence is marked by inauthenticity. Does that mean that Wittgenstein's later philosophy, which emphasizes the importance of our agreement in forms of life, is fundamentally inauthentic?

My response to this challenge will have a double thrust. On one hand, I will argue that, just as we can find parallels in Wittgenstein's later philosophy to Heidegger's ontic–ontological distinction and his treatment of worldliness and being-with, we can also find parallels in Wittgenstein to Heidegger's treatment of anxiety and uncanniness, such that an attendant Wittgensteinian conception of authenticity emerges. And on the other hand, I will argue that we should read Heidegger's account of authenticity, in accord with Wittgenstein's, not as an escape from everydayness but as a reinhabitation of the everyday, one that accepts the everyday *as* the everyday. In this chapter, I show how Heidegger's treatment of anxiety and uncanniness finds parallels in Wittgenstein's later philosophy. And in the next, I develop a conception of 'authentic everydayness' that Wittgenstein and Heidegger share, at least to some extent.

4.1. Heidegger: Inauthenticity and Falling

In the previous chapter, I discussed Heidegger's complicated treatment of *das Man*. Without claiming to eliminate the inconsistencies in Heidegger's treatment, I argued that we could make sense of *das Man* as an existential if we recognize that he pairs it with distantiality: Dasein's existence is constituted by public norms but not exhaustively so. An ineliminable distance separates each individual from all others. Leaving Dasein with some distance from *das Man* is important because, I argued, Heidegger sees absorption in *das Man* as constitutive of an inauthentic mode of existence. If such absorption were inescapable, it would become hard to see how an authentic existence could be so much as a possibility for Dasein.

Although Heidegger does not say that we are necessarily absorbed in *das Man*, he does say that we necessarily have a tendency toward such absorption. He calls this tendency 'falling' (*Verfallen*),[1] characterized by idle talk, curiosity, and ambiguity. As an existential, falling is a constitutive feature of Dasein's existence, and Heidegger protests that the term 'does not express any negative value judgment' (*BT* 175). Like his treatment of *das Man*, Heidegger's treatment of falling is not entirely consistent on this point, nor on its status as an existential.[2] But its existential significance becomes apparent if we see it as a constant tendency that informs our everyday activities. Our existence involves us in a balance between seeing the forest and seeing the trees: it takes a certain degree of disengaged reflection to consider what projects are worth pursuing but we can only actually pursue those projects by re-engaging and focusing on the task at hand.[3] That engagement means that Dasein is 'initially and for the most part *together with* the "world" of its concern [bei *der besorgten »Welt«*]' (*BT* 175; translation modified).[4]

---

[1] Stambaugh translates this term as 'falling prey' or 'entanglement'.

[2] It seems Heidegger wants to treat falling as an existential and flight—which comes to the fore in his discussion of anxiety—as an existentiell, but in *BT* §40 the two are often difficult to disentangle. For instance, he writes of 'the falling flight of Dasein from itself' [*der verfallenden Flucht des Daseins vor ihm selbst*]' (*BT* 186; translation modified), where falling seems to be a modification of flight, and not the other way around. See Dreyfus (1991, chap. 13) for some discussion of Heidegger's inconsistency with regard to his treatment of falling.

[3] Philip Larkin's poem 'To Put One Brick Upon Another' treats this dilemma with his characteristically acerbic wit.

[4] Although Heidegger signals that he will use scare quotes to distinguish the ontic 'world' of present-at-hand beings from the worldly world of Dasein's existence (*BT* 65), he does not use this convention consistently in this stretch of text. We encounter an almost

The world shows up as the worldly whole of Dasein's being-in-the-world because Dasein is engaged in that world. And it is only from this starting point of engagement that disengaged reflection so much as makes sense. Dasein is not necessarily absorbed in *das Man*, but it is necessarily absorbed in its world, and that world shows up initially and for the most part as a world constituted by *das Man*. We only apprehend the forest as a forest to the extent that, initially and for the most part, we are concerned with the trees that constitute the forest.

The existential status of falling can be understood in close analogy to the priority of readiness-to-hand over presence-at-hand that I discussed in section 2.3. Heidegger does not want us to see the tendency toward absorption in *das Man* that is manifest in falling as more primordial than our authentic possibility of being a self, or as exclusive of it, but he rather wants us to see that falling has a hermeneutical priority: falling characterizes how we encounter the world *initially and for the most part*. Dasein is thrown into a world whose intelligibility is shaped by *das Man*, and it is with that shared intelligibility that Dasein begins to make sense of its existence.

The metaphorical connotations of 'falling' suggest two locations: the place fallen from and the place fallen to. Heidegger is explicit in filling out this connotation: 'As an authentic potentiality for being a self, Dasein has initially always already fallen away from itself and fallen into the "world"' (*BT* 175; translation modified). Dasein's absorption in *das Man* comes at the cost of realizing its authentic potentiality for being a self. If we follow through with the metaphor of falling, the latter is diametrically opposed to the former, and our existential gravity pulls us into the world. We are no more fated to absorption in *das Man* than we are unable to resist gravity, but, like climbing a mountain, ascending toward authenticity is hard work—and against our natural inclination.

Falling, then, defines the direction of our existential gravitational pull, but it does not determine the direction in which we actually move. Over the course of *Being and Time*, Heidegger works through two alternatives: downward into inauthenticity or upward to authenticity.

As I noted in section 2.1, Dasein differs from other beings in that its being is an issue for it. It is a self-interpreting being in that its mode of

identical claim to the one quoted here two paragraphs later, and 'world' occurs without scare quotes there.

existence manifests an understanding of the meaning of that existence. As long as it exists, Dasein cannot *not* interpret its own being. In what way and on what basis that self-interpretation takes place, however, is an open question. In particular, beyond the first-order question of how Dasein understands the meaning of its existence is the second-order question of the extent to which it understands itself as a self-interpreting being.[5] Just as the first-order question of Dasein's self-understanding is not necessarily given explicit expression, this second-order question is not settled so much in whether Dasein explicitly says or thinks 'I am a self-interpreting being', but is rather answered in the manner of Dasein's existence. Whether Dasein understands itself as a self-interpreting being is manifest in the way in which it faces up to the task of self-interpretation.

Dasein's authenticity or inauthenticity can be understood in terms of how it addresses this second-order question. An inauthentic mode of existence is one in which Dasein suppresses its own role in interpreting its existence. An authentic mode of existence is one that owns up to its status as self-interpreting. Authenticity is internally related to Dasein's existence in this respect: it is the way of being in which Dasein most fully realizes its status as a self-interpreting being—that is, that it exists.

A central burden of Heidegger's phenomenological project is to recover this authentic understanding of Dasein as a self-interpreting being. Authenticity is not just a matter of Dasein's self-understanding, but also—or rather, consequently—a matter of its understanding of the world. The world of an architect and the world of a botanist show up differently, and they do so in ways that reflect their self-understanding: what stands out as salient in my environment reflects my sense of significance, of what matters to me, and why. And, Heidegger wants to impress upon us, this salience is all the salience there is. '*Dasein is its disclosedness*' (*BT* 133): it is in the 'clearing' (*BT* 133) of Dasein's existential-ontological structure that a world of interpretable beings come into view. Authentic self-understanding, then, is a matter of Dasein

---

[5] Richardson (2012, 167–8) talks about authenticity as a second-order commitment to our first-order projects. I will argue that authenticity is better understood as a particular kind of self-understanding than a particular kind of commitment, but I share his sense that the dynamic of authenticity has this second-order relation to our first-order projects.

recognizing the significance of the world as responsive to its understanding of the meaning of its own being.

Heidegger's account of authenticity bears some important resemblances to Aristotle's account of *eudaimonia*—and, indeed, Aristotle was close to Heidegger throughout the period in which *Being and Time* was germinating.[6] Aristotle treats the question of human flourishing as internally related to the question of human nature. To understand what it means for human beings to flourish, we must understand what it means to be a human being: human flourishing is then a matter of doing the distinctively human activities to an excellent degree. Heidegger's account of authenticity has roughly the same framework as Aristotle's account of human flourishing, but diverges sharply from Aristotle's account of human nature. What is distinctive about human beings for Aristotle is that we are the uniquely rational animal, so that the distinctively human good turns out to be 'activity of the soul and actions in accordance with reason' (*Nicomachean Ethics* 1098a16). Heidegger, by contrast, resists understanding Dasein as a biological organism and disavows thinking of different kinds of beings as species of the genus of being (*BT* 3). What is distinctive about Dasein is not this or that attribute, according to Heidegger, but the fact that it *exists*: Dasein is the being that relates to itself as a question. Accordingly, Dasein's flourishing *qua* Dasein is a matter of fulfilling its nature as self-interpreting.[7] Authentic Dasein explicitly owns up to this task of self-interpretation, whereas inauthentic Dasein hides from it. Inauthentic Dasein does a poor job of manifesting its distinctive Daseinhood.

In avoiding the second-order question of Dasein's own role in interpreting its existence, inauthentic Dasein treats its nature as something already determined, something fixed and obvious. In other words, it interprets itself as having the kind of being of a present-at-hand object. In a fundamental way, inauthentic Dasein fails to treat itself as a self.

The irony of inauthenticity, of course, is that inauthentic Dasein's self-interpretation as a being whose essence is fixed and obvious is a manifestation of precisely the hermeneutic capacity that means that Dasein's

---

[6] See Kisiel (1993, part 2). Wrathall (2015, 354–5) points to evidence that Heidegger saw his conception of authenticity in analogy with Aristotle's conception of *eudaimonia*.

[7] See, e.g., *BT* 221: 'The most primordial and authentic disclosedness in which Dasein can be as a potentiality-of-being is the *truth of existence*'.

nature is open to self-interpretation. Whether or not it acknowledges the second-order question of its status as self-interpreting, Dasein is essentially always engaged with the first-order question of its self-understanding. Heidegger explicitly denies that Dasein can lose its existential status as being-in-the-world:

> Inauthenticity does not mean anything like no-longer-being-in-the-world, but rather it constitutes precisely a distinctive kind of being-in-the-world which is completely taken in [*benommen*] by the world and the Dasein-with of the others in *das Man*. Not-being-its-self functions as a *positive* possibility of beings which are absorbed in a world, essentially concerned with that world.
> (*BT* 176; translation modified)[8]

Inauthenticity is not a failure of self-interpretation but is rather a mode of self-interpretation that defers the interpretive work as much as possible to *das Man*, and reaches for the interpretive resources that are closest to hand. This is the mode of existence that Heidegger characterizes as lost in the one-self—*das Man* is not itself a way of being for Dasein, but the one-self that is lost in *das Man* is.

4.2. Heidegger: Anxiety and Uncanniness

The language of falling and being taken in suggests that Dasein is passive in being pulled into its absorption in *das Man*. Heidegger introduces more active language in characterizing Dasein's '*flight*... from itself as an authentic potentiality for being itself' (*BT* 184). Dasein is not simply pulled away from itself but seems almost repelled by the possibility of a confrontation with itself, such that it flees from itself. Heidegger explores this repulsion in his discussion of anxiety, which for him is a positive and

---

[8] Like so many of Heidegger's crucial terms, *benommen* does not lend itself to easy translation. In non-Heideggerian contexts it means something like 'dazed' or 'stunned'. Stambaugh's rendering as 'taken in' aptly picks up on the etymological link with *nehmen*, or 'take': Dasein's *Benommenheit* implicates Dasein in being taken, or captivated. Macquarrie and Robinson translate the word as 'fascinated', which captures the kind of captivation Heidegger has in mind, especially if we bear in mind the etymological derivation of 'fascinated' from its Latin root meaning 'bewitched': the average everyday understanding of the world casts a spell on us, leaving us stunned or dazed, unable to see ourselves or our circumstances with clear vision. Intriguingly, in *Fundamental Concepts of Metaphysics*, Heidegger takes *Benommenheit* to be characteristic of animals' absorption in the world: they are 'taken in' by their environment and do not stand out from it in the way that Dasein does.

importantly disclosive mood. In anxiety, Dasein is confronted with its existential status as being-in-the-world, and although its habitual response to such a confrontation is a flight into inauthenticity, this confrontation is also a door by which Dasein can be opened up to its authentic potentiality for being a self.[9]

Heidegger treats anxiety as a special kind of fear. Ordinarily, what we fear are beings we encounter in the world—either present-at-hand, ready-to-hand, or other Dasein (*BT* 140). Anxiety, by contrast, is directed not toward innerworldly beings but toward Dasein itself as being-in-the-world: '*That about which one has anxiety is being-in-the-world as such*' (*BT* 186). In this respect, anxiety—which Heidegger says is the condition for the possibility of fear (*BT* 186)—inverts the phenomenology of ordinary fear. Ordinarily we flee from the innerworldly beings that threaten us, but anxiety prompts our flight *toward* innerworldly beings: to escape from anxiety, Dasein typically (but not necessarily) seeks the absorption with innerworldly beings that anxiety disrupts. And where what is fearsome 'shows itself in a context of relevance [*Bewandtniszusammenhang*]' (*BT* 140), what we are anxious about 'essentially cannot have any relevance [*Bewandtnis*]' (*BT* 186). Where fear gives a distinct relevance to certain innerworldly beings, anxiety is precisely the falling away of the relevance of *all* innerworldly beings.

Anxiety is troubling because it brings to awareness the fragility of the significance of the world. Ordinarily, Dasein's world has significance because Dasein is engaged in it in the pursuit of ends-oriented projects. In anxiety, all of those ends suddenly come to seem irrelevant, and so all innerworldly beings suddenly come to seem irrelevant (*BT* 187). The character of innerworldly beings as ready-to-hand equipment dissolves in the face of anxiety. Instead, they show up as present-at-hand 'in just such a way that they are of *no* relevance *whatsoever*, but can show themselves in a barren mercilessness' (*BT* 343).[10]

---

[9] Anxiety gets the lion's share of Heidegger's attention in *Being and Time*, and it seems to have a distinctive importance for him, but he does not single out anxiety as uniquely disclosive in this way. In 'What is Metaphysics?', Heidegger suggests a similar—although importantly not entirely similar—disclosure is possible in boredom and in the presence of a Dasein that we love (*WM* 99), and treats boredom at length in *The Fundamental Concepts of Metaphysics*. At the beginning of *Introduction to Metaphysics*, he gives a similar status to great despair, heartfelt joy, and boredom (*IM* 1–2).

[10] This is the sense in which, as I noted in section 2.3, Fell (1992) argues that presence-at-hand has a kind of priority over readiness-to-hand. I will return to this point shortly.

This idea of a loss of relevance requires further scrutiny. In particular, we should resist the idea that this loss of relevance means that things come to seem entirely meaningless.[11] As McManus (2015a, 163–4) points out, if Dasein is defined as the being that has an understanding of being, the idea that Dasein could have an experience of universal meaninglessness teeters close to a contradiction. Phenomenologically speaking, we should also be wary of pushing the idea of loss of relevance too far: it is unclear what possible experience Heidegger could have in mind if a loss of relevance means something as extreme as no longer being able to see, say, a spoon as a spoon. We do better to see the loss of relevance of innerworldly beings as a consequence of—and hence to be understood in terms of—a loss of relevance of our projects. In anxiety, we come face to face with the recognition that there is *no good reason* for pursuing the projects we pursue. If my laptop shows up to me as ready-to-hand in a particular way to the extent that it serves the project of writing this book, which is in turn a project that expresses a more general understanding of the meaning of my existence, a crisis in which this book-writing project suddenly seems irrelevant to me becomes a crisis in which my laptop suddenly comes to seem useless. But saying that the laptop shows up as useless is not to say that the laptop suddenly becomes a naked object that I can make no sense of at all. I can still grasp what kind of a tool a laptop is, and how it might be of service in various ends, but these ends cease to have the salience that might motivate a project directed toward them. This crisis is not simply a contingent tedium, as if no project that I've considered quite tickles my fancy enough to get me out of bed, but an existential crisis: in anxiety, it ceases to be clear how *any* project could *possibly* be worth pursuing. There is nothing either in the world or in my status as Dasein that can provide a compelling justification for what I ought to do.[12]

The positive aspect of anxiety is that, in anxiety, we come to see more clearly our own role in constituting the significance of our existence. The significance that drains away in anxiety is the shared significance of a world that is constituted publicly by *das Man*. Instead, anxiety leaves

---

[11] For articulations of this view, see Dreyfus and Rubin (1991, 332), Philipse (1998, 395), and Dahlstrom (2013, 208).

[12] Cf. Thomson (2013, 270): '[T]here is ultimately nothing about the ontological structure of the self that could tell us what specifically we should do with our lives'.

Dasein with itself: anxiety 'throws Dasein back upon that for which it is anxious, its authentic potentiality-for-being-in-the-world. Anxiety individuates Dasein to its ownmost being-in-the-world which, as understanding, projects itself essentially upon possibilities' (*BT* 187). What becomes inescapably clear in anxiety is that the significance of the world cannot be grounded in any source outside of ourselves: Dasein is its own ground.[13]

Anxiety discloses the fundamental incompleteness of Dasein's existence. In section 2.1, I argued that Dasein's distinctive status as self-interpreting is a matter of being essentially open-ended. As I put it there, rocks simply are what they are, whereas *what* Dasein is gets articulated in the living out of its life. These two features of Dasein's existence—that it is self-interpreting and that it is essentially open-ended—are importantly linked. Dasein relates to itself and its world as a question *because* it is essentially incomplete. In its incompleteness, Dasein has a kind of openness—one might even say vulnerability—to the world: Dasein is formed by *how* it is in the world. Compare this openness to the closedness of a rock. *How* the rock is in the world has no bearing on *what* it is. It may sit on top of a mountain, fall into a gully, or be used for cracking open nuts, but through all this it remains the same rock. The rock might be broken into pebbles, in which case it would simply cease to be a rock, but as long as it is a rock, its rockness is impervious to the slings and arrows of outrageous fortune.[14] *What* a rock will be from moment to moment is already settled—it will be a rock—and so not open to question. By contrast, *what* Dasein will be is an open question, and for that reason Dasein is a question to itself.[15]

---

[13] Cf. Fell (1992, 68).
[14] To put a Heideggerian spin on Hamlet's famous soliloquy, we could say that suffering the slings and arrows of outrageous fortune is the essential fate of being Dasein. *What* we are is a continuously unfolding project and hence vulnerable to what the world throws at us in the course of its unfolding. The comfort Hamlet finds in the prospect of death is that he could thereby put an end to his essential vulnerability as Dasein precisely by ceasing to be Dasein.
[15] In section 1.5, I introduced Heidegger by touching on Carnap's criticism of Heidegger's expatiation on 'the nothing' in 'What Is Metaphysics?' without saying much about what 'the nothing' means for Heidegger. One of Heidegger's aims in that essay is to draw attention to Dasein's essential incompleteness. Unlike the closed-off rock, Dasein has an opening on to being precisely because of a nullity—a gap, an absence—in its own being.

The term Heidegger gives for this incompleteness is *Unheimlichkeit*, uncanniness or unsettledness: Dasein is fundamentally not at home in the world.[16] This uncanniness is disturbing. It places a continual burden on us (*BT* 134–5): because we are unsettled in our being, we are at every moment faced with the question of how we will articulate that being. In flight, Dasein seeks to flee this burden and find tranquillity in seeing its being as already fixed and settled by the dictates of *das Man*. But Heidegger repeatedly emphasizes that the uncanniness of Dasein's existence is more fundamental than the comforting familiarity of its everyday existence: 'Tranquillized, familiar being-in-the-world is a mode of the uncanniness of Dasein, not the other way around. *Not-being-at-home must be conceived existentially and ontologically as the more primordial phenomenon*' (*BT* 189).[17]

Although this uncanniness is unsettling, owning up to it is crucial to Heidegger's understanding of authenticity. Earlier, I claimed that we could understand authenticity as a second-order form of understanding in which Dasein understands itself as a self-interpreting being. Its existential status as self-interpreting is what gives Dasein the unsettled incompleteness that Heidegger describes as uncanny. And authentic self-understanding essentially involves understanding the uncanniness of Dasein's existence.

4.3. Wittgenstein: Explanations and Rule Following

Dasein's tendency for absorption in its world—what Heidegger calls 'falling'—seems almost synonymous with what Heidegger characterizes as everydayness. For instance, Heidegger introduces falling as 'a basic kind of the being of **everydayness**' (*BT* 175) shortly before saying that

---

[16] *Unheimlich* carries the root word *das Heim*, meaning 'home', a connotation that Heidegger brings out by emphasizing that uncanniness means 'not-being-at-home' (*BT* 188). As Freud ([1919] 2003) famously notes, *unheimlich* is also related to the adjective *heimlich*, or secret, so that the uncanny can also be understood as the revealing of what is secret.

[17] Cf. also *BT* 277: 'Uncanniness is the fundamental kind of being-in-the-world, although it is covered over in everydayness'. Katherine Withy (2015) emphasizes that Heidegger differs from many other theorists of the uncanny—most notably Freud—in that he treats the uncanny not simply as a *feeling* that can overcome us but as something that Dasein *is*. We do not simply *feel* uncanny; we *are* uncanny.

4.3. WITTGENSTEIN: EXPLANATIONS AND RULE FOLLOWING

'Dasein is **initially and for the most part** *together with* the "world" that it takes care of' (*BT* 175). That authentic Dasein breaks free from its absorption in *das Man* might easily be read as authentic Dasein breaking free from its everydayness.

Heidegger's treatment of anxiety and uncanniness sharpens the challenge to Wittgenstein that I mentioned at the beginning of the chapter. Uncanniness reveals a fundamental openness and vulnerability in our forms of life that Wittgenstein might seem to push aside: 'What has to be accepted, the given, is—one might say—*forms of life*' (*PPF* xi §345). Heidegger qualifies the priority he gives to readiness-to-hand: beings show up to us as ready-to-hand initially and for the most part, but, as we saw, anxiety drains the world of relevance so that beings show up in their 'barren mercilessness' as present-at-hand (*BT* 343). Wittgenstein's treatment of our forms of life does not make room in its analysis for anxiety, a Heideggerian critic might claim, and so does not acknowledge the fundamental uncanniness underlying these forms of life.

I glossed the crisis that potentially confronts Dasein in anxiety by saying that there is *no good reason* for pursuing the projects we pursue. Eventually reasons bottom out. The spectre of reasons bottoming out haunts Wittgenstein's later philosophy: 'Explanations come to an end somewhere' (*PI* §1), 'I have exhausted the justifications' (*PI* §217), and so on. In this respect, Wittgenstein is deeply concerned with what Heidegger calls anxiety. This concern enters the secondary literature on Wittgenstein not under the guise of anxiety but as scepticism, primarily in Wittgenstein's reflections on following a rule. And, as it happens, the range of responses to scepticism in this secondary literature bears some resemblance to Heidegger's treatment of flight and resoluteness. Wittgenstein's later philosophy is indeed vulnerable to the charge of inauthenticity, but only if we read him as accepting the sceptic's framing of the problem as a crisis. If we read Wittgenstein as trying to transform the sceptic's self-understanding, we see the possibility of an authentic reading of Wittgenstein, and one that can inform our understanding of Heideggerian anxiety as well.

Let me begin by considering a worry about explanation that makes its first appearance as early as *PI* §1, and that returns in a number of guises throughout *Philosophical Investigations*. Confronted with a series of queries from his interlocutor regarding the very first language-game in the *Investigations*—the story of the shopping trip for five red apples at

PI §1d—Wittgenstein abruptly replies, 'Explanations come to an end somewhere', at a point where a great deal seems unexplained. The spectre of scepticism that haunts Wittgenstein's investigations is intimately connected to the question of where explanations (might, do, can legitimately be said to) come to an end.

Explanation and doubt are closely related. One crude way of putting the relation is to say that explanations close gaps in our understanding and doubts manifest them. We supply or ask for an explanation when we sense that something has not been understood, or when we sense a risk of misunderstanding. And raising a doubt suggests that something wants explaining, or it raises a challenge: if you cannot explain this further, you are not entitled to claim it. This way of stating the relation between explanation and doubt is crude because it might incline us toward a certain picture of understanding that seems innocent enough, but which nudges us in the direction of philosophical confusion.[18] The picture is this: our understanding is an imperfect thing, riddled with holes. These holes are doubts, and the role of explanation is to stop up these holes. Hole by hole, explanation works to render our understanding more perfect.

One potentially misleading aspect of this picture of explanation as filling gaps in the understanding is that it inclines us to think of the gaps as already being there, like holes in a cloth, which we might notice or not notice. Then the doubts that concern me and the doubts that have not occurred to me can seem like essentially the same sorts of thing, like the hole in a shirt that I have noticed and the one I have not noticed. If anything, the unnoticed holes take on greater importance, since my neglect of them might seem more liable to cause problems. And then a crucial task in the perfection of my understanding would seem to be to find all of the holes as a preliminary to the task of stopping them up systematically. Wittgenstein gives voice to this temptation at *PI* §87: 'It may easily look as if every doubt merely *revealed* a gap in the foundations; so that secure understanding is possible only if we first doubt everything that *can* be doubted, and then remove all these doubts'. We see one manifestation of this undertaking in the *locus classicus* of modern scepticism: the methodological doubt of Descartes's *First Meditation*.

---

[18] Cf. *PI* §308: 'The decisive movement in the conjuring trick has been made, and it was the very one that seemed to us quite innocent'.

4.3. WITTGENSTEIN: EXPLANATIONS AND RULE FOLLOWING

When we start looking for doubts, they seem to be everywhere, including in the explanations that aim to resolve the doubts. If we picture the understanding as a cloth riddled with holes and explanations as patches that close up those holes, the explanations themselves turn out to be of the same moth-eaten character as the understanding whose gaps they seek to close. Wittgenstein imagines a signpost, whose purpose is to explain in which direction one ought to go to arrive at a certain destination, and rehearses doubts one might raise about interpreting the signpost:

Does the signpost leave no doubt about the way I have to go? Does it show which direction I am to take when I have passed it, whether along the road or the footpath or cross-country? But where does it say which way I am to follow it; whether in the direction of its finger or (for example) in the opposite one? — And if there were not a single signpost, but a sequence of signposts or chalk marks on the ground — is there only *one* way of interpreting them?   (*PI* §85)

Expanding on that last question, Wittgenstein imagines a schema of arrows that shows how one is supposed to read a chart—and then imagines a further schema of arrows that shows how one is supposed to interpret the first schema of arrows, and a further further schema of arrows for interpreting the further schema of arrows, and so on down.

The prospect of infinitely ramifying doubt leads Wittgenstein's interlocutor to question the very possibility that explanation could lead to understanding: 'But then how does an explanation help me to understand, if, after all, it is not the final one? In that case the explanation is never completed; so I still don't understand what he means, and never shall!' (*PI* §87). The interlocutor has arrived at a characteristically philosophical impasse. What seems like nothing more than rigorous scrutiny of a familiar concept leads us to specify what we think would be required for that concept to reach its proper fulfilment, strictly speaking. And that requirement seems to exceed any practical implementation, casting doubt on the very possibility of that concept's fulfilment.

One consequence of becoming entranced by this idea of a final explanation is that ordinary explanations come to seem not only imperfect in comparison but totally useless. If ordinary explanations leave unresolved gaps and doubts, they provide us not with understanding but at best the illusion of understanding, an illusion born of having given insufficient scrutiny to the latent gaps in the explanation. And if these latent gaps are filled by supplementary explanations that have the same imperfections as the explanations they seek to supplement, then any explanation short of a so-called 'final' explanation will just be one step in an infinite regress that gets us no closer to understanding: 'As though an explanation, as it were, hung in the air unless supported by another' (*PI* §87).[19] If it is part of the logic of ordinary explanations that they can always be misunderstood or doubted, and that a further explanation can always be called for, then any so-called 'final' explanation must somehow be of a different kind from these ordinary explanations. If we imagine each explanation in our chain of explanations as progressively more fundamental and less dubitable, our final explanation is where the fundamentality and indubitability bottom out.

This worry about explanation takes a variety of related guises, but finds its canonical expression in Wittgenstein's treatment of rule following, which becomes the primary focus of *PI* §§185–242. Wittgenstein introduces these passages with his parable of the wayward pupil, in which he imagines a teacher instructing a pupil in various series of natural numbers:

Then we get the pupil to continue one series (say '+ 2') beyond 1000 — and he writes 1000, 1004, 1008, 1012.

We say to him, 'Look what you're doing!' — He doesn't understand. We say, 'You should have added *two*: look how you began the series!' — He answers, 'Yes, isn't it right? I thought that was how I *had* to do it'. ——Or suppose he pointed to the series and said, 'But I did go on in the same way'. — It would now be no use to say, 'But can't you see . . . ?' — and go over the old explanations and examples for him again. (*PI* §185)

To understand the force of Wittgenstein's example here, it is important to note that everything in the training that the pupil was given is compatible with him going on in this way. Wittgenstein imagines the teacher accounting for the pupil's departure from the expected procedure by saying, '[T]his person finds it natural, once given our explanations, to understand our order as we would understand the order "Add 2 up to 1000, 4 up to 2000, 6 up to 3000, and so on"' (*PI* §185). And if, in our training, we had made *that* point clear, there are still infinitely many

---

[19] Wittgenstein's interlocutor expresses a similar worry with similar language at *PI* §198: '[E]very interpretation hangs in the air together with what it interprets, and cannot give it any support'.

other ways in which the pupil might have diverged from us. Because the context in which we learn any practice is finite and the possible extensions of that practice are infinite, no training exhaustively dictates how we should extend the practice in every case.

If no training exhaustively dictates how we should extend the practice in every case, that also means that our own training into our practices is not exhaustive. That we share practices at all is not just a matter of having the same training, but also a matter of taking up that training in the same way. Because I speak and act with certain kinds of regularity, and with complete confidence in these regularities, and others accord with these regularities with similar confidence, there is a powerful temptation to suppose that there is something more guiding me when I follow a rule—as if the training were hinting at something else. In the sections that follow *PI* §185, Wittgenstein's interlocutor shuttles between positing what this *something else* might be—an intuition, a mental act of meaning, a mathematical formula—and the vertiginous anxiety that comes from finding that none of these posited entities does the work she wants them to do.[20]

4.4. Wittgensteinian Scepticism and Heideggerian Anxiety

This dynamic—oscillating between a Platonist insistence on absolute foundations and a sceptical anxiety that there are no foundations—bears a striking resemblance to the dynamic in Heidegger that I discussed above, concerning falling, anxiety, and flight. Heidegger characterizes falling Dasein as having a tendency to unthinking absorption in its practices, just as Wittgenstein draws attention to our tendency to engage unreflectively in practices of explanation or rule following. This worry that none of our ordinary explanations can give us the understanding we seek, that every interpretation of a rule 'hangs in the air together with what it interprets, and cannot give it any support' (*PI* §198), resembles the anxiety that Heidegger discusses, where Dasein is suddenly confronted with the groundlessness of its various projects. And the interlocutor's insistence that *something must*

---

[20] Here and elsewhere in this book, I will use feminine pronouns to refer to Wittgenstein's interlocutor, as it helps to distinguish the voices in Wittgenstein's dialectic.

serve as a ground to our practices resembles Dasein's flight into inauthentic absorption in *das Man*: in the face of destabilizing anxiety, Wittgenstein's interlocutor seeks the tranquillizing assurance that her practices do rest on a stable foundation after all.

At first blush, Wittgenstein and Heidegger might seem to be pursuing radically different quarries. Wittgenstein is concerned with a technical question regarding the justification or grounding of our rule-governed practices whereas Heidegger's concern is explicitly existential: Heidegger is concerned with the possibility that our projects and practices might not have any relevance, and whether we can continue to act in the absence of that relevance. Wittgenstein's concern is theoretical, we might say, while Heidegger's is practical. Heideggerian anxiety raises deep questions about *how to live*, and it is far from evident that Wittgensteinian scepticism does the same.

I do not want to reduce the differences between Wittgensteinian scepticism and Heideggerian anxiety to nothing, but the resemblances are deeper than they may at first appear. In particular, I will spell out three similarities: both problematics exhibit what James Conant (2012) characterizes as Kantian scepticism, both are forms of scepticism concerned with meaning, and finally, Wittgenstein's scepticism can be construed as having a much more existential barb than the previous paragraph allowed.

Conant (2012) distinguishes between two varieties of sceptical problematic—following Cavell (1979, 46), he takes the term 'scepticism' to refer not just to arguments in support of a sceptical conclusion but 'to the wider *dialectical space*' within which sceptical arguments are disputed (Conant 2012, 3)—which he labels Cartesian and Kantian.[21] Roughly speaking, Cartesian scepticism as Conant understands it concerns the possibility of knowledge, whereas Kantian scepticism concerns the conditions for the possibility of knowledge. Consider, for instance (this is Conant's example), the difference between Cartesian scepticism

---

[21] A shorter version of the same paper appears in Conant (2004). Conant insists that these labels are not meant to make strong historical claims—Conant allows that some form of Kantian scepticism precedes Kant, that some form of Cartesian scepticism precedes Descartes, that Kant is also concerned with what Conant calls Cartesian scepticism, and that neither thinker is concerned with all the variants of scepticism to which he gives their name—but rather just provide ease of reference by denoting the thinker who gave each variety of scepticism its canonical expression.

with regard to perception, which asks how I can be confident that the testimony of my senses is veridical, and Kantian scepticism with regard to perception, which asks how my senses can be conceived as providing testimony at all, how perception can be the sort of thing that can provide knowledge in the first place. This broad division into two varieties of scepticism allows for a wide range of distinct if homologous variants, and the history of philosophy furnishes us with a wide range of treatments of these varieties and variants, many of which bleed into one another, sometimes deliberately on the part of the philosopher engaged with the problematic and sometimes not.

Both Cartesian and Kantian varieties of scepticism receive treatment in Wittgenstein's later philosophy, but the problematic of explanation and rule following that I broached above has a distinctively Kantian tenor. Or rather, the Cartesian doubts with which Wittgenstein's interlocutor begins slide ineluctably into Kantian ones. At the beginning of *PI* §186, for instance, Wittgenstein's interlocutor asks, 'What you are saying, then, comes to this: a new insight—intuition—is needed at every step to carry out the order "+n" correctly'. Wittgenstein replies: 'To carry it out correctly! How is it decided what is the right step to take at any particular point?' The interlocutor at this point thinks she is confronted with a Cartesian problem—how can we *know* that we are following a rule correctly?—but Wittgenstein pushes her to see that the problem goes deeper, to the question of the very constitution of correctness. The two aspects of the problem remain intertwined—part of Wittgenstein's treatment of the Kantian problem is to draw attention to the interlocutor's assumption that the ability to follow a rule correctly at every step involves *knowing* or *understanding* something—but the overall shape of the problem is Kantian.

Although Heidegger does not frame anxiety explicitly as a sceptical problem, it has the contours of Kantian scepticism as Conant formulates it.[22] In the grip of anxiety, Dasein's concern is not that she does not *know* what she should do, but she is rather confronted with the question of how *anything* could *possibly* have the required motivational salience.

---

[22] Conant raises the question of whether what he calls the Kantian variety of scepticism is rightly called scepticism at all. One of the burdens of his paper is to provide grounds for thinking so. See especially Conant (2012, 19–22), although his defence of this claim is a theme that runs throughout.

Dasein's crisis in the grip of anxiety exhibits many of the features that Conant identifies with Kantian scepticism.[23] To take three examples, Dasein's anxiety is better characterized as a *boggle* than a doubt, resulting in a state of *despair* rather than disappointment, and the crisis is not that there is something Dasein *cannot* do but rather it seems as if there is *nothing* to do. In anxiety, Dasein confronts the question of the very condition for the possibility of a meaningful existence.

This difference between Kantian and Cartesian varieties of scepticism is worth emphasizing because Cartesian scepticism also animates Division I of *Being and Time*, and Heidegger explicitly addresses the Cartesian problem of external world scepticism at *BT* §43(a). In analysing Dasein as being-in-the-world, Heidegger exposes the inadequacy of the traditional framing of the Cartesian problematic. In conceiving of Dasein as always already coupled with its world, Heidegger rejects what Putnam (1994, 489) calls the 'interface conception' of the relation between mind and world, thereby obviating the whole question of how experience can be veridical. But this rejection of the Cartesian problematic unfolds in a project with a more Kantian shape: Heidegger's analytic of Dasein explores the conditions for the possibility of Dasein's distinctive mode of being, the being of a being that exists.[24]

The Kantian shape of Heideggerian anxiety brings me to its second similarity to Wittgensteinian scepticism. The constitutional question that Dasein confronts in anxiety is a question about meaning. As a being that exists, Dasein is always already taking a stance on the meaning of its being. Anxiety is deeply unsettling because it calls into question the very possibility of taking such a stance. If Dasein's projects lack relevance—and if Dasein consequently encounters beings as inaccessible to meaningful projects, and hence as present-at-hand—there is nothing for Dasein to take a stance *on*. And if leading a meaningful existence

---

[23] See Conant (2012, 30–6) for a discussion of nine salient features of Kantian scepticism, including those discussed in the following sentence.

[24] In saying that Division I of *Being and Time* is pervasively engaged with scepticism, I follow Stephen Mulhall (2001, 263 and 2005b, 114–19). However, Mulhall, following Cavell, gives this scepticism a primarily Cartesian tenor. I think Mulhall is right to find Cartesian scepticism as an animating concern for Heidegger. But, for reasons I am developing here, I think Mulhall's treatment of Heideggerian anxiety as a form of scepticism does not adequately register the difference between Cartesian and Kantian varieties of scepticism. Conant (2012, 65–6) argues that McDowell is more sensitive than Cavell to the distinctively Kantian shape of Wittgenstein's treatment of rule following.

comes to seem impossible, the mode of being of Dasein itself comes to seem impossible. Hence Heidegger's characterization of anxiety as directed toward '*being-in-the-world as such*' (*BT* 186). What it is to be Dasein is to be engaged by the question of its own being, and anxiety raises the prospect that such engagement is impossible.[25]

The sceptical problematic that Wittgenstein engages with in connection with explanation and rule following is also fundamentally concerned with meaning and understanding. At stake, ultimately, is the question of how any of my conventional behaviour—using language, obeying orders, playing games, participating in customs, etc.—can count as correct or incorrect. The standing threat is one of meaninglessness. If there are no grounds for correctness then all we are left with is brute behaviour: we just move about, expel air through our vocal chords, and so on, without these behaviours having any more significance than leaves blowing in the wind. In this respect, the sceptical doubts Wittgenstein engages with also concern anxiety about a global loss of relevance.

Finding echoes of Heideggerian anxiety in the sceptical doubts Wittgenstein considers brings me to my third point of similarity, which is that, like Heideggerian anxiety, Wittgensteinian scepticism broaches existential concerns. But we should not embrace this third parallel too hastily. In saying that Heidegger and Wittgenstein are both concerned with meaning in the moments I have highlighted might feel like a bit of a fudge. To the extent that Wittgenstein is concerned with meaning—both in the rule following sections and in the *Investigations* as a whole—an objector might point out that he is concerned with *linguistic* meaning, whereas Heidegger is concerned with the relevance of beings,

---

[25] Earlier, I cited McManus (2015a, 163-4) in rejection of the idea that anxiety can present Dasein with an experience of total meaninglessness, since Dasein's existence necessarily entails some sort of understanding of being. I think McManus is right on this point, but we can now see that one feature of Heideggerian anxiety is that it calls into question the very possibility of the being that is doing the questioning. That said, I remain unpersuaded by one interpretive response to this idea of anxiety as calling into question the very possibility of Dasein's existence, namely that anxiety in this respect is one face of what Heidegger calls death. This view, espoused in different ways in Blattner (1994), Haugeland (2000), White (2005), and Thomson (2013), distances Heidegger's treatment of death from anything we might ordinarily mean by the word, claiming instead that, by death, Heidegger means something more like this anxious confrontation with the impossibility of the kind of existence that is characteristic of Dasein. This issue is not central to my own reading, so I will not dwell on it here, but I am uneasy with an interpretation of death that distances it so radically from what Heidegger calls demise (*Ableben*).

projects, and the existential 'clearing' in which these beings and projects are connected. This difference diminishes somewhat when we recall that, for Wittgenstein, grammatical investigations are investigations of the forms of life in which language is used, so that a threat to the possibility of linguistic meaning also becomes a threat to the significance of forms of life more generally. But the difference does not disappear altogether. Wittgenstein's interlocutor certainly appears anxious, but it seems a stretch to characterize this anxiety as anxiety about being-in-the-world as such.

One way of accounting for the difference is to return to the distinction I drew earlier: Wittgensteinian anxiety seems more theoretical than practical. Wittgenstein's interlocutor is not immediately concerned with *doing* anything but rather with considering abstractly what significant action consists in. Only a philosopher need share the worries of Wittgenstein's interlocutor, we might say, whereas Heideggerian anxiety afflicts all of us. This distinction is acceptable up to a point, but only if we add the caveat that, for Wittgenstein, we are *all* philosophers. Cavell draws a curious but apt distinction, classing Plato, Nietzsche, and Derrida as philosophers for whom 'philosophy retains a given reality, an autonomous, cultural, intellectual, institutional life', while grouping Wittgenstein with Socrates, Descartes, Hume, Emerson, Thoreau, and Austin as a philosopher for whom 'the mood of philosophy begins in the street, or in doorways, or closets, anywhere but in philosophical schools' (Cavell 1994, 63). Wittgenstein does not treat philosophy as a rarefied intellectual discipline that we can take or—preferably, as some choose to read him—leave. The sorts of temptations and confusions that Wittgenstein characterizes as philosophical await anyone who thinks and speaks. His interlocutors are not professional philosophers—and here it is telling that Wittgenstein rarely engages with the texts of actual philosophers—but simply fellow human beings who are caught in perplexities that Wittgenstein himself shares. In this respect, the anxieties that Wittgenstein confronts are, every bit as much as Heidegger's, anxieties to which all of us are subject.

Nevertheless, Wittgenstein's anxieties do have a distinctly philosophical tenor that is lacking in Heidegger's treatment. Here I think Mulhall is right to see scepticism not as equivalent to Heideggerian anxiety but rather as a distinct manifestation of anxiety. For Mulhall, 'scepticism just *is* how [anxiety] makes itself manifest in philosophy' (Mulhall 2001, 263).

Although philosophizing in Wittgenstein's (and, I think, Heidegger's) sense is an inescapable feature of being human, that does not mean that we are always engaged in philosophizing. Philosophical scepticism, then, is a distinct manifestation of anxiety, one that treats the uncanniness of Dasein's existence as principally an intellectual concern. To appropriate a phrase of Cavell's, scepticism construes 'a metaphysical finitude as an intellectual lack' (Cavell 1976d, 263).[26] However, as I have noted above, 'intellectual lack' gives the affair a colouring that is too Cartesian. What is at issue in anxiety is not an epistemological problematic but a constitutional one: what is at stake are the very conditions for the possibility of existence.

In Part One, I argued that Wittgenstein's grammatical investigations shared many important features with Heidegger's analysis of Dasein's average everydayness. In this chapter I have extended the parallels further. Heidegger's discussion of anxiety in §40 of *Being and Time* is an important pivot toward Division II, where Dasein's average everyday understanding is revealed to be existentially limiting, and where the possibility of an authentic existence comes into clearer focus. If we find in Wittgenstein's later philosophy not just a number of parallels to Heidegger's treatment of average everydayness but also, in Wittgenstein's engagement with scepticism, something homologous to Heideggerian anxiety, the next question is whether we can extend the parallels even further, so that we find something akin to Heidegger's appeal to authenticity in Wittgenstein's later philosophy. The short answer is that I think we can, although the story is not quite as straightforward as that. And that is the story I turn to in the next chapter.

---

[26] Cavell uses this phrase in his treatment of scepticism about other minds, which he characterizes as a failure of acknowledgment. The matters I discuss here are concerned with a different kind of scepticism, and so my appropriation of Cavell's phrase about construing a metaphysical finitude as an intellectual lack should be taken somewhat loosely. That said, I think Cavell's discussion of acknowledgment is pertinent to this cluster of issues. I touch on its pertinence in section 5.5.

5
Authenticity and the Everyday

5.1. Kripke's Wittgenstein

Like Heidegger's engagement with anxiety, Wittgenstein's engagement with scepticism induces a recognition of the uncanniness of our ordinary practices, an underlying unsettledness in what we want to regard as secure. Among Wittgenstein's readers, Cavell has done the most to draw attention to the sense of uncanniness that pervades his work, one that is deeply woven into Wittgenstein's engagement with ordinary language. From the very beginning, Cavell claims, Wittgenstein's investigations are shot through with a feeling of precariousness, where our ease in our ordinary language and practices can be destabilized at any moment. Cavell sees such a characteristic moment in the engagement with the passage from Saint Augustine at the very beginning of the *Investigations*. On Cavell's reading, we should be struck by the very fact that Wittgenstein is struck by this passage. It is not obviously philosophically problematic—it is not obviously philosophical at all—and Wittgenstein does not so much want to advise us of Augustine's error as to draw our attention to the way that philosophical anxiety can grip us at any moment:

One observes, 'What could be less remarkable than Augustine's remark about his elders moving around and uttering sounds?' Another retorts, 'Less remarkable—when we are in a maze of unanswered questions about what *naming* is, what it *is* to call a thing or a person, what constitutes an *object*, *how* we (with certainty) grasp one idea or image or concept rather than another, what makes a pointer *point*, a talker *mean*!' Nothing is wrong; everything is wrong. It is the philosophical moment.   (Cavell 1990, 98–9)[1]

---

[1] See also Cavell (1989, 60–4), (1988, 166–7), and (1995) for other passages in which Cavell examines the interplay between the ordinary and the strange in the opening passages of the *Investigations*.

5.1. KRIPKE'S WITTGENSTEIN 111

For Cavell, this oscillation between a sense of ordinariness and a sense of strangeness is at the heart of Wittgenstein's engagement with philosophy.[2] And he connects this uncanniness to scepticism: '[F]or me the uncanniness of the ordinary is epitomized by the possibility or threat of what philosophy has called skepticism, understood... as the capacity, even desire, of ordinary language to repudiate itself, specifically to repudiate its power to word the world, to apply to the things we have in common, or to pass them by' (Cavell 1988, 154).

If I was right in the previous chapter to find the parallels I did between the sceptical worries that animate Wittgenstein's *Investigations* and Heidegger's treatment of anxiety, the question of whether Wittgenstein's emphasis on our everyday practices should be read as inauthentic hinges considerably on how Wittgenstein responds to the threat of scepticism. And, as it happens, the secondary literature offers us divergent responses to this question.

Kripke famously finds in Wittgenstein's treatment of rule following a novel formulation of a sceptical problem with regard to meaning, and a novel response to the problem.[3] Wittgenstein presents us with a dilemma between Platonism and scepticism and, on Kripke's reading, grasps the sceptical horn of the dilemma. To the question of what justifies us in saying that, for instance, the correct continuation of the rule 'Add 2' beyond 1000 is 1002, 1004, and so on, Kripke's Wittgenstein endorses the sceptic's answer: nothing. The scepticism at work here cuts deep. At issue, Kripke insists, is not merely the epistemological question of how I might *know* what someone—or even I myself—means by the word 'plus'. At stake, rather, is the very question of whether there is any fact at all regarding the meaning of the word 'plus' that could be known, even by an ideal knower.[4] 'There can be no fact as to what I mean by "plus", or any other word at any time', Kripke concludes (Kripke 1982, 21).

---

[2] In Chapter 8, I consider in more detail Wittgenstein's use of imaginary scenarios to unsettle our confidence and to provoke us to see the familiar in a strange new light.

[3] Because its fidelity to Wittgenstein's own text is questionable, Kripke's reading has been dubbed 'Kripkenstein'. Kripke himself is refreshingly candid in admitting that exegetical accuracy is not his primary concern. His argument, he claims, 'should be thought of as expounding neither "Wittgenstein's" argument nor "Kripke's": rather Wittgenstein's argument as it struck Kripke, as it presented a problem for him' (Kripke 1982, 5).

[4] In this respect, Kripke endorses the reading of Wittgenstein's treatment of rule following as manifesting a Kantian rather than a Cartesian variety of scepticism, to use the distinction of Conant's that I discussed in section 4.4. In section 3.2, I classed Kripke and Wright (1980) together in offering variants of a conventionalist reading of Wittgenstein. One point at which

Kripke's Wittgenstein provides what he calls, following Hume, a 'sceptical solution' to the sceptical problem as presented. That is, rather than arguing that the sceptical conclusion—in this case, that there are no facts with regard to meaning—is unwarranted, a sceptical solution 'begins on the contrary by conceding that the sceptic's negative assertions are unanswerable', but that 'our ordinary practice or belief is justified because—contrary appearances notwithstanding—it need not require the justification the sceptic has shown to be untenable' (Kripke 1982, 66). The sceptical solution that Kripke provides to this Wittgensteinian puzzle about meaning is to jettison the idea of truth-conditions in favour of assertion or justification conditions, which are licensed by the collective behaviour of a community. There may be no fact about the 'correct' continuation of a rule, but there are facts about how a community of language-users proceeds, and provided this community does not fall into discord, we are no worse off than the Humean sceptic whose worries dissolve into nothing when he leaves off his philosophical speculations.[5] What it means to engage in rule-following behaviour correctly is to find one's inclinations on how to follow a given rule to be in accord with others. On Kripke's reading of Wittgenstein, our behaviour is licensed not by its accord with a standard of correctness in the rule itself, or in the mind of the rule-follower, but by its accord with the behaviour of our fellows.

5.2. An 'Authentic' Alternative

On Kripke's reading, Wittgenstein presents us with a choice—scepticism or Platonism—and rejects Platonism. A common criticism of Kripke's

---

they diverge is this one here. Wright seems more concerned than Kripke with the epistemological question of how I *know* that I am going on in the right way, whereas Kripke is more concerned with the question of what, if anything, constitutes the facts that would determine what is right and wrong in the first place.

[5] Hume famously reconciles himself to his sceptical solution at the end of Book One of his *Treatise on Human Nature*, 1.4.7: 'Most fortunately it happens, that since reason is incapable of dispelling these clouds, nature herself suffices to that purpose, and cures me of this philosophical melancholy and delirium, either by relaxing this bent of mind, or by some avocation, and lively impression of my senses, which obliterate all these chimeras. I dine, I play a game of back-gammon, I converse, and am merry with my friends; and when after three or four hour's amusement, I wou'd return to these speculations, they appear so cold, and strain'd, and ridiculous, that I cannot find in my heart to enter into them any farther'.

reading—and one with which I am in sympathy—is that it fails to register that Wittgenstein rejects scepticism as well as Platonism.[6] The problem, on this alternative reading, is not the Platonist response to the sceptical dilemma but the sceptical dilemma itself. Kripke is right to think that Wittgenstein wants us to feel the force of this sceptical dilemma, but he does not see that Wittgenstein thinks this force comes from the sceptic's misapprehension of the situation. What Wittgenstein calls for is not a way *through* the sceptical dilemma to a sceptical solution but rather a way of shifting our apprehension of the sceptical dilemma so that it loses its force.

In section 4.3, I presented a picture of explanations as filling gaps in understanding. This picture allowed us one perspective on the sceptical problematic: since every explanation can be multiply interpreted we seem to face an infinite regress of explanations of explanations of explanations unless we can find a 'final' explanation that definitively closes every possible gap in our understanding. What Kripke (1982, 66) calls a 'straight' solution to this problem would be a satisfactory account of how such 'final' explanations operate so that we see that our anxieties were misplaced. Kripke's sceptical solution finds a way to live without a final explanation. What I will call, for reasons that will become clear shortly, an 'authentic' response to the problem seeks to dislodge the picture that fed the problem in the first place. The way out of the paradox is not to realize that we can live without a final explanation but to realize that the very idea of a final explanation is incoherent, so that there is nothing we are learning to live without.

At *PI* §§198–201—the core sections of Kripke's reading of the sceptical problem—Wittgenstein adverts several times to the concept of interpretation. The problem as posed by his interlocutor begins: 'But how can a rule teach me what I have to do at *this* point? After all, whatever I do can, on some interpretation, be made compatible with the rule' (*PI* §198). The problem, as Wittgenstein's interlocutor perceives it, is a variant on the story I told about explanation: following a rule means interpreting the rule, but interpretations themselves can be multiply interpreted so that we face a regress of interpretations of interpretations of interpretations. At *PI* §198, and again at *PI* §201, the primary force of Wittgenstein's

---

[6] This criticism finds varied expression in McDowell (1984), Goldfarb (1985), Diamond (1989), Cavell (1990), and Stone (2000).

response is to re-situate the concept of interpretation within the forms of life in which it has a use. 'Interpretations by themselves do not determine meaning', he replies at PI §198, and he elaborates on this point at PI §201:

> That there is a misunderstanding here is shown by the mere fact that in this chain of reasoning we place one interpretation behind another, as if each one contented us at least for a moment, until we thought of yet another lying behind it. For what we thereby show is that there is a way of grasping a rule which is *not* an interpretation, but which, from case to case of application, is exhibited in what we call 'following the rule' and 'going against it'.
>
> That's why there is an inclination to say: every action according to a rule is an interpretation. But one should speak of interpretation only when one expression of a rule is substituted for another.

The interlocutor's confusion arises from expecting of interpretation something other than what it provides. There are occasions on which we do interpret a rule—a signpost indicating that my destination is on the right at an intersection where I have the choice between a hard and soft right might involve me in interpreting the sign as pointing to one of the two plausible alternatives—but the idea that *every* instance of following a rule involves an interpretive act is precisely the kind of philosophical wheel-spinning Wittgenstein wants to overcome. By reminding us of how interpretations are *used*, Wittgenstein encourages us to resist the pursuit of idealized concepts that have no application in our language-games.

Kripke adverts to the idea of communally-licensed inclinations in rule following on the basis of Wittgenstein's emphasis on custom at PI §198 and §199. But he misunderstands Wittgenstein's emphasis, I think, in reading custom as part of a sceptical solution to a sceptical paradox rather than as a way of side-stepping the paradox altogether. The notion of a custom enters the discussion at a point where Wittgenstein's interlocutor is troubled by the very constitution of correctness in following a rule—if interpretations do not tell me how to follow a rule correctly, what does? As I read him, Wittgenstein is not saying that customs *determine* or *constitute* what is correct—'custom' is not the answer to the question of what constitutes the correctness of our behaviour—but rather that, when we see rule-following behaviour as part of a custom, the question of correctness or constitution loses its grip on us. The concept of correctness has a role *within* certain language-games, and examining those language-games gives us a clearer picture of the way that the concept of correctness engages with other concepts within those language-games. But that means that it makes no sense to inquire about the correctness of the given language-games themselves. It makes sense to say that following the sign '→' by going right is the correct way of following that sign. It makes no sense to ask further whether that language-game is the correct one to be playing. It is not, *pace* Kripke, that there is no general *fact* about whether we are following the rule correctly but rather that talk of facts and correctness have no place outside specific language-games.[7]

Both Kripke's sceptical solution and the Platonist insistence that *something* must ground our rule-following practices assume that there is a coherent question to be asked about what justifies us in playing the language-games that we do. But Wittgenstein, as I understand him, wants to challenge precisely that assumption. A sceptical solution wants to make do with the discovery that there is 'something one *couldn't* do' (*PI* §374).[8] But in recovering an ordinary conception of interpretation, Wittgenstein wants us to see that this perceived dilemma is illusory: we only seem unable to do something when we detach the concept of interpretation from the language-games in which it has a use.

5.3. Kripke's Heidegger

If I am right in seeing parallels between Wittgenstein's treatment of rule following and Heidegger's treatment of anxiety, our interpretive responses to the two can inform one another. On one hand, as I have been hinting, seeing the interpretive debate surrounding Wittgenstein's treatment of rule following with a Heideggerian eye helps us see that Cavell, McDowell, Diamond, and others are pushing for a reading of Wittgenstein that could be construed as envisioning an authentic understanding of our practices. And, on the other hand, the parallel will help us understand Heideggerian authenticity not as a transcendence of the everyday, but as an investment in it.

---

[7] Stone (2000, 99) diagnoses the problem with talk about facts about meaning nicely: 'If there is something amiss—some cause for philosophy—in talk of "facts" about meaning, how could denying the proposition that such facts exist be any less problematic than asserting it?'

[8] I discuss this remark in section 1.3.

As a starting point for unfolding these interpretive moves, consider a salient similarity between Wittgensteinian scepticism and Heideggerian anxiety: both crises are prompted by the discovery of the publicly-constituted nature of our practices and projects. Wittgenstein reminds us that 'it's not possible to follow a rule "privately"' (*PI* §202), and Heidegger concludes that '[t]he world of Dasein is a *with-world* [*Mitwelt*]' (*BT* 118). For both, it is not simply that I *happen* to share the world with others, but that this sharing is manifest in the broad range of sense-making activities that give my life the coherence it has.

In related ways, Wittgensteinian scepticism and Heideggerian anxiety confront a worry about the disclosure of what Heidegger calls the with-world. One way to put the worry is this. With the disclosure that my practices have coherence by virtue of being shared with others comes the worry that I have no better reason for doing the things that I do—following rules the way I do, using words the way I do, pursuing the projects that I pursue—than 'that's just how everyone does it'. And phrased like that, it seems like a very weak reason indeed. Both the sceptical problematic and the problematic of anxiety are prompted by a need to find better reasons for doing the things that we do, and by the growing alarm that adequate reasons might not obtain.

On this framing, we can map the three responses to Wittgenstein's sceptical paradox that I rehearsed above—the 'straight' solution, the Kripkean sceptical solution, and my preferred 'authentic' response—on to Heidegger's problematic of anxiety. A 'sceptical' reader of Heidegger—call him Kripkendegger—might interpret the problematic as follows. Anxiety presents Dasein with an existential crisis: there is no reason that can ultimately justify my choice to pursue any projects, and so all my possible projects suddenly show up as irrelevant. This crisis presents Dasein with a dilemma. One horn is the 'straight' solution of insisting that there are good reasons for doing the things that I do after all—either because the authority of *das Man* is sufficient or for some other reason. Heidegger characterizes this response as an inauthentic flight from anxiety into absorption in the one-self. As an alternative, Kripkendegger presents us with a sceptical solution. There is indeed no good reason for doing the things that I do, Kripkendegger tells us—the existential crisis is real and cannot be escaped—but it turns out that things are not as dire as we had feared. We simply act without reasons, and because our actions seem to cohere with the actions of others, these actions gain a kind of emergent significance.

This way of interpreting Heidegger finds more currency among his critics than his defenders,[9] but I think elements of Kripkendegger's response to anxiety make their way not only into some interpreters of Heidegger but also into Heidegger himself. I will say something about the former in this section and return to Kripkendegger in section 5.7, where I argue that Heidegger is more willing than Wittgenstein to accept the sceptical framing of the problematic.

The 'attestation of Dasein of an authentic potentiality-for-being' that is the focus of the second chapter of Division II of *Being and Time* culminates in a discussion of resoluteness in §60. What it means to be resolute is central to understanding what it means to be authentic. The crucial move in Kripkendegger's dialectic—accepting the sceptical conclusion that there is no good reason for any of the choices I make—presents resoluteness as making a self-consciously groundless choice. This way of interpreting Heidegger has achieved some currency. For instance, Dreyfus and Rubin (1991, 316) accept a conception of the world 'as offering no basis for rational choice and no basis on which to construct *my* world', and treat resoluteness as making a choice from *within* this problematic. Relatedly, Michael Friedman talks about an authentic existence as one 'in which Dasein's own choices and decisions rest on no taken for granted background framework at all' (Friedman 2000, 51), and characterizes a 'resolute' decision as 'a decision that goes all the way down, as it were' (Friedman 2000, 52). This notion of action bottoming out in a radically unconstrained choice bears some resemblance to Dummett's (1959) interpretation of a radical conventionalism in Wittgenstein's philosophy of mathematics, which in turn occupies similar conceptual territory to Kripke's sceptical reading. What this cluster of interpretive moves—Kripke's and Dummett's with regard to Wittgenstein and Dreyfus and Rubin's and Friedman's with regard to Heidegger—shares is the idea that the problematics of scepticism and anxiety expose our choices as fundamentally groundless.

The idea that authentic Dasein resolutely makes a groundless choice in full awareness of the groundlessness of that choice should give us cause

---

[9] Burch (2010, 211–12) presents what he calls the 'Decisionism Critique' of Heidegger and finds versions of it in Löwith, Habermas, Levinas, Ricoeur, and Tugendhat.

for concern. Such a choice would amount to no more than heeding one's inclination, willy-nilly. An existential choice, on this reading, is not the point at which Dasein's existence is staked most resolutely but the point at which Dasein's stake simply gives out. McManus (2015a, 166) calls this 'the Motivation Problem': if I have no good reason for making my choices, it becomes unclear what motivates my choices, and how they can be meaningful at all. This reading holds on to a sceptical framing of human motivation that leaves us with an unappealing dilemma: every action either has a rational grounding or it is simply brute behaviour. If we accept this dilemma, anxious Dasein is left with no option besides brute behaviour.

The notion that our choices are groundless is key here. It implies a lack: we search for grounds but, we discover, there are none. I think the real Heidegger differs from Kripkendegger in precisely the way that I think the real Wittgenstein differs from Kripkenstein: rather than offer a sceptical solution to a sceptical (or anxious) paradox, he finds a way of framing our engagement in our practices such that the paradox need not arise. In particular, rather than confronting the alleged fact that we have no good reason for the choices we make, he presents reasoned choice as unfolding *within* an understanding of our existence and presents that understanding as itself not the kind of thing about which we can coherently talk in terms of reasons and choices. In other words, finding good reasons for pursuing my projects at a fundamental level is not something I *cannot* do because it makes no sense to think of it as something I *could* do.

To illustrate what I mean, I will apply this way of reading Heidegger to the crucial second chapter of Division II. Then I will turn back to the question of how we should understand authenticity in relation to the everyday.

5.4. Conscience and Resoluteness

Although the theme of authenticity comes to its climax in Chapter Two of Division II of *Being and Time*, the groundwork is laid early in Division I when Heidegger characterizes the being of Dasein as 'always *mine*' (*BT* 41), or having 'the character of *always-being-my-own-being*' (*BT* 42).[10]

---

[10] This mouthful, which both Stambaugh and Macquarrie and Robinson normally translate more simply as 'mineness', is a clunkier but more accurate attempt to render Heidegger's coinage *Jemeinigkeit*. The *je* prefixed to the first personal possessive pronoun

5.4. CONSCIENCE AND RESOLUTENESS

The mineness that distinguishes Dasein's existence from other modes of being means that Dasein is constantly engaged in, and concerned with, understanding the meaning of its own being. As being-in-the-world, Dasein's self-understanding is also an understanding of its world. Dasein is not simply the being to which beings are disclosed but also, as Heidegger puts it, '*Dasein is its disclosedness*' (*BT* 133). Other beings are disclosed *to* Dasein, but the very phenomenon of disclosedness—that there is a world at all—is a manifestation of the being of Dasein. We do not have a world full of significant things and then subsequently determine what we will do with all this significance. The world only has significance in the first place because we are always already investing it with significance.

As I noted earlier, all of this is equally true of inauthentic and authentic Dasein: as Dasein we cannot *not* engage with concern and understanding in our world. But we can lose sight of our own place at the heart of this significant whole, and this is where Heidegger distinguishes authentic and inauthentic modes of existence. Schematically put, what keeps us from losing sight of our place at the heart of this significant whole is what Heidegger calls the call of conscience, what we do not lose sight of is what Heidegger calls guilt, and not losing sight of it is what Heidegger calls resoluteness. And this resoluteness, I will argue, should be understood not as freedom from the with-world of the everyday, but rather as an investment in it—a recognition of and a commitment to the stake we have in our world.

Heidegger treats conscience itself as a distinctive form of disclosure. He characterizes conscience as a call that summons Dasein to its '*own self*' (*BT* 273). But Heidegger also emphasizes the purely formal nature of this call: 'The call does not say anything, does not give any information about events of the world, has nothing to tell' (*BT* 273). The use of negation here recalls his treatment of anxiety in 'What Is Metaphysics?' In that essay, he writes that, in anxiety, 'man is brought before the **nothing** itself' (*WM* 100), and that '[a]nxiety reveals the **nothing**' (*WM* 101). We see similar language in his treatment of the call of conscience: '*What* does conscience call to the one summoned? Strictly speaking—**nothing**.... "Nothing" is called *to* the self which is

---

mein suggests an 'always' in connection with mineness. Indeed, when Heidegger characterizes the being of Dasein as 'always *mine*', the German is '*je meines*'.

summoned' (*BT* 273).[11] The point in both cases is to distinguish ontic and ontological forms of disclosure. The relation between fear and anxiety is similar to the relation between disclosure and the call of conscience. Disclosure brings before us ontic facts and the call of conscience brings before us the ontological structure of disclosure itself. There is no 'what' in the call of conscience because the call of conscience does not disclose this or that fact. The call of conscience is not the disclosure of some*thing* but the disclosure of Dasein as the clearing in which disclosure is possible. Heidegger says that, hearing the call of conscience, Dasein 'is *summoned* to itself, that is, to its ownmost potentiality-of-being' (*BT* 273). 'What' we learn in hearing the call of conscience is 'what' we are—namely Dasein. Ultimately, Heidegger concludes that conscience '*reveals itself as the call of care*':

[T]he caller is Dasein, anxious in thrownness (in its already-being-in...) about its potentiality-of-being. The one summoned is also Dasein, called forth to its ownmost potentiality-of-being (in its already-ahead-of-itself...). And what is called by the summons—out of falling into *das Man* (already-being-together-with-the-world-taken-care-of)—is Dasein. The call of conscience, that is, conscience itself, has its ontological possibility in the fact that Dasein, in the ground of its being, is care. (*BT* 277; translation modified)

The call of conscience reminds Dasein that the world is significant because it has significance to Dasein, because 'Dasein, in the ground of its being, is care'.

Heidegger tells us that the call of conscience is 'something that *we ourselves* have neither planned, nor prepared for, nor willfully brought about.... The call comes *from* me, and yet *over* me' (*BT* 275). What we plan, prepare for, and wilfully bring about are our projects. Having a conscience is not a project because it is not a factical state of affairs that we can bring about. It is not a particular worldly achievement so much as an orientation toward all worldly achievements. I can *want* to pursue an academic career because pursuing an academic career is a project that has a place within a broader understanding of my being. But I cannot *want* to have a conscience in the same sense because having a conscience is not a project that has a place within an understanding of being but is rather an inflection of that understanding of being itself.

---

[11] See also *BT* 276: 'In its who, the caller is definable by *nothing* "worldly"'.

And yet Heidegger not only talks about wanting to have a conscience but assigns to it supreme importance: he introduces it as what it means to understand the call of conscience (*BT* 288) and later says that it involves 'understanding one's ownmost and constant being-guilty' (*BT* 292). Wanting to have a conscience, then, is closely connected with understanding: it is not so much a matter of wanting this or that outcome but a matter of understanding what it means to want outcomes at all, what it means, that is, to be a being that projects possibilities.

This understanding is closely connected to being-guilty because projecting possibilities also means closing off others. Pursuing a career as an academic philosopher, with the possibilities for disclosure and understanding that that life entails, paradoxically seems to preclude a life of quiet contemplation, with the possibilities for disclosure and understanding that *that* life entails. How the world is disclosed to me is a function of the circumstances I am thrown into and the projects I pursue. And that means that other circumstances and other projects are closed off from me in this disclosure. An inauthentic self-understanding according to which Dasein is plunked down in a ready-made 'world' of present-at-hand beings places the burden of disclosure squarely on this 'world': what the world shows me or does not show me is simply a question of what is already there in the world to be shown. But if Dasein is its disclosedness, what is and is not disclosed to me is a function of how I give expression to my understanding of my own being. Whatever disclosures my way of being affords necessarily negate other possible disclosures. That Dasein is the ground of this negation is what Heidegger characterizes as guilt. As Heidegger has it, Dasein is necessarily 'the (null) ground of a nullity [*Das (nichtige) Grund-sein einer Nichtigkeit*]' (*BT* 285).

We see one manifestation of an inauthentic self-understanding, according to which the burden of disclosure rests squarely on the 'world', in Heidegger's characterization of inauthentic Dasein as sharing common entertainments, tastes in literature, and the like. If this film won an Oscar, if that album hit number one, if that novel won the Booker, it *must be* good—its goodness is elevated to the status of a fact, as if some common currency of approval settles these questions once and for all. But we also see a subtler denial of Dasein's existential status in our way of treating certain measures and modes of description as fixed and objective. McManus (2012, 154–62) offers an illuminating discussion of what he calls 'methodological fetishism', whereby 'we unwittingly cling to particular modes of description beyond the point at which our use of those modes does for us what we take it to do' (McManus 2012, 161). McManus offers as an example the fetishization of quantitative measures in empirical psychology, but his point applies well beyond questions of appropriate scientific method. Whether we are concerned with research methods, tastes in literature, or conversational style, we risk getting entangled in certain procedures in a way that obscures the fact that those procedures are *ours*, that they have been adopted by us or by others because they serve our needs, and that other procedures might turn out to serve us better, or serve us better *now*, if only we attend more carefully to ourselves and our needs. If we lose sight of the ways in which our modes of description serve us, McManus warns, they risk becoming empty, and this emptiness manifests 'a kind of *self*-obscurity—a misunderstanding not "of the world" but of what *we* are trying to do: a loss of an overarching sense of where what we are doing fits within the rest of what we are doing' (McManus 2012, 160).

Wanting to have a conscience represents an authentic response to what I earlier (in section 4.1) called the second-order question of Dasein's understanding of itself as a self-interpreting being. It amounts to recognizing that the meaning of my existence is internally related to my understanding of my existence. Heidegger also characterizes wanting to have a conscience as 'a readiness for anxiety' (*BT* 296), which is one component of resoluteness.[12] Inauthentic Dasein confronts anxiety as an existential crisis because it expects its world to provide it with adequate grounds for its projects. In effect, as I noted earlier, it treats itself as a present-at-hand being whose nature is fixed and defined by its situation in the world. Anxiety confronts Dasein with its existential status as being-in-the-world, and hence with the inadequacy of an inauthentic understanding of its being as something fixed and definite. If authentic Dasein, in wanting to have a conscience, already apprehends itself as being-in-the-world, then the disclosure of anxiety does not come as a crisis: authentic Dasein is ready for it.

Resoluteness—which is the key concept in Heidegger's conception of authenticity—involves understanding the call of conscience, understanding

---

[12] The other two components are reticence and projecting oneself upon one's ownmost being-guilty (see *BT* 295–7).

5.4. CONSCIENCE AND RESOLUTENESS

'one's ownmost and constant being guilty', and hence understanding that Dasein, as being-in-the-world, is the existential ground of the world it finds itself in. This characterization differs from treatments of resoluteness and authenticity that portray them primarily in terms of choice and decision. Such treatments might encourage the kind of Kripkendeggerian reading I sketched above, according to which authentic Dasein resolutely makes a groundless choice in full awareness of its groundlessness. Heidegger certainly emphasizes choice—especially early on in Chapter Two of Division II[13]—but, as I read him, this theme of existential or identity-defining choices is not the deepest stratum of his investigation. What characterizes resoluteness, on my reading, is not primarily a particular *kind of* choice but rather an understanding of what it means to be a being that makes choices in the first place. Heidegger distinguishes authentic and inauthentic modes of existence not in terms of a change in circumstance but in terms of a different orientation toward those circumstances:

> The ready-to-hand 'world' does not become different [in authenticity] as far as 'content', the circle of others is not exchanged for a new one, and yet the understanding, concernful being toward ready-to-hand things, and the solicitous being-with with others is now defined in terms of their ownmost potentiality-of-being-a-self. (*BT* 297–8; translation modified)

What changes, on this account, is not the character of our choices but the character of our concern for things and our solicitude for other Dasein. To the extent that authentic Dasein's choices also differ from those of inauthentic Dasein, that is because, with an authentic understanding of its being, 'resolute Dasein frees itself for its world' (*BT* 298) and inhabits that world clear-sightedly.

In Chapter 3, I investigated the extent to which *das Man* entangles us in conformity or conformism. On the reading I have presented here, the difference between authentic and inauthentic modes of existence is not primarily a question of what we *do*—and hence of whether what we do represents a kind of conformity or conformism—but rather a question of how we understand what we do, how we understand what it means to be the kind of being that can *do* things. An authentic understanding of our

---

[13] See, for instance, *BT* 268, where Heidegger talks about 'choosing to make [the] choice' of a potentiality-of-being.

existential status no doubt affects the way we make decisions but, on this reading, authentic choice is a manifestation of authentic understanding.

Coming to a clearer understanding of what it means to be the kind of being that can *do* things is also a central feature of Wittgenstein's investigations. The aspiration for authenticity that I find in both of these writers is an aspiration to get into clearer view what it means to be the kind of being that we are. A central feature of this kind of being is what I have called our attunement: the world of our everyday practices and ordinary language is a world we share with others, and this attunement is not itself the sort of thing that can be regarded as either justified or unjustified. In the remainder of this chapter, I will articulate and defend the idea that our everydayness is not in conflict with what Heidegger calls authenticity.

5.5. Wittgenstein's Bedrock

Although Heidegger maintains that Dasein is essentially being-with, the public aspect of Dasein's existence seems to fall out of the picture in his treatment of authenticity.[14] In his analysis of anxiety, death, and the call of conscience, Heidegger repeatedly emphasizes that Dasein is individuated, singled out, drawn away from its absorption in the one-self. This picture of the singled out individual might be read as indicating a disinvestment in the shared practices of *das Man* and, accordingly, a rejection of the everydayness that we encounter in Division I. That Heideggerian authenticity does not entail a rejection of the everyday will be easier to see by investigating further what I called the 'authentic' response to Wittgenstein's problematic of rule following.

The Kripkean framing of Heideggerian anxiety presented a dilemma: either we inauthentically ground our choices in the 'that's how one does things' of *das Man* or we commit ourselves to a groundless choice, which is hardly better. Wittgenstein also seems to give some credence to the idea of a groundless choice at *PI* §211: in asking for my reasons for continuing a pattern in a given way, Wittgenstein remarks: '[M]y reasons will soon give out. And then I shall act, without reasons'. I can only justify my actions—even to myself—so far, Wittgenstein tells us, and

---

[14] An interesting exception to this pattern is Heidegger's treatment of history in Chapter 5 of Division II, and especially his treatment of destiny in §74.

eventually these justifications bottom out. 'Once I have exhausted the justifications, I have reached bedrock, and my spade is turned', he famously remarks. 'Then I am inclined to say: "This is simply what I do"' (*PI* §217). No set pattern prescribes what happens when our attempts at explanation or justification give out. The bedrock Wittgenstein alludes to at *PI* §217 is not a fixed ground to our reasoning, but simply the point at which we find ourselves unable to say or do anything to breach a particular impasse in understanding.

I want to return again to a problematic picture of explanation as filling gaps in understanding, which I broached in section 4.3 and returned to in section 5.2. I found this picture problematic because it fed the sceptical worry that no explanation could serve as a 'final' explanation that definitively fills every gap in understanding. This picture of explanation as filling gaps in understanding risks obscuring an important aspect of these gaps: the gaps in understanding that explanations try to bridge are also gaps between particular people. I want to explain something to you because I feel a gap between you and me: there is something—about me, about the world, about you—that I think I understand and you do not. My explanation aims to bring us closer together, to help you see things as I see them. This explanation presupposes a distance between us, but it also presupposes a finite distance: I could not begin trying to explain something to you if we did not share some common ground from which to start. To teach a child subtraction, I have to be confident that the child already knows how to count; to explain why your sister is upset with you, I have to assume we share some understanding of the emotional lives of others. We tailor our explanations to the particular route we need to travel from our shared common ground to cover the gap between us. The demand for a 'final' explanation seems impossible because, in its aspiration to absolute generality, it aims to bridge every conceivable gap in understanding, and so, in effect, reach out to every conceivable person, all at once. This demand presupposes no common ground and so would have an infinite distance to travel.

I have been calling this common ground our attunement. The sceptical problematic, which conjures up the demand for a 'final' explanation, is, in effect, a denial of this attunement. It manifests, one might say, dissatisfaction with the ground we stand on. The requirement that, if I want to be understood, I must share some common ground with others raises the worry that it might not exist, or might be rejected. And this worry pushes us to seek an ideal form of explanation, one that covers all possible questions and compels understanding. This ideal form of explanation aspires to bypass the need for a common ground by giving reasons that do not require it, reasons that could compel anyone, and so establishes the fiction that common ground is a convenience for communication, but not a necessity. In short, the demand for a 'final' explanation denies the need for a common ground, and so effectively denies the common ground itself. The worry that I might not share a common ground with others feeds its denial by demanding that our explanations not rely upon it. Like with the builders of the Tower of Babel, the anxiety that we *might* not share a life together brings it about that we *do* not.

One way of characterizing the difference between a sceptical reading and an authentic reading of Wittgenstein is to say that, on the former, the bedrock of *PI* §217 is our inclinations and, on the latter, the bedrock is our attunement. Once reasons give out, on the sceptical reading, there is just brute behaviour. This reading aligns significant action with justified action: either I have reasons for what I do or what I do is meaningless brute behaviour. This dilemma supposes that it makes sense to ask of this bedrock whether it is rationally justified, so that if the answer is 'no' then we have an *irrational* or *unjustified* action. In other words, it supposes that we can apply to the very practice of asking for and giving reasons the question of whether this practice has a rational foundation. It amounts to an attempt to look in on the life we live with language from the outside, as it were, or from sideways on. If we resist this impulse to try to look at our lives from sideways on, we no longer face the dilemma of characterizing every action as either rationally justified or as brute behaviour. On the authentic reading, significant action does not have to be justified action.

Cavell (1990, 70–1) distinguishes his reading of *PI* §217 from Kripke's in part by noting the different inflections they give to Wittgenstein's response to reaching bedrock. Kripke, as Cavell reads him, takes Wittgenstein to be saying: 'Then I am licensed to say: "This is simply what I am inclined to do"'. Kripke sees a fixed answer to what happens when justifications give out: we fall back on our inclinations, and the normative heft of our inclinations comes with our sharing these inclinations with others. On this reading, 'This is simply what I do' stands as a kind of ultimatum: do as I do or you do not belong to our community.

On Cavell's reading, the *inclination* to say, 'This is simply what I do' stands as an invitation: with the failed attempts at explanation and justification, the teacher offers herself and her conduct as a sample, which may or may not bridge the gap between teacher and pupil. Wittgenstein's 'This is simply what I do' is an expression of the speaker staking herself, of showing where she stands, and soliciting in her interlocutor a response by which they can discover how far her 'I' might become a 'we'. That this is what I do is not something I can further explain or justify any more than I can explain or justify my existence.

Against a tradition that often treats assertion as the primary form of expression, so that language can come to seem primarily—or even exclusively—a matter of exchanging information in an impersonal manner, Cavell works to remind us of the extent to which we stake ourselves in our speech, and the extent to which our speech makes claims on others—and on ourselves. Wittgenstein's inclination to say 'This is simply what I do' could also manifest itself as the inclination to say 'This is simply (or rather, not simply at all) who I am'. In Kripke's telling, nothing more of me is at stake than my inclinations, and those inclinations are no more *mine* than, say, my reflexes. Wittgenstein's moment of bedrock is, for Kripke, the place at which my stake in my words and actions gives out, whereas for Cavell it is the place at which my stake stands out most prominently.

5.6. Authentic Everydayness

A Kripkean reading of Heidegger, according to which resoluteness bottoms out in a choice that is unmotivated because groundless, derives from what I think is a misunderstanding of the difference between the resoluteness of authentic Dasein and inauthentic Dasein's absorption in the one-self. As social beings, this misunderstanding goes, we run the constant risk of allowing others to dictate to us the meaning of our lives, but an authentic being steps forward in its individuality, charting its own course. What keeps us from becoming our authentic selves is our bondage to others. Inauthenticity, then, is a matter of allowing others to matter too much.

I propose, on the contrary, that inauthenticity is a matter of not allowing others to matter enough, or allowing them to matter only in the wrong way. Inauthenticity is a misguided attempt to outsource

Dasein's work of self-interpretation, of seeking the significance of our lives in something external to us. In its absorption in *das Man*, Dasein misunderstands its true nature not because it allows its self to be constituted by others—as being-with, Dasein's constitution by others is inescapable—but because it does not see itself among those others. Because it sees *das Man* as an impersonal 'one' or 'they' rather than as a collaborative 'we'.

Lost in the one-self, Dasein disowns or refuses its stake in its own words. Heidegger emphasizes inauthentic Dasein's unreflective assent to what 'one' says in idle talk. The characteristic features of idle talk—another aspect of Dasein's existential constitution that Heidegger dubiously insists is not to be understood in a disparaging sense (*BT* 167)—are '*gossiping* and *passing the word along*', which he contrasts with communicating 'in the mode of a primordial appropriation of' the being that is talked about (*BT* 168). Heidegger emphasizes the 'complete groundlessness' of idle talk (*BT* 168): in idle talk, words are circulated between people without being grounded in the things that are talked about. We accept a claim as true because it is what 'one' says, and we pass it on to others not as something to which we are personally staked, but as what 'one' says.

Idle talk forecloses the possibility that my words might matter to you, or yours to me, because the words that we speak are not properly *mine* or *yours* but belong to something more impersonal. In its absorption in *das Man*, inauthentic Dasein closes out the others it shares a world with by allowing them to make no more than conventional claims upon one another. In idle talk, inauthentic Dasein contrives to exchange words where nothing is at stake. To the extent that they fall back on inclinations in which Dasein has no stake, both Kripkenstein and Kripkendegger represent inauthentic modes of existence.

Conceiving Wittgensteinian scepticism as motivated by the worry that nothing guarantees my attunement with others adds a wrinkle to Heidegger's account of anxiety as individuating Dasein to its ownmost being-in-the-world (*BT* 187). If this individuation manifests a loss of confidence in the shared world of being-with, it is closely related to the loss of significance that befalls Dasein in anxiety. Untethered from our connection to others, we emerge not as sovereign individuals but as bereft of our capacity to make sense—not just to one another, but also to ourselves. An authentic investment in the work of self-understanding requires not a declaration of independence from the publicly-constituted with-world of the everyday but an investment in it.

This investment means seeing our shared world as structured not by what 'one' says and does but rather by what *we* say and do. But that also means that our shared world is no more stable and secure, no more coherent and rational in its structure, than we ourselves are. Just as the question of *what* Dasein is gets articulated in the living out of its existence, so the question of *what* our shared world is gets articulated in the living out of our shared existence. In other words, the structure of our shared world is fundamentally uncanny.

Both Heideggerian flight into the one-self and the Wittgensteinian temptation to find some external justification for our practices represent a denial of this uncanniness. The embrace of the one-self represents a yearning for stability, for seeing this attunement as secure beyond doubt. There is nothing insidious about following a rule in the way that everyone else follows that rule, but we get ourselves into trouble when we take the further step of assuming or theorizing that some independent standard of correctness compels our and everyone else's conformity to the rule. Conforming to what *one* does, then, is not so much the problem. The problem rather lies in supposing that this conformity is grounded in a source more stable and absolute than our mutual attunement. Here Wittgenstein and Heidegger are agreed. For the most part, we tend to accept both our conformity to norms and the conformism of received opinion with an air of necessity and inevitability. Because this is the way things are done, surely they could not be done in any other way. Because just *this* is how we live, we want the security of seeing our forms of life as grounded on the most solid bedrock.

Of course, even the most solid bedrock is afloat upon a sea of magma. Even the firmest foundations are unstable. Recognizing the instability of attunement induces anxiety: if nothing guarantees our attunement, our words might not reach others. In Division I of *Being and Time*, Heidegger explores anxiety as a crucial mood that discloses the absence of any deeper foundation for our forms of life. We find a similar mood of anxiety pervading Wittgenstein's investigations. Readings of Wittgenstein that place too much emphasis on the shared norms of an established community risk missing the precariousness of many of the scenarios Wittgenstein explores. Wittgenstein's writings are peopled with a variety of strange creatures, from the wood-sellers (*RFM* I §149) to the wayward pupil

(*PI* §143 and §185) to the talking lion (*PPF* xi §327). These bizarre examples dislodge the impression of absoluteness that sometimes attaches to our practices, and remind us that our normal attunement with one another is an achievement, and not a matter of course.[15] His language-games and imagined scenarios are rife with misunderstandings, breakdowns, failures of people to make sense of one another. Wittgenstein's investigations induce the vertiginous discovery that our lives literally depend upon an attunement that comes with no guarantees.[16]

Wittgenstein's emphasis on ordinary language does not represent an evasion or suppression of uncanniness. Instead, he sees uncanniness inscribed in our inhabitation of the ordinary. The ordinary is our home in the sense that ordinary language is the language that speaks to and from the particular situation we find ourselves in. Concepts articulate the interests and needs of the people who use them, and they are useful to the extent that they are usable. We find it useful to price cheese according to its weight, but this practice would lose its point if the weight of cheese were constantly fluctuating (*PI* §142). If everything were in a continual flux of rapid growth and shrinking, our concept of weight would have no use, or would have radically different applications, whereas other concepts would become useful to us that have no application in the language-games we play at present. Our concepts are responsive to our circumstances in their particularity. Wittgenstein's appeal to ordinary language thus acknowledges the impossibility of a godlike—or sideways—perspective for which, as Wittgenstein puts it, 'certain concepts are absolutely the correct ones' (*PPF* xii §366). Wittgenstein does not mean that, in our finitude, we fail to grasp the absolutely correct concepts, but rather that it is of the nature of concepts to belong to forms of life that are themselves neither correct nor incorrect.

If I am right in tracing these parallels between Wittgenstein and Heidegger, Heidegger's exhortation to authenticity in Division II no more repudiates the everydayness of Division I than Wittgenstein's reminders of ordinary language repudiate the ordinary. Living authentically does not require some sort of extra-ordinary, non-everyday way of

---

[15] Cf. Mulhall (2001, 216): 'Wittgenstein's conception of ordinariness is no less receptive to the idea that its structures may become fixated or frozen, expressive of the human flight from ordinariness as it might otherwise be, than is Heidegger's'.

[16] McDowell (1981, 149–53) also discusses this experience in terms of vertigo.

living. What it requires is an acknowledgment and acceptance that my way of living—however mundane or zany—is something I am responsible for, something that expresses me, that *is* me. Authenticity then calls not for an escape from the everyday but, as Heidegger puts it, mastery of the everyday: 'But existence can also master the everyday in the Moment [*Augenblick*], and of course often only "for the moment", but it can never extinguish it' (*BT* 371). Inauthentic Dasein is 'mastered' by *das Man*, allowing its inhabitation of the everyday to be subjected to an authority other than its own, but authentic Dasein turns the tables on *das Man*, so to speak, asserting its own mastery over the everyday.

Mulhall (1994) emphasizes that Heidegger's analysis of inauthentic Dasein is an analysis of Dasein in its *average* everydayness, raising the question of whether there are other ways of inhabiting the everyday. Mulhall answers that authentic Dasein repudiates inauthentic Dasein's averageness—its subjecting of itself to the average—and not its everydayness: 'Authentic Being-in-the-world is not a transcendence of or escape from everydayness but a mode of everydayness; it is not an extraordinary mode of Being, but a mode of inhabiting the ordinary' (Mulhall 1994, 151).[17] The contrast with average everydayness for Mulhall is authentic everydayness. Authentic Dasein does not move beyond the everyday, but accepts the everyday without becoming lost in it.[18]

This contrast echoes Cavell's (1989, 46) contrast between the 'actual' and 'eventual' everyday. The actual everyday is the 'scene of illusion' (Cavell 1989, 46), the average everydayness of the one-self in which we find ourselves initially and for the most part. However, the actual everyday requires not rejection but reconfiguration: Wittgenstein's appeal to ordinary language neither endorses the actual everyday nor

---

[17] Here again, we find inconsistency in Heidegger's handling of everydayness. Mulhall marshals evidence to support his reading: '[A]uthentic existence is nothing which hovers over entangled everydayness, but is existentially a modified grasp of everydayness' (*BT* 179). On the other hand, in the initial discussion of *das Man* Heidegger says: 'The self of everyday Dasein is the *one-self*, which we distinguish from the *authentic self*' (*BT* 129; translation modified), making no allowance for the self of an *authentic* everyday Dasein as distinct from an *average* everyday Dasein. I find Mulhall's reading compelling, and consonant with what I think is the stronger way of reading through Heidegger's inconsistencies, so I feel comfortable following it despite textual evidence to the contrary.

[18] Blattner (2015, 131) makes a similar claim: 'A life...inflected by authenticity [is] still lived within the everyday. One must return authentically to the everyday, for there is nowhere else to live'.

rejects the everyday, but rather appeals to the eventual everyday. This eventual everyday, as I understand it, resembles Heidegger's authentic Dasein. It calls not for a change in our outward forms of life but for an inward change in our relation to them.

Both Wittgenstein and Heidegger style this inward change not as a matter of grasping something new but as a matter of recovering something we have always had but have somehow lost sight of. This recovery does not require new truths or new theories, but rather helps us inhabit where we are without self-deception. Despite vast stylistic differences, both Wittgenstein and Heidegger characterize this call in terms of bringing back: 'What *we* do is to **bring words back** from their metaphysical to their everyday use', Wittgenstein says (*PI* §116), while in heeding the call of conscience, Heidegger tells us, 'Dasein explicitly **brings itself back** to itself from its lostness in *das Man*' (*BT* 268). Philosophy, for both Wittgenstein and Heidegger, is not a matter of moving forward to the new discovery that will ground our practices, but rather a matter of calling us back to the uncanniness that we have always already known and always already forgotten.

5.7. 'Therapeutic' and 'Existential' Wittgensteins

What it means to do philosophy on the uncanny ground of the everyday is a question I will turn to in Part Three, where the differences I perceive between Wittgenstein and Heidegger become most pronounced. But even at this stage, I should be careful not to overstate the similarities between these two thinkers even as I argue that those similarities go deeper than is commonly acknowledged. Let me begin to articulate an important difference between Wittgenstein and Heidegger by giving voice to an objection that may have been building in the minds of some readers, especially over the course of the last two chapters.[19]

The objection is this. On my reading of his approach to philosophical criticism, especially as I presented it in Chapter 1, Wittgenstein aims not at refuting the metaphysician but at disarming her. The endgame is not

---

[19] These readers do not exist only in my imagination. I am grateful to one of the anonymous readers of this manuscript for articulating this objection incisively.

5.7. 'THERAPEUTIC' AND 'EXISTENTIAL' WITTGENSTEINS

to reach a point where Wittgenstein's interlocutors have come to see the wrongness of their views but rather to reach a point where the interlocutors no longer think that they have a substantive view that can be distinguished from substantive opposing views. In the case of the anxiety of the rule-following sceptic, the endgame is, in effect, the discovery that there was nothing to be anxious about. Our ordinary ways of following a rule are fine as they are and the sceptic's anxiety was a misapprehension. By contrast, Heidegger thinks anxiety reveals something profound and important. There is *something* we discover in anxiety about the groundlessness of our everyday practices and assimilating the truth of this discovery calls for a profound transformation in our self-understanding.

One way to see this difference between the two philosophers is to return to Heidegger's play on 'nothing' in 'What Is Metaphysics?': Wittgensteinian criticism and Heideggerian criticism agree that the targets of their criticism are wrong about *nothing*, but this 'nothing' takes on sharply different inflections. We might say, borrowing terms from the secondary literature on the *Tractatus*, that Wittgenstein has an *austere* conception of this 'nothing' whereas Heidegger has a *substantial* conception of the 'nothing'.[20] Unlike Wittgenstein, Heidegger thinks that inauthentic Dasein overlooks something deeply important in neglecting the nothing. This difference between them is particularly pronounced when we consider the different ways that they invoke images of covering, uncovering, and discovering. Heidegger frequently appeals to more authentic modes of apprehension as being 'covered up' (*verdeckt*) and looks to what phenomenological investigation can 'uncover' (*entdecken*) whereas what Wittgenstein aspires to uncover is not a more primordial understanding but nonsense: 'The results of philosophy are the **discovery** [*Entdeckung*] of some piece of plain nonsense and the bumps that the understanding has got by running up against the limits of language' (*PI* §119). In describing his phenomenological method, Heidegger claims that '[B]eing covered up [*Verdecktheit*] is the counterconcept to "phenomenon"' (*BT* 36), and says that the phenomenon 'is something that is concealed [*verborgen*]' (*BT* 35), whereas, for Wittgenstein, 'nothing is concealed [*verborgen*]' (*PI* §435). As Heidegger figures it, there is *something* more primordial that we need to uncover, whereas for

---

[20] Conant (2000, 2002) distinguishes between 'substantial' and 'austere' conceptions of nonsense in his interpretation of the *Tractatus*.

Wittgenstein, discovery consists in exposing *nothing* where we thought we saw *something*.[21]

The force of this objection is not simply that Wittgenstein and Heidegger are more different than I have been letting on. The objection also suggests a tension within my reading of Wittgenstein. Can I have it both ways, presenting a 'therapeutic' Wittgenstein, who thinks that the metaphysician's dissatisfaction with our ordinary forms of speech is a result of simple confusion, and an 'existential' Wittgenstein, who shares Heidegger's apprehension of the ordinarily overlooked uncanniness of our forms of life? I think I can, provided I emphasize that the metaphysician's dissatisfaction with our ordinary forms of speech is not a result of a *simple* confusion.

To begin with, let me draw attention to a further difference between what I have been calling 'sceptical' and 'authentic' readings of Wittgenstein on rule following. On Kripke's reading, the sceptical paradox disrupts a Platonist assumption about meaning that a 'straight' solution to the paradox would try to restore. That is, the sceptical doubt is a challenge to a prior Platonism. One feature of the 'authentic' response is that our ordinary way of following a rule harbours no Platonist assumption. On this reading, the Platonist insistence on a 'final' explanation that provides a secure grounding for our practices is a subsequent response to a prior sceptical worry. In a sense, Wittgenstein more closely resembles the Platonist than the sceptic. Like the Platonist, he too wants to say that explanations come to an end. The difference is that he does not accept the sceptic's hyperbolic requirement for what it must mean for an explanation to come to an end.[22]

This point dovetails with one I developed in Chapter 1—section 1.4 in particular—where I claimed that ordinary language does not encode metaphysical assumptions. The Heraclitean philosopher I engaged with there wanted to say (a) that ordinary language encodes the metaphysical assumption that rivers are perdurable objects and (b) that this assumption is mistaken. Kripke's sceptical reading presents a similar pair of

---

[21] Consider also *PI* §133: 'The real discovery [*Entdeckung*] is the one that enables me to break off philosophizing when I want to', or *PI* §126: 'The name "philosophy" might also be given to what is possible *before* all new discoveries [*Entdeckungen*] and inventions'. I return to these differences in their modes of criticism in section 8.1.

[22] Stone (2000) also discusses the idea that the sceptical reading gets things backwards by presenting the sceptical dilemma as engaging with a prior Platonist assumption.

claims: (a) in our everyday practices, we hold a Platonist assumption that our rule-following practices are justified by some 'final' explanation and (b) this assumption is wrong. I want to refigure Kripke's reading of the sceptical problematic in a manner similar to my refiguring of the Heraclitean philosopher's framing of the metaphysics of ordinary language. In both cases, metaphysical or Platonist assertions are not the starting point but rather one direction our thinking might go if we accept the force of the sceptic's challenge at face value.

Heidegger's diagnosis of anxiety sometimes seems closer to Kripke's diagnosis of the sceptical paradox than it is to my preferred 'authentic' alternative. Pre-anxious Dasein is absorbed in a world constituted by *das Man* in a way that suppresses its authentic potentiality-for-being-a-self. Heidegger looks more favourably on anxiety than Wittgenstein does on scepticism because it disrupts this absorption, and he styles flight as an inauthentic re-absorption in the world of the one-self. As Heidegger presents it, average everyday Dasein is not guilty of holding bogus metaphysical presuppositions but something parallel, what we might call bogus hermeneutical presuppositions about the ground of intelligibility of its world.

Heidegger's analysis of average everydayness is not quite so cut-and-dried as to leave us with a dilemma between an inauthentic Dasein absorbed in the one-self and an authentic Dasein that resists this absorption. At a number of points, he characterizes average everyday Dasein not as inauthentic but in an indifferent mode that is neither authentic nor inauthentic.[23] But this third option of indifference sometimes falls out of his discussion, and even when it does not, it can be difficult to distinguish it from what Heidegger characterizes as inauthentic. He certainly does not regard indifferent Dasein the way Wittgenstein regards our ordinary forms of language: indifference, as much as inauthenticity, is something to be overcome in Heidegger's account of authenticity.

For Heidegger, in other words, we should mistrust our habitual modes of speech, thought, and behaviour. For Wittgenstein, by contrast, we should mistrust our mistrust. In the story I have been telling about rule following, we are led astray by a loss of confidence in our attunement,

---

[23] See, for example, *BT* 232: 'But this *potentiality-of-being* that is always *mine* is free for authenticity or inauthenticity, or for a mode in which neither of these has been differentiated'. See similar claims at *BT* 43, 121, and 331.

which prompts a search for firmer ground that in turn ushers in the sceptical problematic. What we need, on Wittgenstein's diagnosis, is 'to recognize the ground that lies before us as the ground' (*RFM* VI §31). But this loss of confidence is not a simple, avoidable error. For Wittgenstein, our propensity to lose confidence in our attunement is as deeply rooted in our nature as our propensity to fall into absorption in the world is for Heidegger.[24] And like Heidegger, Wittgenstein sees this propensity as a response to the uncanniness of the ordinary.

The different levels of trust our two authors exhibit in the everyday is evident in the differing structures of their *magna opera*. Average everyday Dasein and authentic Dasein are distinct enough for Heidegger that he can analyse them in the two distinct Divisions of *Being and Time*. *Philosophical Investigations*, by contrast, has no break in its analysis: even in editions in which it is divided into two parts, 'Part II' is not presented as a deepening of the analysis of 'Part I', even if in some respects that is in fact what it is. The structure of *Being and Time* figures authenticity as a single big achievement. *Philosophical Investigations* figures it as hundreds of small achievements, fallen away from and re-secured on every page.

As I have read them, both Wittgenstein and Heidegger conceive authenticity not as an escape from the everyday but as a reinvestment in it. However, the differences I have remarked upon here indicate a greater whole-heartedness on Wittgenstein's part in that project of reinvestment. And this whole-heartedness in turn gives Wittgenstein's criticism its therapeutic inflection: he holds unflinchingly to the conviction that we already have at our disposal the resources we need to overcome our propensity for self-bafflement.

The seeming tension between a 'therapeutic' and an 'existential' Wittgenstein arises, I think, from a view of our attunement as fixed and stable. If the 'therapeutic' Wittgenstein wants to return us to a stable home, he would find himself at odds with an 'existential' Wittgenstein who finds an uncanny openness in our attunement. But if Wittgensteinian therapy is meant precisely to disabuse us of the aspiration to find firm footing and to recognize our attunement as labile, the tension disappears.

---

[24] Cf. Cavell (1979, 207): '[Wittgenstein] never, I think, underestimated the power of the motive to reject the human: nothing could be more human'.

5.7. 'THERAPEUTIC' AND 'EXISTENTIAL' WITTGENSTEINS

It also refigures what resoluteness calls for: not standing firm—this is precisely what gets us into trouble—but nimbleness and improvisation. Wittgensteinian authenticity, in other words, calls upon us to play. In the next chapter I develop a conception of authenticity as play, and then in Part Three I consider how this ludic conception of authenticity informs Wittgenstein's method.

6
Authenticity and Play

At the end of the previous chapter, I considered the tension between two versions of Wittgenstein I have been giving voice to: a 'therapeutic' Wittgenstein, who wants us to see metaphysical and sceptical concerns as ultimately empty, and an 'existential' Wittgenstein, who follows Heidegger in seeing the problematic of scepticism (or anxiety in Heidegger's case) as disclosing something profound and important, namely the uncanniness of our being-in-the-world. I argued that this uncanniness does not lend substance to the sceptic's doubts but it does inform our understanding of the nature of the ordinary to which Wittgenstein wants to return us. In particular, in seeing the ordinary as founded in nothing more stable than our attunement, I noted that resoluteness—at least as understood through a Wittgensteinian lens—calls not for steadfast constancy but for the nimbleness and improvisation of play. My aim in this chapter is to expand on Wittgenstein's thinking about play and to articulate and defend a conception of authenticity in terms of play.

6.1. Wittgenstein's Language-Game Analogy

We find Wittgenstein thinking about play most overtly in his treatment of language-games. The coinage 'language-game' first enters *Philosophical Investigations* at §7, and it is multi-faceted from its inception. Wittgenstein introduces the term to model the ostensive teaching by which a child learns a language, but immediately adds that he will use the same expression to describe the sorts of primitive languages he uses as objects of comparison.[1] He also declares that he will 'call the whole,

---

[1] See *PI* §130 for this use of 'objects of comparison'. I explore the idea of objects in comparison in more detail in Chapter 8.

consisting of language and the activities into which it is woven, a "language-game"'. At *PI* §23, he calls the various sectors of natural language language-games, with the emphasis on 'game' suggesting 'that the *speaking* of language is part of an activity, or of a form of life'. Starting at §65, Wittgenstein develops a further analogy between language and games, claiming that neither the word 'language' nor the word 'game' has fixed boundaries, and that their various instances are connected not by sharing a set of necessary and sufficient conditions, but by family resemblances.

Wittgenstein often speaks about meaningful utterances as moves in a language-game,[2] and his primary analogy here is chess: utterances form the same sorts of discrete units in language that moves do in chess, units that we do not find in free-flowing games. Associating utterances with moves in a game brings out the way in which speaking is a matter of doing something, and if we are to avoid a stalemate, it is a matter of doing something that changes the state of the language-game. The analogy with games helps us to see a number of contrasts in language that we risk passing over due to similarities in grammatical structure. At *PI* §49, for instance, Wittgenstein rejects the view that naming is a special kind of description, saying that describing is a move in a language-game, but that naming is not itself a move but a precondition for making a move: 'Naming is so far not a move in the language-game—any more than putting a piece in its place on the board is a move in chess'. Naming and describing can be expressed in sentences with identical grammatical structures—indeed, with identical wording (e.g. 'The bishop moves diagonally' could either be used to define how a bishop moves or to describe the latest move in a game in progress)—but the analogy with moves in a game brings out a crucial difference. Thinking of language in analogy with games shows that our words gain meaning by being put into play in a language-game. Any other use of words is either a preparatory step toward playing a language-game, or it is simply idling.

In addition to chess, Wittgenstein often appeals by analogy to another form of play that is far removed from the structured play of chess. He alludes to the kind of free play most characteristic of children in order to emphasize that language users do not need to consult or obey rules in

---

[2] See e.g. *PI* §§22, 31, 33, and 49.

order to speak and that our criteria for the use of words are fluid. Wittgenstein tells us that 'one can also imagine someone's having learnt the game without ever learning or formulating rules' (*PI* §31) and returns to this point at *PI* §54. At *PI* §83, he claims that games can evolve without anyone ever formulating rules:

We can easily imagine people amusing themselves in a field by playing with a ball like this: starting various existing games, but playing several without finishing them, and in between throwing the ball aimlessly into the air, chasing one another with the ball, throwing it at one another for a joke, and so on. And now someone says: The whole time they are playing a ball-game and therefore are following definite rules at every throw.

And is there not also the case where we play, and make up the rules as we go along? And even where we alter them—as we go along.

One of the guiding themes of *On Certainty* is the mutability of our fundamental rules of thought and language. *OC* §95 likens the 'propositions describing [our] world-picture' to the rules of a game, and claims that we need never learn these rules explicitly. The following two sections present the famous riverbed analogy, in which Wittgenstein claims that these propositions are subject to gradual change.

The sort of free-flowing play Wittgenstein describes at *PI* §83 is very different from chess. We might reasonably wonder whether Wittgenstein can help himself to two such very different points of reference when comparing language to a game without getting himself into trouble. Roy Harris (1988) raises precisely this objection, and frames it as a dilemma. On one hand, he notes, the openness of criteria in the use of language differs markedly from games like chess, where the rules are formulated explicitly. The rules of a game, Harris claims, are explicitly and exhaustively formulated, and must already be in place and agreed upon by all players before the game can begin. By contrast, the diversity of idiolects and the gradual and unlegislated change of languages suggest that language does not follow the dictates laid down by pre-set rules, but that we rather formulate rules to track a language that evolves independent of those rules. On the other hand, if we liken language to the sorts of openended games where innovation *is* possible, we lose the institutional character of language:

The whole point of the chess analogy is that the rules *do* determine in advance all the possible moves, and that the grammar of the game is *not* decided by individual players as the spirit moves them. Games which are not like chess in this respect, although they may have every right to count as games, simply do not supply the right model for explicating the institutional character of language, its regularity and its autonomy. Once we come to games where play is an improvised free-for-all, there is not only no guarantee that different players are not playing by different rules but no clear way of making good the claim that there are any rules at all. (Harris 1988, 91–2)

As Harris sees it, the appeal to rules is supposed to explain the regularity of language, but this same appeal to rules disables the open-endedness of language that permits change and innovation.

Wittgenstein appeals to his two different kinds of analogy for two different purposes. The analogy with chess characterizes language in use between speakers who are already attuned in the language they use. The analogy with free play explores how this attunement evolves. In other words, the regulated attunement of chess players builds on the unregulated attunement of free play, and so the two are not so far apart as Harris supposes.

Wittgenstein can happily grant that chess and free play are different kinds of activities as long as we grant two further points. First this difference is one of degree rather than of kind,[3] and second, the regularity of the former builds on our capacity for coordinating ourselves without regulation as manifest in the latter. These two points become evident when we see the connection between chess and free play in Wittgenstein's thought as a special case of a connection between two larger themes that run throughout Wittgenstein's later philosophy. The first is the theme of rules, rule following, and game playing. The second is the theme of teaching and learning. We misapprehend the importance of this first theme if we do not consider its connection with the second.

6.2. The Scene of Instruction

On a fairly standard interpretation, the primary purpose of Wittgenstein's analogy with games is to facilitate a certain way of thinking about rules and rule following. Both Baker and Hacker (2005) and Kenny (2006, chap. 9), for instance, place their primary emphasis on three points: the

---

[3] To borrow a distinction from Roger Caillois ([1958] 2001, chap. 2), chess and free play fall on opposite ends of a spectrum running from the rule-governed play of *ludus* to the unregulated play of *paideia*.

rule-like structure of games and language, the fact that we can learn both games and language without explicitly learning the rules, and the autonomy of both games and language in the sense that they are not constrained by any external purpose—at *Z* §320, for instance, Wittgenstein contrasts games and language with cookery, where the aim of cookery constrains what rules we can follow when cooking.[4] But this standard interpretation tends to underplay or leave out the point that I take to be most important, which is our own role as 'players' of a language-game. The language-game analogy, as I will show, draws attention to the responsiveness of our concepts to the forms of life in which they find application, and hence to the way in which our language is *ours*.

In section 3.1, I emphasized the centrality of attunement in Wittgenstein's later philosophy—the idea that we share a broad range of agreement in our practices that precedes any kind of explicit agreement to agree—and argued that our attunement is not subject to justification. This attunement is manifest in the language-games we play together—not just sharing a vocabulary, but sharing what Cavell (1976b, 52) calls the 'whirl of organism' of the forms of life in and through which these language-games are played. Grasping the use of a word means understanding the forms of life in which it finds application (cf. *PI* §19). This point may be clearer in the case of 'hope' or 'understanding' than in the case of 'cat' or 'tree', but it applies generally. Examples involving chairs recur throughout the *Investigations*, with Wittgenstein showing how this mundane concept relates to various other concepts—like sameness, simple/composite, belief, and so on—such that its use is embedded in our broader life with words.[5]

If understanding a word also means understanding the forms of life in which it finds application, learning language is also a process of acculturation, where we are inducted into the forms of life that involve language. Wittgenstein shows a deep interest in what Cavell (1990) calls 'the scene of instruction', where an act of teaching or learning takes place.[6] A scene of instruction builds on a common ground shared

[4] We find an earlier version of this discussion at *PG* 184–5.
[5] Examples involving chairs occur at *PI* §§1, 35, 47, 60, 80, 253, 356, 361, 368, 486, and 575.
[6] Besides the opening sections of the *Investigations*, which consider Augustine's child and the tribe of builders, see also *PI* §§27, 31, 32, 35, 49, 53, 54, 77, 85, 86, 143, 144, 145, 156, 157, 159, 162, 179, 185, 189, 197, 198, 206, 207, 208, 223, 224, 232, 233, 237, 244, 249, 250, 257, 282, 308, 320, 328, 340, 361, 362, 375, 376, 378, 384, 385, 386, 441, 495, 535, 590, 630,

by the teacher and the learner. Most learning takes place within a framework that the learner already shares with the teacher. High school mathematics, for instance, follows a linear progression because topics build on one another successively. Students need a foundation in coordinate geometry before they learn trigonometry, and a teacher can explain to students the principles of trigonometry by drawing on that shared framework of coordinate geometry. The scene of instruction resembles scenes of explanation more generally, and the shared framework need not be so academically oriented. If I want to explain to you why I would prefer to stay home this evening, I need to share with you (among other things) at least a rough sense of what passes for worthwhile ways to spend one's time. If we are different enough, it might take considerable effort on my part to find an explanation that will make sense to you.

As the example of trigonometry illustrates, what is explained can become the shared framework for further explanations: trigonometry builds on the framework supplied by coordinate geometry, which in turn builds on the framework supplied by Euclidean geometry, algebra, and the Cartesian coordinate system, and these frameworks in turn build on more elementary frameworks, and so on down. But how far down? How, for instance, can we speak of learning the practice of learning without circularity?

The work of establishing fundamental shared frameworks, Wittgenstein tells us, is a matter of training. The teaching of language, for example, involves 'not explaining, but training' (*PI* §5). If we do not already share a language, I cannot *explain* anything to you. First, I must train you (or you me, or each of us reciprocally) to the point where we share enough that we can take up one another's explanations. When his interlocutor asks how we can explain the use of a sign if that explanation itself stands in need of explanation, Wittgenstein says that we are trained in the use of the sign (*PI* §86; see also *PI* §198). Ultimately, there is no *reason* why we read an arrow as pointing in one direction rather than the opposite direction—or why we read it as pointing at all. We are simply *trained* in the practice of using arrows in this way, and with this practice in place,

---

636, and 693. As Cavell (1989, 75) puts it: 'In the culture depicted in the *Investigations* we are all teachers and all students—talkers, hearers, overhearers, hearsayers, believers, explainers; we learn and teach incessantly, indiscriminately; we are all elders and all justices'.

we can use arrow signs to explain other things—how to read a table, how to get from one place to another, and so on. With regard to various rule-governed practices—most notably mathematics—Wittgenstein affirms that we explain things *within* the practice, but the basic techniques of the practice itself are given not by explanation but by training.[7]

A natural objection to this emphasis on the scene of instruction is that Wittgenstein himself denies that the way we learn a concept plays any role in its subsequent application:

> Teaching as the hypothetical history of our subsequent actions (understanding, obeying, estimating a length, etc.) drops out of our considerations. The rule which has been taught and is subsequently applied interests us only so far as it is involved in the application. A rule, so far as it interests us, does not act at a distance. (*BB* 14)[8]

This denial is of a piece with Wittgenstein's insistence that his grammatical investigations are different in kind from empirical or factual investigations. No empirical data, from child psychology or elsewhere, should be relevant. He makes this point explicit at *Z* §412, while clarifying the role of these scenes of instruction in his work: 'Am I doing child psychology?—I am making a connection between the concept of teaching and the concept of meaning'.[9] Wittgenstein is making a logical or grammatical point: we speak with meaning *within* a language-game, but the language-game itself is something we are first trained into. And because giving reasons, explanations, and justifications are moves made within language-games, that means the training is logically prior to any reason, explanation, or justification that could be given for the training proceeding in the way that it does.

I draw three principal lessons from this emphasis on the logical priority of training to reasons at the scene of instruction. The first is that it reminds us that we learn language together with the forms of life in which we use language. The scene of instruction is a scene of teaching someone to *do* something. The words of the language-game find their use as part of a larger activity and we learn the words and the activity together. In the variations on the theme of the builders in the opening

---

[7] See, e.g., *PI* §§189 and 206, *RFM* I §1, *RFM* IV §30, *RFM* VI §§16 and 31, and *RFM* VII §§27 and 40.

[8] See also *PI* §495 and *PG* 81. I am grateful to P. M. S. Hacker for pressing this objection on me.

[9] The same remark appears at *RPP* II §337.

sections of *Philosophical Investigations*,[10] Wittgenstein explores the way that we might distinguish different kinds of words based on the different uses they have and the correspondingly different ways in which they are taught. One aim of this exploration is to dislodge the presupposition that the kinds of words are given in advance of the uses we have for them. This presupposition is one aspect of the 'picture of the essence of human language' that Wittgenstein finds in Saint Augustine's account of how he learned language (*PI* §1). The Augustinian picture treats language learning as primarily an activity of attaching names to things, since it assumes that language learning is simply a matter of finding the right words to give voice to a thinking that is already in place (*PI* §32). Or, to assimilate the thought at *PI* §19 that 'to imagine a language means to imagine a form of life', the problem with Augustine's scenario is that it imagines the pre-linguistic child as already sharing its elders' forms of life, so that all it must learn are the names attached to various things and practices, all the while presupposing a ready familiarity with these things and practices.

The second lesson is the one I drew in the previous chapter when advocating what I called an authentic response to the seeming paradox of rule following, and which I returned to above. We could frame that paradox in the language of training as follows. I follow the rule 'Add 2' after 1000 by writing 1002, 1004, 1006, and so on. But if it turns out that there is no *reason* for following the rule in this way beyond the mere fact that I was trained to follow the rule in this way, I might worry that I have no reason for saying that I am following the rule *correctly*. Wittgenstein's investigation of scenes of instruction distinguishes the correctness of practices into which we have been trained from the correctness of the training itself. There are legal and illegal moves in a chess game but the rules of chess are themselves neither legal nor illegal—they constitute legality and illegality within this particular game. Likewise, there are correct and incorrect ways of playing language-games, but the language-games themselves are neither correct nor incorrect. In this light, the answer to the rule-following paradox is not that we *lack* reasons for following rules in the ways that we do, but rather that questions of right and wrong apply only *within* a practice we have been trained into, and such questions simply do not apply to the training itself.

---

[10] We find an even richer set of variations in the opening pages of the *Brown Book*.

The third lesson, which draws from the first two, and which I will develop further in what follows, is that this emphasis on training brings to the fore the joint importance of attunement and play. The force of Wittgenstein's parable of the wayward pupil at *PI* §185 comes from the fact that the pupil's response can be understood as according with everything the teacher has explained. The rule-following paradox arises when we expect that the training must be able to compel accord between teacher and pupil on its own. But the accord that develops—when it develops—is a manifestation of the attunement between teacher and pupil that underlies the explicit teaching. What is required for successful teaching is not just the teacher's explicit instructions but also the pupil taking up those instructions in the way that the teacher intends. This uptake manifests an untaught attunement between teacher and pupil.

The idea that uptake manifests attunement can be misunderstood. It might seem as if the problem is that there is a shortcoming in training, or in human communication, such that the teacher's instructions can only get her so far, but for the pupil to understand what the teacher means, the pupil must have some additional thing called 'attunement', which, mysteriously, cannot be taught. This misunderstanding supposes that the teacher has *something*—some ground or reason—that determines her own accord with the rule, but that this something cannot be communicated without deterioration.

In a series of remarks starting at *PI* §208, Wittgenstein pushes back against the idea that there is *something* guiding even the teacher. When I teach a pupil by means of examples and exercises, Wittgenstein says, 'I do not communicate less to him than I know myself' (*PI* §208). In response to his interlocutor's worry that, in teaching, the teacher leaves it to the pupil 'to *guess* the essential thing' (*PI* §210), Wittgenstein replies: 'Every explanation I can give myself I give to him too' (*PI* §210), adding that the interlocutor's 'guessing' is like the earlier confusion with 'interpretation'. We guess or interpret someone's intention in specific cases of ambiguity, not in all instances. These reflections foreshadow the bedrock remark of *PI* §217: even in my own case, Wittgenstein says, reasons do not reach all the way down. '[M]y reasons will soon give out', he remarks. 'And then I shall act, without reasons' (*PI* §211).

If, ultimately, there is no reason for taking up the training in one way rather than another, what ensures that we do? One answer is: nothing. This training is not the kind of thing that can—or is expected to—provide rock-solid guarantees. But, for all that, for the most part we *do* succeed in learning new language-games and teaching them to others. This success is owed to a shared attunement, or, as Wittgenstein occasionally puts it, to a shared sense of what is natural. In trying to account for the waywardness of the pupil of *PI* §185, for instance, Wittgenstein proposes that 'we might perhaps say: this person finds it **natural**, once given our explanations, to understand our order as we would understand the order "Add 2 up to 1000, 4 up to 2000, 6 up to 3000, and so on"' (*PI* §185). To the extent that our own scenes of instruction and subsequent participation in language-games do not careen off into waywardness, this security comes not so much from sharing the same reasons but from sharing the same sense of what is natural. Another way to put the same point is to say that we are creatures that are naturally disposed to share forms of life with one another.

6.3. Play and Projection

Yet another way of putting the same point is to repeat the classic kindergarten commendation: we play well with others. Our capacity for play is closely connected to our capacity to learn by imitation, to follow the example of others, and even more basically to understand what a game is, to recognize a game as a game, to find the game worth playing, and so on. If you know what a game is, I can teach you to play *this* game. If you do not know what a game is, or do not understand why anyone would want to play games, I will find myself at a loss fairly quickly.

Successful play requires not that players all grasp the same exhaustive set of rules but simply that they be sufficiently attuned to respond to one another in a way that perpetuates the play. The common ground of our attunement is both discovered and created in interplay with others. In dealing with others, we learn how those others behave, how they react, how and toward what they register interest, surprise, fear, and so on. We learn to interact with others or calibrate ourselves to others partly through imitation and partly through finding our own ways of behaving, reacting, and so on. This interaction or calibration does not itself follow set rules, since rules only emerge as a consequence of this interaction or calibration. It is an unregulated activity that nevertheless gives rise to regularity. As Johan Huizinga ([1938] 1995, 10) remarks, play 'creates order, *is* order'. Our ordered world of forms of life and language-games is something we play our way into.

Consider a game where a parent teaches his child 'please' and 'thank you' by ritually passing an object back and forth between them. The parent cannot explain to the child how the game will run—that is part of what he is teaching—but rather relies on his attunement with the child, in both capacities and responses, which he hopes will ensure that the child will respond in certain expected ways. The child may need a bit of prompting at first—and again, this prompting cannot take the form of established rules or norms of explanation, since these rules and norms are part of what is being established—but, most of the time, the child will gradually grasp the game and start playing along. Nothing guarantees that parent and child will fall into accord such that they manage to play happily together. That they do for the most part is a manifestation of their attunement.

This teaching only serves its purpose if the child grasps that it can play this game in other contexts too. It is not just this one object that can be exchanged with a 'please' and a 'thank you' but also other objects: toys, cutlery, toothbrushes, and so on. In learning what sorts of things can be exchanged with a 'please' and 'thank you', the child also learns something about the things. A toothbrush and a spoon are similar in at least the respect that both can be exchanged in the same way, and both have enough in common with a kiss that this, too, can be exchanged with a 'please' and a 'thank you' but differently enough that playing the 'please-and-thank-you' game with kisses carries a touch of humour that registers the oddness of projecting the game into this new context.

In playing these games with the child, the parent teaches the child no less than he knows himself. There is not some deeper rule that determines for the parent that *these* are the contexts where the 'please-and-thank-you' game is standardly played, *these* are the contexts where it can be played, but in a way that is somewhat odd or unusual, and *these* are the contexts in which it is not played. Because the context in which we learn words is finite and the possible contexts in which we can use words is infinite, no set of rules exhaustively dictates how we should use words in all contexts. Cavell speaks of 'projecting' words into new contexts to describe how we apply and extend the criteria for using words in this non-rule-governed manner: his example is a child unproblematically understanding what it means to 'feed the meter' having already learned what it means to 'feed the kitty' (Cavell 1979, 181). That we project words in ways that others understand, and that we understand

6.3. PLAY AND PROJECTION

the projections of others, manifests the shared 'modes of response' (Cavell 1976b, 52) that characterize our attunement. This projectability is not something we need to be *taught* because without it there is nothing to learn: it is part of what teaching *is* that the teaching can be applied in new contexts that differ in unanticipated ways from the scene of instruction.

These projections are not always straightforward. Consider Wittgenstein's example of 'A rose has no teeth' (*PPF* xi §314). Rather than judge this statement obviously true, Wittgenstein insists that its meaning is far from clear. Because it is such a peculiar thing to say, the appropriate route of projection is also unclear: if someone were to say 'A goose has no teeth', we would know how to check: we look in the goose's mouth. But where do we look for the teeth of a rose? Because we have no clear picture of what it would mean for a rose to *have* teeth, many possible projections present themselves. Wittgenstein imagines one projection in which it could make sense to say that a rose does indeed have teeth: '[S]uppose one were to say: the cow chews its food and then dungs the rose with it, so the rose has teeth in the mouth of an animal. This would not be absurd, because one has no option in advance where to look for teeth in a rose' (*PPF* xi §314). Wittgenstein thinks philosophical missteps often take this form: philosophers assert what seems to be obvious, but the seeming obviousness of the assertion disguises the fact that no clear sense—no clear method of projection—has been given to the words. The discussion of private language that begins at *PI* §243 frequently addresses this sort of confusion.

Wittgenstein's attention to language-games, and to the scenes of instruction in which they are taught, reminds us that the concepts that we have are not 'absolutely the correct ones' (*PPF* xii §366) but are rather the concepts that belong to—and give expression to—our forms of life. They have a use to the extent that they have a role in language-games we play. Wittgenstein gives striking expression to this idea at *Z* §351, in which he imagines an interlocutor insisting: 'If humans were not in general agreed about the colours of things, if undetermined cases were not exceptional, then our concept of colour could not exist'. Wittgenstein's reply is terse and subtle: 'No: — our concept *would* not exist'.[11] The interlocutor's 'could'

---

[11] Cf. also *RPP* II §393. Wittgenstein similarly challenges an interlocutory 'could' at *PI* §497.

affords our concept of colour an existence independent of the lives in which it has a use, as if our concept of colour were already there waiting for us, but required our agreement in order to come into view. Wittgenstein's shift to 'would' reminds us that our concept of colour is a manifestation of this agreement. There is no concept of colour independent of that agreement, and nor is there that particular agreement independent of our concept of colour.[12]

The interlocutor of Z §351 might well think she shares Wittgenstein's thought that concepts are only at home in the language-games in which they are used. But for Wittgenstein, this way of characterizing the relationship between concepts and language-games is still too loose because it supposes that the concepts are intelligible at all apart from the language-games in which they have a use. Although he clearly has many affinities with Kant and the post-Kantian tradition, it would miss the mark to characterize Wittgenstein as delineating the conditions for the possibility of the concepts that we have precisely because such delineation engages with the question of the conditions under which we *could* have such-and-such a concept.[13]

I am in a position to judge which projections of the word 'feed' are natural, which odd, which surprisingly appropriate, and which inappropriate because the concept has a place in a life that has significance for me. If you take up my projection of a word in a way that perpetuates the language-game we are playing, that is not because my projection is in accord with a rule about the use of the word, or a rule about the legitimate projections of that word, but because we are in accord with one another. Or to put the point differently, being in accord with a rule means being in accord with other people. This accord is not, as I discussed in the previous chapter and *pace* Kripke, an accord in inclinations but an accord in forms of life. We *play* language-games in the sense that they call for a responsiveness and attunement between

---

[12] Diamond (1989, 19–20) discusses this section in a way that informs my own treatment.

[13] We find a similar remark at *PI* §142, where Wittgenstein imagines lumps of cheese regularly growing or shrinking without obvious cause. In such cases, rather than say that we *could not* measure the weight of cheese as we currently do, we should say simply that we *would not*: our current language-game of measuring cheese would simply have no point in such circumstances.

players that is not compelled by any necessity beyond the needs of the players themselves.

At the beginning of section 6.2, I noted that the standard interpretation of Wittgenstein's language-game analogy focuses on the analogy between the way rules operate in games and in language without extending this analogy to consider our status as players. One casualty of this neglect is that it does not consider the analogy between how we learn games and how we learn language. The scene of instruction is important because it shows that learning involves play, and this play teaches us not just how to use concepts but how we make them our own. To treat our language-games as fixed and given to us in advance, as the standard interpretation does, manifests what we might call an Augustinian conception of games, according to which a child that learns a language-game already knows how to play language-games, only not this one (cf. *PI* §32). One consequence of this interpretation is that it limits the extent to which our language-games might be subject to further innovation and improvisation as we use them responsively in ever new circumstances. In other words, it limits the extent to which we make our language-games our own through play.[14]

Put another way, the standard interpretation sees play as something that happens *within* language-games whereas I see language-games unfolding within a broader field of play. That is, we only have language-*games* and the scenes of instruction in which they are taught because we have this underlying capacity for unregulated or free play. Our capacity to respond generatively to one another outside the strictures of any particular game is what enables us to develop more regular language-games in the first place.[15]

---

[14] Neglecting the ludic aspect of the scene of instruction also has an impact on how we understand Wittgensteinian criticism. One significant fissure between the later work of Gordon Baker (2004) and the interpretive line of the commentaries he co-authored with P. M. S. Hacker concerns the appropriate diagnosis of philosophical nonsense. If the rules of our language-games are clear and fixed in advance, we can simply point out when the targets of our criticism have broken the rules of the language-game and that is the end of the matter. But if language-games are open to innovation and improvisation, the matter becomes considerably more complicated. Sensitive criticism would first require understanding what one's interlocutor is trying to do in using words in an unusual way, without being able to assume in advance that any departure from the expected use constitutes a mistake.

[15] In his criticism of Wittgenstein, Harris reads Wittgenstein as advocating a variant of the standard interpretation, and reads Wittgenstein in this respect as having many affinities with

6.4. Improvisation as a Model of Authenticity

At this stage, I am ready to offer a preliminary account of how Wittgenstein's sensitivity to play in language and the scene of instruction is part of a distinctively Wittgensteinian conception of authenticity. In section 4.1, I characterized Heideggerian authenticity as a second-order kind of self-understanding. As Dasein, we are always already giving an answer to the question of the meaning of our existence: that answer is the manner in which we are living. Inauthentic Dasein is engaged in this self-interpretive activity every bit as much as authentic Dasein is. Where they differ is that authentic Dasein exists in resolute awareness that its manner of being constitutes a distinct interpretive response to its circumstances, and one through which it manifests its understanding of its being.

We can extract a similar distinction between authentic and inauthentic self-understanding from the discussion of Wittgenstein and play in this chapter. As language users, Wittgenstein tells us, we are always already playing language-games, 'inauthentic' no less than 'authentic' speakers of language. But we differ in the extent to which we recognize ourselves as *players* in these games. We might regard our concepts as disclosing an objective reality—we might regard our concepts as 'absolutely the correct ones'—and the rules of our language-games as inviting participation only through rigid obedience. Wittgenstein encourages a different understanding of our relationship with our language by considering the irreducible role of play at the scene of instruction. With this understanding, we recognize our language-games as tools for giving expression to our distinct response to our distinct circumstances, tools that are as flexible or inflexible as we ourselves are.

Saussure ([1916] 2011). Saussure's structural linguistics distinguishes between the structure of signs and the play of signs within that structure. However, I think Wittgenstein's affinities are deeper with one of Saussure's most infamous critics, Jacques Derrida. In tune with my criticism of the standard interpretation of Wittgenstein's language-game analogy, Derrida argues that the structure itself requires some degree of play in order to enable the play of signs. Derrida's engagement with Saussure is ubiquitous in his early work, but see especially Derrida ([1966] 1978) and ([1967] 1976, 27–73). Henry Staten provides a rich exploration of the similarities between Wittgenstein and Derrida, arguing that Wittgenstein is unique among Derrida's predecessors in 'having achieved . . . a consistently deconstructive standpoint' (Staten 1984, 1).

6.4. IMPROVISATION AS A MODEL OF AUTHENTICITY 153

I have developed these conceptions of authenticity by setting them against what I argued are analogous moments in Wittgenstein and Heidegger: Wittgenstein's investigation of rule following and Heidegger's investigation of anxiety. In both cases, we confront the worry that we have no good reason for going on as we do. For Heidegger, this was what McManus (2015a, 166) calls the 'Motivation Problem' that confronts Dasein in anxiety: in the absence of compelling reasons for pursuing projects, my choices, far from being resolute and authentic, seem either groundless and arbitrary or inauthentically grounded in *das Man*.

Here is one way of framing that dilemma. Inauthentic absorption in the one-self unduly constrains my responsiveness to my circumstances whereas the voice of scepticism or anxiety makes that responsiveness seem radically unconstrained: 'Anything—and nothing—is right' (*PI* §77). Responding authentically to our uncanniness means finding in ourselves a way of responding to our circumstances that is neither so sharply constrained as to be inauthentic nor so radically unconstrained as to be arbitrary. What does such responsiveness look like? Although Wittgenstein does not give Heidegger's explicit attention to the concept of authenticity, I think we find in his attention to unregulated play a model for thinking about the kind of responsiveness that authenticity requires.

We find a real-world model for this kind of responsiveness in musical and theatrical improvisation.[16] Improvisers untether themselves from scripted instructions for how they should proceed but this does not leave them radically unconstrained: *pace* Harris (1988, 91), free play does not entail a 'free-for-all' in which any move is as good as any other. Actual improvisation is an exquisitely delicate balancing act that can collapse into chaos or banality unless players allow themselves to be guided by the continuously evolving play. The twin threats of chaos and banality are essentially the threats of the dilemma I framed in the previous paragraph. The improviser who falls back on merely

---

[16] Another model for this kind of constrained responsiveness is sporting excellence: see Mulhall (2001, 79) for one example. However, athletes pursue goals that are set for them by the rules of the game: what counts as athletic 'success' is ultimately constrained by the outcomes of victory or defeat. By contrast, what counts as success in improvisation is itself something that is open to the inventiveness of the improvisers.

conventional responses is boring and the improviser whose responses are entirely arbitrary turns the performance into an incoherent mess.

Performing the balancing act successfully requires responsiveness rather than control. Accomplished jazz musicians seem less to be *making* music than they are *listening* to the music that is flowing through them and their fellow musicians. Theatrical improvisers also place a high value on listening and discourage as destructive the ambition to control the direction of a scene.[17] This kind of deep listening allows improvisers to avoid the twin threats of banality and chaos. Their attunement allows them to find responses to the state of play that are neither conventional nor arbitrary but rather answer inventively to the particularities of the situation.

The conventional responses of inauthentic Dasein manifest a coarse-grained responsiveness to its situation. At a high enough level of definition, every situation is unique, so falling back on what 'one' does manifests an impulse to assimilate this situation to ones that are similar to it. Skilled improvisers see what is similar while also being alive to the uniqueness of the situation.[18]

What emerges from this model is an account of authenticity in which we are not so much *agents* as *players*. Responding to the challenge of scepticism or anxiety requires not a satisfactory account of the sovereign individual that exists independently of socially constituted practices but rather from a satisfactory account of how we find ourselves—and not just the impersonal norms of *das Man*—*within* our socially constituted practices. The account I have been developing here emphasizes improvisation and responsiveness. We make our circumstances and our selves our own by attending to them carefully and calibrating our responses accordingly.

This conception of authenticity might sound appealing in the abstract but what sense can we make of it at a mundane level? What kind of

---

[17] I am far more familiar with theatrical improvisation than with musical improvisation. Jagodowski, Pasquesi, and Victor's (2015) *Improvisation at the Speed of Life* is one notable recent example of a text on theatrical improvisation that emphasizes listening. See especially Part Two of that book.

[18] I should note that improvisation and conventional response are not the only two options. Ritualized activities are not improvisatory but nor are they necessarily emptily 'going through the motions'. Ritualized activities often help participants become acutely alive to the particularities of the moment. I am grateful to Priya Nelson for pressing this point on me.

improvisatory responsiveness is called for when I sit in a chair or follow a road sign? In many circumstances, being alive and responsive to the particularities of our circumstances does not call on us to *do* anything particularly unusual. But recall how both Wittgenstein and Heidegger approach the world holistically: every item of equipment is essentially part of a larger totality and every concept has a use in language-games in coordination with other concepts. A chair shows up as a chair because it has a place within a larger whole of significant action. In its authentic moments, Dasein understands the significance of that whole as something to which it is responsive, and whose continued significance is shaped by Dasein's responses. Occasionally, that responsiveness might involve an unconventional projection of the handiness of a chair—it might become a makeshift oratorical soapbox, a subtle obstacle that keeps an unwanted suitor at arm's length, or a potent emblem of past disappointments that allows me to see, suddenly and for the first time, the possibility of renewal—but more often, a keen responsiveness to my present circumstances does not require unusual projections of this sort. Nevertheless, this keen responsiveness means being alive to the possibilities of projection, and to the fact that my circumstances do not prescribe the appropriate projections.

6.5. Sophistry and Spoilsports

In articulating a Wittgensteinian conception of authenticity, I have leaned heavily on connections with games and play. This emphasis invites an understandable concern: am I treating language and life as 'just a game', with no more weight or significance than a whimsically chosen amusement? We do not need to have an uncharitable disposition toward Wittgenstein to see something potentially troublesome in the prominence he gives to play. One of his most faithful students, Rush Rhees, objects to the notion that language might be composed of a collection of independent and distinct games, and he voices this objection in terms that have a somewhat Heideggerian flavour.[19] His central concern is that, unlike games, language has a point—it is *about* something. Rhees affirms the 'reality of language' in its capacity to induce

---

[19] Rhees first gives voice to these concerns in Rhees (1970b) and works through them at greater length in Rhees (2006).

learning, understanding, and growth.[20] What we learn from or through language is not limited by the rules of a game, but only by our own limitations. Language is open-ended: it does not have a particular subject matter, but is rather the medium in which we can talk about anything.

In questioning Wittgenstein's ability to account for the reality of language in his analogy with games, Rhees takes himself to be engaging in Plato's ancient battle against sophistry. If the words we speak are just moves in a game, skilful deployments of a technique, then 'the growth of understanding could only mean the growth of a skill (efficiency, I suppose) or the multiplication of skills' (Rhees 2006, 3) and the only value of the words we speak would be their efficacy in achieving the desired ends. If speaking is simply a means to a desired and predetermined end, language becomes a sophistical battlefield, the site where orators spar and determine whose rhetoric wins out. If the object of every conversation is to 'win', then we can never truly learn from a conversation, since the only conclusion to a conversation will be the result of victory or defeat.

Rhees's concern about sophistry resonates with concerns that animate *Being and Time* from its outset.[21] Like Rhees, Heidegger is concerned with the threat of sophistry, or the danger that our discourse might amount to nothing more than idle talk (although, as I will soon show, sophistry and idle talk are not quite the same thing). If our forms of discourse are just isolated games, undertaken for their own sake, then they lack genuine worth.

Rhetorical exchanges between sophists have many of the characteristics of a game, but what concerns Rhees, as well as Heidegger and Plato, is the challenge sophistry presents to any discussion whatsoever. In Book I of the *Republic*, Thrasymachus does not treat as a game what the others take seriously; he denies the possibility of taking a discussion of justice seriously in the way that Socrates wants to. As far as Thrasymachus is concerned, justice is unreal: high-minded talk about justice is just empty

---

[20] Rhees uses the expression 'reality of language' at Rhees (2006, 33, 85, 119, 125, 131, and 138).
[21] Mulhall (2001) discusses how the epigraph to *Being and Time*, from Plato's *Sophist*, orients the work as a whole, and announces as a central concern the distinction between sophistry and philosophy. Mulhall (2007b and 2013) also explicitly links Rhees's concerns with Heidegger's.

chatter, and we could excise the word 'justice' from our vocabulary entirely by substituting talk about power. Rhees has this sort of challenge in mind when he talks about the reality of language.

But if Thrasymachus trivializes discussions of justice by treating them not as games but as unreal, then the contrast between sophistry and philosophy is not one of play and seriousness. Nor should we find this surprising: play and seriousness are not opposites. In one sense play contrasts with seriousness, but in another sense, seriousness is absolutely essential to play. Playing a game in a spirit of what in some contexts we call sportsmanship requires total commitment to the goals and rules of that game. Huizinga ([1938] 1995, 5) recognizes this point, and Gadamer—who acknowledges his debt to Huizinga—links this point to a deeper contrast between sophistry and philosophy: '[S]eriousness in playing is necessary to make the play wholly play. Someone who doesn't take the game seriously is a spoilsport' (Gadamer [1960] 1989, 102). Sophistry is not a matter of playing where others are serious, but rather a matter of playing the spoilsport where others play seriously.

Bernard Suits ([1978] 2014, 51) draws a helpful distinction: '[T]riflers recognize rules but not goals, cheats recognize goals but not rules, players recognize both rules and goals, and spoilsports recognize neither rules nor goals'.[22] We may not engage in conversations with the goal of 'winning' in mind, but conversations do usually have goals, or at least a point: one reason for engaging in conversation, according to Rhees, is so that we can grow in understanding. A sophist both refuses to recognize this goal and denies its very possibility, thereby rejecting the framework within which these conversations take place. In these respects, a sophist does not resemble a trifler—someone who fails to take the conversation seriously—so much as a spoilsport. The discursive trifler is closer to the

---

[22] Suits draws these distinctions in the context of a book-length conceptual analysis of games of precisely the necessary-and-sufficient-conditions kind whose possibility Wittgenstein denies. In this respect, Suits poses a direct challenge to Wittgenstein's argument about family resemblance—or, as Thomas Hurka delicately puts it, Suits's book is 'a precisely placed boot in Wittgenstein's balls' (Hurka 2014, xiv). Although I find Suits's book rich and illuminating, I do not think it undermines Wittgenstein's argument about family resemblance in the way that Hurka supposes. I will not flesh out my response to Suits here, but probably the most important point for the present argument is that Suits takes the distinction between rule-governed games and free play to be sharper than I do. See also Tasioulas (2006) for some powerful challenges to the necessity and sufficiency of Suits's definition.

sort of person who engages in Heidegger's 'idle talk',[23] whereas the cheat relies on specious reasoning or false evidence to win an argument. Unlike the spoilsport/sophist, the cheat is fully invested in the reality of the discussion, but takes illegitimate shortcuts.[24]

The analogy between language and games does not license sophistry but rather provides within it the tools for thinking about the distinction between sophistry and philosophy, and it does so more cleanly than Rhees's somewhat vague talk about the reality of language. The analogy between language and games indicates that language derives its reality from being 'in play' in discussion. Conversation falls prey to sophistry not when the people engaged in conversation allow the conversation to move according to the dynamic of play, but precisely on the contrary, when one or more people reject the very grounds for holding the conversation, behaving like spoilsports.

Spoilsports come in different guises. Consider first the spoilsport who simply brings the game to a halt: 'I'm taking my ball and going home'. As both Huizinga ([1938] 1995, 11) and Caillois ([1958] 2001, 8–9) note, spoilsports have a corrosive effect on games by highlighting their artificiality. Commitment to a game requires commitment to the rules of the game, but those rules command no independent authority. There is no reason why the knight in chess should move as it does beyond the fact that these movements enable the game as it is played.[25] 'It's just a piece of wood and I can move it however I like' draws attention both to the arbitrariness of the rules of the game and to the indifference of the world beyond the game to our fealty to these rules.

---

[23] Harry Frankfurt (2005) colourfully describes talk undertaken without any particular concern for its truth or falsity as 'bullshit'.

[24] If the 'goal' of a conversation is the growth of understanding, does a cheat still recognize that goal if she employs methods, like specious reasoning and false evidence, whose illegitimacy rests on the fact that they do not lead to genuine understanding? I think so, to the extent that the cheat, unlike the spoilsport, still recognizes growth in understanding through the conversation as a worthwhile goal. When we converse, we have all sorts of goals, of which growth in understanding is just one. We are also concerned with the impression we are making on our interlocutors, exchanges in status between interlocutors, wanting to respond to the human needs behind the words of our interlocutors, and so on. The goal of impressing others sometimes trumps the goal of growing in understanding, but this latter goal may still be sincerely held even if it is betrayed.

[25] Suits ([1978] 2014, 43) defines the 'lusory attitude' that accompanies all games as 'the acceptance of constitutive rules just so the activity made possible by such acceptance can occur'.

6.5. SOPHISTRY AND SPOILSPORTS

Thrasymachus is arguably this kind of spoilsport, calling our discourse about justice artificial and arbitrary and thereby attempting to disable any serious conversation about justice. We find another manifestation of this kind of spoilsport in the gnawing voice of scepticism or anxiety. What is corrosive about the spoilsports who draw attention to the artificiality of the rules of a game is that they are right: there *is* no reason beyond the game itself for why we should respect its rules. Similarly, scepticism and anxiety can paralyze us by revealing that we have no independent reason for going on as we do—that is, no reason that stands outside and undergirds our commitment to going on as we do. But scepticism, like anxiety, can also be productive precisely in drawing our attention to the uncanniness of our language-games. Our language-games are playable because they are *played*, and they have significance to the extent that we invest them with significance.

But there is another kind of spoilsport who offers a more productive form of dissent. Rather than taking the ball and going home, this is the spoilsport who—in the spirit of William Webb Ellis's 'fine disregard for the rules'—catches the ball and runs with it.[26] Deviation from the rules and goal of a game can bring it grinding to a halt or it can constitute an inventive departure that initiates something new. Huizinga remarks that spoilsports draw more ire than cheats because cheats at least allow the game to continue, whereas spoilsports '[threaten] the existence of the play-community' (Huizinga [1938] 1995, 11). However, Huizinga sees in discursive spoilsports more noble possibilities than sophistry:

> In the world of high seriousness, too, the cheat and the hypocrite have always had an easier time of it than the spoil-sports, here called apostates, heretics, innovators, prophets, conscientious objectors, etc. It sometimes happens, however, that the spoil-sports in their turn make a new community with rules of its own. The outlaw, the revolutionary, the cabbalist or member of a secret society, indeed heretics of all kinds are of a highly associative if not sociable disposition, and a certain element of play is prominent in all their doings. (Huizinga [1938] 1995, 12)

The sophist and the revolutionary both reject certain operative modes of discourse as unreal, thereby rejecting or defining away key terms in these modes of discourse: compare 'Justice is the advantage of the stronger'

---

[26] According to legend, Ellis invented rugby football by catching the ball and running forward with it in flagrant violation of the rules of the game of football that he was allegedly playing.

and 'Property is theft'. Revolutions—political or intellectual—generally have a positive intent as well: they reject as illegitimate some language-games but seek to establish others in their place.

A discursive spoilsport, then, is not necessarily contemptible. No clear criteria distinguish the sophist from the revolutionary, nor the revolutionary we admire from the revolutionary we condemn. Rather than think of spoilsports as people who simply disrupt the game, we might think of them as people who make bold and unexpected projections that radically alter the state of play. The questions of which language-game we are playing and which language-game we should be playing are not questions we can settle in advance, but are rather themselves open to debate and discussion. Nor is there any principled means for settling definitively the question of which language-game we should be playing. Ultimately, the upshot of the spoilsport's deviance hinges on how we respond to it. In Chapter 1, I argued that Wittgenstein responds to the Heraclitean philosopher—who insists that one cannot step into the same river twice—not with dogmatic rejection but with patient engagement. If our language-games are not rigidly fixed we cannot straightforwardly dismiss anyone who deviates from the rules. Instead, we have to ask ourselves what this deviation is for, what new game this person is trying to play, and whether we can find ourselves in it if we play along.

This route to accepting the spoilsport indicates the possibility of transformation if we are open to it. We cannot step outside our language-games and assess them from sideways on, but we can work at them transformatively from within. This point, however, requires that we see language-games as fluid and based in play, and not fixed in advance, as the standard interpretation of language-games has it. If we neglect this fundamental element of play in Wittgenstein's language-game analogy, we risk developing a conception of discourse that is indeed subject to Rhees's criticism.

6.6. Receptivity and Responsiveness in *Being and Time*

In arguing that we find a model of authenticity in the flexibility and nimbleness of improvisation, I have focused primarily on Wittgenstein, whose thinking about language draws considerably on analogies with games and play. Heidegger gives less explicit attention to play, but we find a strong emphasis on receptivity and responsiveness that finds many echoes in the Wittgensteinian account of play I have articulated in this chapter.[27]

To begin with, if the connections I drew in Chapter 2 between Heidegger's totality of equipment and Wittgenstein's language-games hold, then what I said in section 6.3 about the projectability of concepts should apply also to equipment. No exhaustive set of rules fixes the proprieties for using equipment and creative projections can always generate new uses. And indeed, English translations of Heideggerese give a prominent place to 'projection' as well, as a translation of Heidegger's *Entwurf*. What Heidegger means by projection is different from the sense I gave to the word in section 6.3, but it is not entirely unrelated. One meaning of *Entwurf* is 'draft': we are, as it were, constantly drafting and re-drafting ourselves, sketching out new versions of ourselves in response to our changing circumstances.

We find a deeper and more pervasive emphasis on Dasein's receptivity and responsiveness in Heidegger's underlying interest in the grammatical middle voice. Only some Indo-European languages have a middle voice—Ancient Greek notably among them—but we find something semantically similar in English sentences like 'The dishes are drying' or 'Dinner is cooking', which are neither quite active nor passive. Heidegger's rather tortuous retrieval of the etymological roots of 'phenomenology' in §7 of *Being and Time* aims to unfold the middle voiced way in which beings 'show themselves'.[28] Heidegger also aims for a middle ground between active and passive voices with the reflexive German verb *sich verhalten*— generally translated as 'comport', 'behave', or 'relate'—in talking about Dasein's relation to itself and the world. For example, Heidegger tells us that 'Dasein is a being which **is related** understandingly in its being toward that being [*Dasein ist Seiendes, das sich in seinem Sein verstehend zu diesem*

---

[27] Although Heidegger himself does not treat play explicitly, it figures in the work of a number of his pupils who see themselves as extending his work, most notably Gadamer ([1960] 1989) and Fink ([1960] 2016). Gadamer (1976, 173–7) also remarks on his affinity with Wittgenstein in the emphasis he places on play. And Withy (2015, 233–7) characterizes uncanniness in terms of play. The idea that authenticity calls for the kind of receptivity and responsiveness I articulate here finds neighbour notions in the secondary literature. For example, Blattner (2015, 130–2) characterizes authenticity in terms of flexibility.

[28] See Scott (1988) for a discussion of this point.

Sein verhält]' (*BT* 52-3). Dasein is neither straightforwardly active nor passive in its relation to its being but rather something in between.

Let me draw attention to two moments in *Being and Time* where Heidegger's emphasis on this agential middle ground is particularly salient. The first comes at the beginning of Chapter Five of Division I with Heidegger's proclamation that '*Dasein is its disclosedness*' (*BT* 133). In introducing the 'there' of Dasein's being-in, Heidegger wants to steer between a realist thesis that the world is already objectively 'there' independent of Dasein's access to it and an idealist thesis that the world is constituted by Dasein and is 'there' only insofar as Dasein is.[29] A great deal of the language in §28 of *Being and Time* seeks a middle ground between passive spectation and active constitution. Heidegger uses imagery of light [*Licht*] to say that Dasein 'is cleared [*gelichtet*] in itself *as* being-in-the-world, not by another being, but in such a way that it *is* itself the clearing [*Lichtung*]' (*BT* 133). Dasein is both what is cleared and what does the clearing, and the imagery of light and clearing itself suggests not so much an act of creation or constitution but one of making visible or accessible. That Dasein is its 'disclosedness' [*Erschlossenheit*] perpetuates this theme: Dasein both does the disclosing and is what is disclosed. Heidegger repeatedly emphasizes that Dasein's essential openness to being does not simply disclose a world that is already there but rather clears or discloses the space in which beings show themselves as the beings that they are.

The second moment where Heidegger's emphasis on Dasein's agential middle ground is particularly salient is his discussion of the call of conscience. Heidegger claims that '*Dasein calls itself in conscience*' (*BT* 275), but then goes on to complicate that claim by arguing that the call comes neither from a present-at-hand entity in the world nor quite from Dasein itself, at least not in a manner over which Dasein exercises volitional control:

> The call is precisely something that *we ourselves* have neither planned, nor prepared for, nor willfully brought about. 'It' calls ['*Es*' *ruft*], against our expectations and even against our will. On the other hand, the call without doubt does not come from someone else who is with me in the world. The call comes *from* me, and yet *over* me. (*BT* 275)

---

[29] I discuss Heidegger's response to the problematic of realism and idealism—which I ultimately find unsatisfying—in more detail in the next chapter.

6.6. RECEPTIVITY AND RESPONSIVENESS 163

The 'it' of '"it" calls' is a dummy pronoun, similar to 'it's raining', where the subject of the sentence is deliberately skirted.[30] The call comes to Dasein not through any exercise of Dasein's agency but it also does not come from any source other than Dasein. Hearkening to the call is not something Dasein *does* so much as something Dasein is receptive to. And, as with my discussion of improvisation in section 6.4, this receptivity essentially requires the capacity to listen.

These two moments indicate a conception of resolute Dasein not as stepping into a fully autonomous agency but rather as being receptive and responsive, neither quite active nor passive. In section 6.4, I noted that sensitive improvisers exhibit a fine-grained responsiveness to their situation in contrast to the coarse-grained conventional responses of inauthentic Dasein. Heidegger identifies this fine-grained responsiveness in resolute Dasein's inhabitation of what he calls the 'situation' [*Situation*]. Inauthentic Dasein 'knows only the *"general situation"* [*allgemeine Lage*]' (*BT* 300) whereas, by contrast,

Situation [*Situation*] is the there disclosed in resoluteness—as which the existing being is there.... The actual factical relevant character of the circumstances is disclosed to the self only when that relevant character is such that one is resolute for the there which that self, in existing, has to be. (*BT* 299–300)

Resoluteness opens a space for significant action precisely because it manifests an acute sensitivity to the situation Dasein finds itself in. Heidegger characterizes resoluteness not primarily as a capacity to act but rather as a capacity to attend to our circumstances so that we can hear what they solicit from us.

On the other hand, Heidegger's emphasis on the 'actual factical relevant character of the circumstances', and, slightly earlier, on 'definite, factical possibilities' (*BT* 299) upon which Dasein projects itself suggests one way in which his account of Dasein's existential situation falls short of the responsiveness I identified with improvisers. Heidegger is not entirely clear on this point, but he seems to indicate that *what* possibilities are open to Dasein are already factically there, so that resoluteness amounts to seeing clearly the full range of possibilities in their full salience. Similarly, Heidegger characterizes the mode of authentic

---

[30] Heidegger also presumably intends an echo with '*es gibt*', literally 'it gives', which is the German equivalent of 'there is'.

temporality in which the present reveals itself in visual terms. The 'Moment' [*Augenblick*: *BT* 338] is literally the 'eye-look': Heidegger figures Dasein's authentic temporalizing of the present in terms of clear seeing. But skilled improvisers do not simply see more clearly than others a set of possibilities that are already there. Their artistry is manifest in their ability to *create* possibilities, to set new patterns that cast what came before in a new light.[31] This point is not simply incidental. As we will see in the coming chapters, Heidegger's phenomenological method focuses on disclosing what is already there, whereas Wittgenstein uses objects of comparison to destabilize and play with any presupposition that we can definitively characterize a given phenomenon.

6.7. Authentic Philosophy

As I have presented it, Heideggerian authenticity entails a clear-sighted apprehension of Dasein's existence as being-in-the-world. In other words, being authentic means understanding our existence along the lines elaborated in a book like *Being and Time*. In this respect, *Being and Time* does not simply contain a *description* of an authentic mode of existence but also constitutes a call to such a mode of existence. We find a hint of this purpose when Heidegger remarks that '[r]esolute Dasein can become the "conscience" of others' (*BT* 298). If the writing of *Being and Time* is itself a performance of authentic understanding, then that text can also serve as a call to the conscience of others.[32] And if the parallels I have drawn between Heidegger and Wittgenstein hold so far, then what I have just said about *Being and Time*—that it serves as a kind of performance of authentic understanding that calls its readers to such an understanding—should be true of *Philosophical Investigations* as well.

If Heidegger's and Wittgenstein's texts enact an authentic understanding, then doing philosophy is at least one way of realizing an authentic understanding. For both Wittgenstein and Heidegger, however, philosophy is also one of the primary culprits in covering over authentic understanding. The activity of giving thought to our lives is fraught with difficulty and prone to misunderstanding and they present this

---

[31] I am grateful to Florian Klinger for suggesting to me this distinction between *seeing* possibilities and *creating* them.
[32] Mulhall (2001, 279–80) argues this point in more detail.

misunderstanding as motivated. In his analysis of falling, Heidegger characterizes Dasein as for the most part turning away from itself and toward the world and Wittgenstein speaks of 'an urge to misunderstand' the workings of our language (PI §109). Both authors speak of misunderstandings as temptations.[33]

What stands between us and what we need to be reminded of, then, is we ourselves: we are complicit in a kind of blindness that prevents us from seeing clearly what we already know, and part of the trouble is that we do not even notice that we are blind. For Heidegger, we have lost sight of the question of the meaning of being and relate ourselves to the world around us, toward each other, and toward ourselves, in a way that forecloses the possibility of raising this question. For Wittgenstein, we persistently talk nonsense without noticing that we are talking nonsense. For both, traditional forms of philosophical investigation and expression are deeply implicated in this blindness, such that the problem is not simply that philosophy has traditionally provided the wrong answers to its questions, but that it has framed its investigations in such a way that it has asked the wrong questions.

What Heidegger and Wittgenstein try to do is quite radical, and very difficult: if they think there is something wrong with philosophy to the extent that we have to ask behind the traditional ways of framing problems, they need not only the insight to see behind these framings, but also the language to get behind them. If their aim is not to tell us anything new, but rather to remind us of what we already know, what stands between us and the proper acknowledgment of these reminders cannot be a lack of information, the sort of thing that could be straightforwardly supplied by assertions. The language of traditional philosophical argumentation would seem to be inadequate to their task: that language would embroil them in the philosophical problems from which they seek extrication.

Furthermore, they need language that will bring their readers with them. There is a frequent temptation—I speak from my own experience as a reader as much as in criticism of anyone else—to try to understand them in terms that are more familiar, more easily grasped, and this temptation often results in assimilating them to particular positions

---

[33] See, e.g., BT 177, 253, 330 and 387, and PI §§20, 39, 143, 159, 182, 254, 277, 288, 334, 345, 374, 402, 520, and 588.

within the philosophical dialectic they are trying to get behind. Their philosophical aims are inseparable from their philosophical style: they have to find a form of expression to get behind the problems they have inherited, and it has to be a form of expression that tempts neither them nor their readers into interpreting them as contributing to these problems instead.

Resisting this model of what philosophy is meant to do requires not just novel insights, then, but a novel method: Wittgenstein and Heidegger need to find a way of doing philosophy that does not *tell* us something new but rather helps us to recover what we already know. The final chapters of this book are concerned with this challenge: what is involved in doing philosophy authentically? And this is the point on which the parallel paths I have drawn for Wittgenstein and Heidegger come apart most clearly. Although I think they exhibit striking similarities in their aims, they differ in a number of important respects in their methods. And, as we will see, that difference consists to a considerable extent in the greater emphasis Wittgenstein places on play—not just as a theme in his philosophy, but as a mode for enacting that philosophy.

PART THREE

The Pursuit of An Authentic Philosophy

PART THREE

7
Heidegger's Pursuit of Authenticity in Philosophy

7.1. The Problematic of Realism and Idealism

In Part One of this book, Chapter 1 in particular, I outlined an approach to philosophy beginning from the everyday that we find in both Wittgenstein's later philosophy and in the existential phenomenology of *Being and Time*. A crucial feature of that approach is the recognition of what Heidegger calls the 'ontological difference' between ontic and ontological investigations, and which finds congruent expression in Wittgenstein's distinction between grammatical and factual investigations. For both philosophers, we go astray when we pursue philosophical investigations in the same way that we might pursue ontic or factual investigations. In particular, what philosophy discloses is not some realm of facts—call them metaphysical facts—that constitute a bedrock of facthood that underlies the regolith of empirical facts. Doing philosophy is a very different *kind* of activity from doing science. Geology and meteorology seek to uncover different kinds of facts and so require different methods, but philosophy differs from both insofar as it does not seek to uncover *facts* at all.

Metaphysics, as Wittgenstein construes it, is a consequence of mistaking grammatical and factual investigations—when we '[predicate] of the thing what lies in the mode of representation' (*PI* §104). That is, we go wrong by mistaking features of our grammar for features of the world. In the hindsight of the discussion of Part Two, we can see this confusion not simply as a case of intellectual negligence but rather as the quintessential manifestation of inauthentic understanding. Inauthentic Dasein accepts received forms of thought and behaviour as fixed, as simply 'the way things are'.

Another name for that inauthentic understanding might be realism. 'Realism' is not the name of a philosophical position so much as of a whole group of philosophical poses clustered around a certain form of what David Cerbone (2005, 250) calls 'transcendental-epistemological' explanation. It is one approach to explaining how a particular domain of objects—or knowledge in general—is so much as possible. A realist explanation emphasizes the mind-independence of the objects of knowledge such that the epistemic goal of the knowing subject is to align her mind in such a way that it accurately mirrors or represents those objects. Realism, in its various guises, is effectively the view that things are the way that they are independent of whether anyone does, or even can, know about them.

Metaphysical realism lacks the intuitive inauthenticity of the trend follower who regards certain received forms of thought and behaviour as 'the way things are' but it manifests a similar stance of regarding the way things are as external to the lives to which these things are significant. In drawing attention to the readiness-to-hand of equipment, Heidegger wants us to recognize that the 'way' of 'the way things are' is *our* way. *Things* do not have *ways*—we do. What is inauthentic about the follower of cultural trends is that she disclaims her capacity to manifest responses to artworks that are properly her own and she does this, more or less explicitly, by treating matters of cultural taste and opinion as matters for which there are 'right' and 'wrong' responses, as if artworks call for us to align ourselves with the 'right' answers in an impersonal way. This attitude diminishes how much of *me* there can be in my responses to artworks: what matters is not how the artwork touches me but whether I respond to it correctly. Similarly, the realist regards reality as having a fixed character that we cognize either rightly or wrongly such that reality calls for us to align our thoughts and responses with it in an impersonal way. In the realist's view, the particular salience the world might have to *me* is a subsequent imposition that can be abstracted away as 'merely' 'subjective'.

To push back against the realist by insisting that there is *not* a 'way things are' independent of us might seem like the authentic response to the inauthentic realist. But this response, by presenting itself as a counterpart thesis to a realist thesis, misfires in two ways. First, it construes realism as asserting something that is *false*. That is, it accepts that what the realist wants to say is clear enough, just that it is wrong. And second,

7.1. THE PROBLEMATIC OF REALISM AND IDEALISM

it construes itself as having a positive thesis of its own to advance, namely the contrary of the realist thesis. This way of framing the problematic shares with the realist the view that, in addition to all the empirical or ontic facts about the world, there is some further fact—namely a fact about the nature of these facts—about which there is room for disagreement. It tries to supplant one transcendental-epistemological explanation with another.

The Buddhist tradition teaches that the four *Brahmaviharas*, or divine abidings, have both a 'far enemy' and a 'near enemy', the former being the opposite of the virtue and the latter being something similar enough that we are liable to mistake it for the virtue. The far enemy of compassion is cruelty, for instance, and the near enemy is self-indulgent pity. If the far enemy of an authentic philosophy is the realist impulse to insist on a world of present-at-hand objects whose being is essentially independent of our own, then the near enemy is the anti-realist impulse to construe realism in terms of a metaphysical thesis that it must refute. Pity remains an enemy to compassion because it holds on to the fantasy of the otherness of the suffering of others that is most clearly manifest in cruelty. Likewise, the anti-realist recoil exhibits the same fantasy of self-alienation as the far enemy of realism. Both parties to this dispute suppose that we can get sufficient distance from ourselves that we can characterize in a general way how self and world are related to one another. And just as pity is dangerous in part because it is easily mistaken for compassion, an anti-realist interpretation of our protagonists is dangerous in part because it seems so plausible.[1]

We saw one version of this problematic in the discussion of scepticism in Chapters 4 and 5. The problematic of realism and idealism is a distinct but related guise. Both Heidegger and Wittgenstein explicitly address this problematic as an example of philosophical confusion, and both respond to the problematic by arguing that the very idea that there are rival positions here between which we might adjudicate is illusory. Both of them, that is, reject the idea that there is some additional fact about the

---

[1] Dummett (1959), Wright (1980), and Kripke (1982) all offer anti-realist interpretations of Wittgenstein. The contrast between realism and anti-realism is notably explored in a number of the essays collected in Dummett (1978). Braver (2007), drawing primarily on Dummett and Putnam (1981) to trace the contours of the debate, offers a history of post-Kantian philosophy in terms of a tension between realism and anti-realism. In his telling, Heidegger represents an important turning away from anti-realism.

nature of empirical facts as a whole. Like the investigations of the realist or the idealist, Wittgenstein's grammatical investigations and Heidegger's ontological investigations aim to understand, as Wittgenstein puts it, 'the foundations, or essence, of everything empirical' (*PI* §89). But they do so in a way that refigures what that understanding consists in.

However, the way in which they do that refiguring differs in a number of respects. To begin with, my presentation of the problematic of realism and idealism above betrays a Heideggerian orientation in presenting idealism as an anti-realist recoil against a realist thesis. In section 5.7 I argued that Wittgenstein sees things the other way around—and we will see in section 8.3 that Wittgenstein's investigation of the same problematic begins with his interlocutor manifesting an anti-realist impulse. In this chapter and the next, I will take their different treatments of this problematic as case studies for examining more generally the different methodological approaches Wittgenstein and Heidegger take to pivoting our philosophical orientation.

7.2. Heidegger and the 'Problem of Reality'

The final chapter of Division I of *Being and Time* has a peculiar structure. Ostensibly, this chapter brings to its completion Heidegger's analysis of average everyday Dasein as being-in-the-world. After insisting that we understand being-in-the-world as a '*unified* phenomenon' (*BT* 53), Heidegger examines distinct aspects of this unified phenomenon in Chapters Three through Five—the worldliness of Dasein's world, the 'who' of Dasein as being-with and *das Man*, and being-in as such—before synthesizing these aspects under the phenomenon of care. But this synthesizing work only really occupies one section of Chapter Six, §41, which itself feels somewhat anti-climactic in its predictability. The anti-climax is more pronounced because §41 follows the discussion in §40 of anxiety, the yin to the yang of care, so that already when we reach the synthesis of §41, we are looking beyond it to Division II. And then in §42, Heidegger seems to interrupt the phenomenological flow of his analysis to offer a reading of an 'old fable' (*BT* 197) concerning care. To my ear, this turn to myth echoes the myths that conclude a number of Platonic dialogues—notably *Republic*,

7.2. HEIDEGGER AND THE 'PROBLEM OF REALITY'   173

Gorgias, *Phaedo*, and *Phaedrus*. Having concluded his formal analysis, the author gives mythic expression to the fruits of that analysis that both completes the foregoing account and gestures at a mode of apprehension beyond the philosophical.

If this reading is correct, the discussion of reality and truth in §§43–4 is not the culmination of Division I but something more like a pair of appendices, tacked on after the main event to clarify some technical matters that fall outside the principal discussion. These sections read as a kind of settling of accounts, in which Heidegger shows how his analysis provides a novel response to certain fundamental and perennial problems in philosophy. Both sections are divided into three parts, in which the first presents how the problem has been handed down by the philosophical tradition, the second shows how the analysis of Dasein as being-in-the-world resolves tensions in that tradition, and the third elaborates on some of the consequences for that problem given Heidegger's analysis. And in both §43(c) and §44(c), Heidegger says some very strange things. At the very moment at which he tries to explain how he has extricated himself from the traditional problematic, Heidegger seems to get himself into trouble. I think this is no accident, nor is it a coincidence that both subsections have passages that are troubling in similar ways. But before I press on this point, I want to consider the dissolution Heidegger claims to effect of the problematic of realism and idealism in §43(a)–(b) and how he thinks his phenomenological method enables him to effect this dissolution.

Heidegger introduces '"the problem of reality"' (*BT* 201) in §43 in scare quotes, indicating that the alleged problem lies primarily with how it has been framed. Having presented his own phenomenological analysis of the everyday existence of Dasein, Heidegger tells us that this analysis, and more generally 'the development of the question of the meaning of being...must be wrested from a one-sided orientation toward being in the sense of reality' (*BT* 201). This orientation toward being, as Heidegger sees it, is a fundamental obstacle to an authentic understanding of Dasein's existence.

Heidegger regards this 'problem of reality' as a cluster of related questions:

(1) whether the beings which are supposedly 'transcendent to consciousness' *are* at all; (2) whether this reality of the 'external world' can be sufficiently *proven*; (3)

to what extent this being, if it is real, is to be known in its being-in-itself; (4) what the meaning of this being, reality, signifies in general. (*BT* 201)

Heidegger introduces realism and idealism as proposed solutions to this cluster of questions, most directly to the second one. These solutions accept at face value a problematic that sets the self against the world and undertake to explain how the two are related. A realist explanation insists on the independence of objects of knowledge from the knowing subject and so needs to account for how the subject can reach out epistemically across the gap between itself and its objects of knowledge. An idealist explanation sees the objects of knowledge as in some way constituted by the knowing subject and so needs to account for how these objects of knowledge are nevertheless sufficiently independent of the knowing subject that the subject can also be wrong—without the possibility of fallibility, it is unclear that we have an achievement worth calling knowledge.

Both of these forms of explanation operate within the dialectical space of the sceptical problematic. In section 4.4, I noted that Cavell—and following him, Conant—regards scepticism not simply as the position that knowledge in a given domain is impossible but rather as the entire problematic that puts the possibility of knowledge into question. Cavell characterizes scepticism about the external world thus:

I do not...confine the term ['scepticism'] to philosophers who wind up denying that we can ever know; I apply it to any view which takes the existence of the world to be a problem of knowledge. A crucial step for me, in calling an argument skeptical, is that it contain a passage running roughly, 'So we don't know (on the basis of the senses (or behavior) alone); then (how) do we know?' (Cavell 1979, 46)

Heidegger shares this orientation toward the 'problem of reality', seeing the appropriate response not as a realist or an idealist account of how knowledge is possible but as a rejection of the sceptical problematic altogether. This problematic presupposes a world made up of independently subsisting beings (the *res* of 'reality'), and then asks about the relation between one of these beings—the subject—and the others.

From such a starting point, any subsequent characterization of Dasein as embedded in its world 'always already comes "too late"' (*BT* 206): such characterizations fumble toward an appropriate epistemology from within the wrong ontological framework. Heidegger claims that the Cartesian cogito gets things backwards in taking the '*cogito*' as the basis for the '*sum*' (*BT* 211). Only once we have recognized Dasein's existence as being-in-the-world (its '*sum*') are we in a position to investigate the nature of this being's epistemic relation to the world (its '*cogito*'). Heidegger couches this form of encounter within a broader context of engagement with the world that radically rethinks the traditional conception of the subject—and hence of objects as well. The theoretical attitude that strips objects of their context of use and reveals them as present-at-hand objects of inquiry involves a withdrawal of the concern that discloses them to Dasein in the first place. The sorts of investigations in which we conceive ourselves as knowing subjects probing the nature of distinct objects are possible only within the worldly world of a Dasein that is concerned with the outcome of these investigations.

Ontology precedes epistemology for Heidegger: speculations about the self's relation to the world are idle if we have not given an adequate analysis of the nature of that self and that world. And once we have, we see that the problematic of external world scepticism gets no purchase: 'The question of whether there is a world at all and whether its being can be demonstrated, makes no sense at all if it is raised by Dasein as being-in-the-world—and who else should ask it?' (*BT* 202). An analysis of Dasein as being-in-the-world does not decide the dispute between realism and idealism, but rather shows that the dispute is founded 'on the basis of a neglect':

> In elucidating these positions [of realism and idealism] it is not so much a matter of clearing them up or of finding one or the other to be the solution, but of seeing that both can exist only on the basis of a neglect: they presuppose a concept of 'subject' and 'object' without clarifying these basic concepts with respect to the basic composition of Dasein itself. (*HCT* 222–3)

If we do not neglect the existential analytic of Dasein that Heidegger pursues in *Being and Time*, the 'problem of reality' cannot find expression.

7.3. The Problem with Assertions

How do we come to be ensnared in this 'neglect' in the first place? One main culprit in Heidegger's diagnosis is our language itself. Our primary way of talking about the world is by means of assertions, but the form of the assertion can distort our sense of what we are talking about. Assertion constitutes a step back from concernful engagement with beings: 'Something *ready-to-hand with which* we have to do or perform something, turns into something "*about which*" the assertion that points it out is made' (*BT* 158; translation modified). As soon as we speak *about* a being, we cease to be as deeply absorbed in the activity we were engaged in *with* that being. Its readiness-to-hand becomes 'veiled' (*verhüllt*), and presence-at-hand takes precedence over readiness-to-hand: 'this discovering of presence-at-hand... covers over readiness-to-hand' (*BT* 158). Furthermore, the act of predication focuses our attention solely on the being and a particular property or set of properties we predicate of it, withdrawing our attention from its more holistic 'totality of relevance' (*BT* 158). Simply by dint of its form, assertion inclines us toward an understanding of the world in terms of present-at-hand beings that are related to one another only accidentally.

The difficulty, then, is how to pursue an ontological project that avoids the deficient understanding that the very form of the assertion seems to entangle us in. Wittgenstein grapples with a similar difficulty regarding propositions early in his career, and the comparison illuminates the challenge Heidegger faces. A central tenet of the *Tractatus* is the bivalence of propositions: all propositions with a sense can be either true or false. That means that the negation of any proposition with sense also has sense. True sensical propositions are true accidentally: they describe the way the world happens to be, but it also makes sense to suppose the world might have been otherwise. What is essential, by contrast, cannot find expression in bivalent propositions, but rather shows itself in the form propositions must have in order to have sense. But because the *Tractatus* itself purports to speak not of what is accidentally the case but of the essential structure of language and the world, Wittgenstein famously concludes that the propositions of the *Tractatus* are themselves nonsensical.

The proposition is itself an inadequate tool for the kind of philosophical work Wittgenstein wants to do in the *Tractatus*. He signals this difficulty early on, in a letter to Russell dating from 1912: 'Logic must turn out to be a *totally* different kind than any other science' (*NB* 120). The sciences express knowledge in the form of propositions, and Russell thought of logic as a supremely general science, dealing in the most general propositions.[2] But if these propositions have sense, no matter

---

[2] Ricketts (1996) provides a particularly helpful discussion of Frege's and Russell's universalist conception of logic, and Wittgenstein's rejection of it.

how self-evident, their negations must also have sense. For logic to be truly foundational, it cannot have even a residue of the accidentality that the bivalence of propositions entails. By the time of the *Tractatus*, Wittgenstein came to regard logical propositions as tautologies whose senselessness shows the limits of thought. Attempts to exceed those limits and speak about the world as a whole or about what is 'higher' (*TLP* 6.42) result in nonsense. Anything that is true of the world is accidentally true, and whatever is non-accidental cannot be given propositional expression (*TLP* 6.41).

I will touch on some important differences shortly, but first let me consider how the difficulty of expression that is so central to the *Tractatus* has resonance with Heidegger's difficulty in *Being and Time*. The *Tractatus* sees the role of propositions as describing some aspect of the world, and similarly Heidegger sees assertion as meaning "[p]rimarily... "*pointing out*"' (*BT* 154). Assertions are problematic for Heidegger's fundamental ontology for similar reasons that propositions are problematic for the philosophy of the *Tractatus*: Heidegger is not trying to point out this or that accidental aspect of the world but rather to help us apprehend the general framework in which these accidental aspects are visible to us in the first place. The readiness-to-hand of equipment is not a particular something that we can point out or see but is rather the way things in general show up under a distinctive kind of 'seeing', namely circumspection.

Heidegger's conception of assertions is not as austerely limiting as the Tractarian conception of propositions. Where Wittgenstein delineates a single task performed by propositions, Heidegger talks about 'many interim stages' between concernful understanding and the 'extreme opposite case' of theoretical assertion (*BT* 158). In particular, *Being and Time* is a book full of assertoric sentences and Heidegger does not throw away any ladders at the end of it.[3] Heidegger is not guilty of a

---

[3] I should add two caveats here. First, unlike the *Tractatus*, *Being and Time* is unfinished: we have only the first two of a projected six divisions of the project. Not only do we not know how Heidegger might have brought that work to completion, but we could reasonably read his abandonment of the *Being and Time* project as a kind of ladder-throwing, or at least a recognition that taking this project further would require giving a radically new form to the expression of his thoughts. And second, we could arguably identify something like a ladder-throwing gesture in *Being and Time* as we have it. Mulhall (2005b, 120–1) argues that Division II does not simply deepen our understanding of the themes introduced in Division I, but calls that very understanding into question. Once we have done the

performative contradiction here, and he is aware of the difficulty: 'It is possible for every phenomenological concept and proposition drawn from genuine origins to degenerate when communicated as an assertion' (*BT* 36; translation modified). But the difficulty is there: if the language we use to talk about the world is complicit in covering over the primordial understanding Heidegger wants to retrieve, how can we use language to access that primordial understanding?

7.4. Formal Indication

Three stylistic features of Heidegger's writing reflect the difficulty of what he writes about. Perhaps the most obvious is his distinctive jargon, coining terms like *Dasein*, *Zuhandenheit*, and *Befindlichkeit* to pick out features of this ontological structure that we have failed to notice. The second is Heidegger's pervasive use of scare quotes. He acknowledges this stylistic feature most explicitly at §14 of *Being and Time*, where he distinguishes his use of 'world' with and without scare quotes, the former denoting the ontic concept of 'the totality of beings which can be present-at-hand within the world' (*BT* 64; translation modified), and the latter denoting the pre-ontological, existentiell sense of the world in which Dasein dwells. More generally, Heidegger seems to use scare quotes to denote usages that betray an ontic understanding. In this regard, we can understand the ubiquitous scare quotes in *Being and Time* as seeking to draw attention to ontological assumptions built into our language. Heidegger at once disowns these words as inadequately expressing his meaning, while also suggesting through citation that this is how 'one' tends to use such words: he alerts us to the inescapable shadow of *das Man* lurking in our language.[4]

---

phenomenological work to understand Dasein in terms of care, we can start our phenomenological investigation anew from the standpoint of care, and apprehend death, guilt, and conscience in a way that destabilizes and subverts the analytic of Dasein's average everydayness presented in Division I. We could identify another such gesture in §§63–5 of *Being and Time*, where Heidegger turns from anticipatory resoluteness to call the hermeneutics of his investigation into question in a way that leads, in Chapter Four of Division II, to a reassessment of the tripartite structure of care in terms of temporality.

[4] All that said, it might be risky to rely too heavily on Heidegger's use of scare quotes in interpreting his meaning. As Dreyfus (1991, 354n10) points out, he is maddeningly inconsistent in his use of scare quotes when talking about the world (or 'world').

The third stylistic feature is related to Heidegger's use of scare quotes: rather than coining neologisms, he often uses a familiar word to gesture at the ontological structure that underlies the ontic features of the world denoted by that word. For example, Heidegger's coinage of 'Dasein' is a way of turning our attention from the ontic being described by biology, anthropology, and psychology, and toward the being of that being whose being is an issue for it. And that means that 'death' understood as the cessation of biological function is inadequate for thinking about the finitude of Dasein. Underlying the prospect of biological cessation is an ontological understanding of death as 'the possibility of the absolute impossibility of Dasein' (*BT* 250).

All three of these stylistic features use words to help us apprehend the ontological features of our world that our everyday modes of speech and comportment cover over. Especially in his lectures before *Being and Time*, Heidegger refers to such gestures as 'formal indications' (*formale Anzeigen*), which contrast suggestively with the pointing out (*aufzeigen*) of assertion. A number of scholars find in formal indication the hidden key to understanding what, if not making assertions, Heidegger is doing with the words of *Being and Time*.[5] Formal indication acts as a kind of 'phenomenological definition' (*PIA* 17), where phenomenology points not to 'this or that being but rather... the *being* of beings' (*BT* 35). But the being of beings is not itself a being (*BT* 6), so we cannot point it out the way we might point out a being.[6]

Formal indication is 'formal' in the sense of being empty, very much in the way that I presented the call of conscience as formal and empty in section 5.4. The call of conscience 'does not say anything, does not give any information about events of the world, has nothing to tell' (*BT* 273),

---

[5] See, for example, Kisiel (1993), Dahlstrom (1994), and Streeter (1997). I have also benefited from reading an unpublished paper on formal indication by Stephen Reynolds. Kisiel (1993, 19) cites a letter in which Heidegger insists that formal indication remains crucial to *Being and Time* even though it receives less explicit attention there than in his earlier lectures.

[6] To extend the parallels between *Being and Time* and the *Tractatus*, Heidegger's formal indications resemble Wittgenstein's elucidations [*Erläuterungen*]: both seem to be ways of gesturing at something that cannot be formulated in straightforward assertions. Both are also subject to considerable discussion and interpretive disagreement in their respective secondary literatures. The parallel is far from perfect—no one claims that Wittgenstein's elucidations gesture at our original comportment toward beings—but both can be read as ways of investigating the essence of the world while being mindful of the difficulties we face in trying to speak meaningfully about the essence of the world.

Heidegger says, because the call of conscience does not disclose this or that being within the world but rather discloses Dasein as the clearing within which disclosure is possible. The call of conscience calls Dasein back to its authentic potentiality-for-being-a-self—in other words, it formally indicates the being of Dasein as a being that exists.

Heidegger's use of familiar words like 'death' and 'guilt' are meant, then, not to point out particular events or experiences we might have but rather to encourage us to look behind those particular events or experiences to the ontological structure within which those particular events or experiences have the distinct salience that they do. In formally indicating death, for instance, Heidegger wants us to consider not a particular moment in our lives—namely the last one—but rather the way in which *every* moment is given a particular shape and salience by the finitude of Dasein's existence. Formal indication does not indicate a specific content, Heidegger tells us, but rather points 'the "way", the "approach"' by which we might uncover 'the mode *in which the object is originally accessible*' (*PIA* 17). For Heidegger, beings are originally accessible to us not through some sort of cognitive grasping, but through our comportment toward them (*PIA* 46): formal indication, then, does not *assert* anything about beings, but rather directs our attention to the way that we originally comport ourselves toward those beings.

For instance, in characterizing Dasein as 'in each case mine', he claims that he has given 'the formal indication of the basic characteristics of Dasein.... This determination *indicates* an *ontological* constitution, but no more than that' (*BT* 114). Heidegger is not trying to fix Dasein in a definition, but wants to direct our attention to the way that, as Dasein, our existence is essentially a matter of concern for us. Reflecting on our relation to ourselves, we come to see that we do not relate to ourselves as to a present-at-hand being, and that some more fundamental account of our existence is required than the one traditionally provided. Heidegger does not *tell* us what Dasein *is* in the manner of assertion, but rather hopes that his words direct us to recover an ontological understanding that will dislodge deeply held prejudices, but for which we lack a clear vocabulary.

This project of recovery is important precisely because the prejudices are so deeply held and the ontological understanding is thereby so thickly obscured. Consider a simple sentence like 'I'm going to die'. This is such an obvious commonplace that it can be hard to say it without sounding trite. And yet—and it is hard to say *this* without sounding trite too—to actually live in the shadow of this knowledge, to keep it constantly close, is the rare achievement of saints and poets. It is easy—and sometimes not inappropriate—to respond to a sentence like that one with a knowing shrug: yes, I know, so what? But in the right circumstances, the same sentence can hit us with the full force of a hurricane. The fact that I am going to die can sit unperturbingly within a staid understanding of my existence and then, all of a sudden, the seemingly same fact can turn that understanding upside down.[7] What changes? Not my understanding of the meaning of the word 'death'. In terms of what philosophers of language call its intension and extension, I use the word just as I did before. I have acquired no new information that I did not already have. And yet the hold that thought has on me—the thought that I am going to die—is different. What has changed is not my understanding of the word, but my understanding of what it means to exist in a world in which that word has a use. What has changed is not the meaning of a word but the meaning of the world.

In this discussion of formal indication we have one explanation for Heidegger's notoriously difficult prose style. If he were to talk straightforwardly about human beings, death, moods, and the like, he would risk being mistaken for talking about an array of familiar ontic phenomena. But he is also not talking about something *other than* human beings, death, moods, and the like. Even his coinages—like almost all coinages, really—are not entirely new made-up words but rather retoolings of familiar words that he wants us to see in a new light. Heidegger uses the method of formal indication to get us to look at the being of beings, but this means looking not at *something else* but at the same familiar world in a different way. As a result, he needs a style of writing that will jolt us out of our complacency, defamiliarize the familiar, and push us to confront our understanding of being at its deepest level.[8]

---

[7] The classic literary treatment of these two understandings of death is Tolstoy's novella, *The Death of Ivan Ilyich*, to which Heidegger alludes in a footnote (*BT* 254n). Consider, for instance, Ivan Ilyich's reflection on a familiar syllogism: 'The example of a syllogism he had studied in Kiesewetter's logic—Caius is a man, men are mortal, therefore Caius is mortal—had seemed to him all his life to be correct only in relation to Caius, but by no means to himself. For the man Caius, man in general, it was perfectly correct; but he was not Caius and not man in general' (Tolstoy [1886] 2009, 32).

[8] In Chapter 1 I made much of what I called a 'Heraclitean philosopher' announcing the 'discovery' that one cannot step into the same river twice as if it were the discovery of a

7.5. Truth and Untruth

So far, I have tried to explain what Heidegger *wants* to do in his use of various stylistic innovations: he wants to eschew the potentially misleading form of assertion—which might seduce us into engaging with his text as a series of claims to ontic truth—and find a manner of expression that draws our attention to the ontological ground of *all* ontic truth. Now I want to look more closely at how exactly he goes about doing this and ask the question: does it work? This question will not lend itself to a tidy answer. After all, the difficulty of Heidegger's undertaking lies precisely in the fact that standard modes of assessment—Is the argument valid? Does it make claims that are true?—do not apply. In particular, Heidegger's investigation calls for a reassessment of the concept of truth itself. As I noted in section 7.2, Heidegger's treatment of truth sits alongside his treatment of the problematic of realism and idealism at the end of Division I of *Being and Time*, and the two discussions share a number of parallels. Most notably, the third subsection of both §43 and §44 see Heidegger making some perplexing and troubling claims. I turn now to his discussion of truth before returning to the related puzzles in §43(c).

In §44(a) of *Being and Time*, Heidegger tells the story of how the concept of truth has been hardened by the philosophical tradition into a conception of correspondence between mind and world. This conception of truth as '*adaequatio intellectus et rei*' is closely tied to the idea of the assertion as the locus of truth (*BT* 214).[9] An assertion is true, on this conception, if what it represents corresponds to a state of affairs in the world.

Heidegger does not reject this account of truth. He thinks it provides an acceptable account of ontic truth, but adds that this account is derivative of a more primordial conception of truth. In particular, this conception of truth presupposes the intelligibility of beings in their

---

heretofore undisclosed fact. We could more charitably think about what Heraclitus himself was up to in terms of Heideggerian formal indications. Heraclitus is not trying to make a metaphysical claim about the nature of rivers (or anything else) but is rather trying to jolt us into a more primordial understanding of sameness and change. That is, we could read him not as announcing a metaphysical discovery but as issuing a phenomenological reminder. In the remainder of this chapter, I will question the success of Heidegger's strategy of using formal indications. A similar line of questioning might apply to this more sophisticated version of Heraclitus.

[9] Heidegger also notes the traditional assignment of the assertion as the locus of truth at *BT* 154.

being. If I am to be able to make an assertion about a chair, the chair has to be available *as* a chair—that is, it has to be disclosed as ready-to-hand equipment—and that disclosure cannot itself be cashed out in terms of a correspondence between one thing and another. More primordial than the conception of truth as *adaequatio intellectus et rei* is the conception of truth as discoveredness—as *aletheia*, says Heidegger, reappropriating the concept at its Greek roots. Dasein is able to make assertions—true and false—about beings because it has already discovered those beings in their being. The site of this discovering is the disclosedness of Dasein so, says Heidegger, '*Dasein is "in the truth"*' (*BT* 221).

This conception of truth as discovering 'has an ontological meaning' (*BT* 221), says Heidegger: to say that Dasein is 'in the truth' does not conflict with the fact that, on the level of ontic truth, Dasein sometimes says things that are false. Furthermore, this ontological conception of truth also has a kind of bivalency: Heidegger later adds that Dasein is equiprimordially in the truth and untruth (*BT* 222–3): Dasein is just as much the site of beings being covered over in their being as it is the site of their discovery. The possibility of inauthenticity is one manifestation of this untruth: as falling, Dasein has a tendency to cover over the truth about its own being. But this untruth is not a matter of saying something false. Heidegger's aim in *Being and Time* is not to counter the false assertions of the philosophical tradition with true assertions but rather to reframe what those assertions are about.

I will have much more to say in the next chapter about the later Wittgenstein by way of comparison, but let me now draw out two near similarities in Wittgenstein that I hope will clarify the tension I see in Heidegger's account of truth. First, Heidegger's conception of discoveredness as an ontological ground for assertoric truth finds a neighbour notion in Wittgenstein's situation of the concept of truth within language-games. At *PI* §136, Wittgenstein considers a variant of the claim that assertion is the locus of truth: 'a proposition is whatever can be true or false'. Wittgenstein cautions against taking this claim as having

determined what a proposition was, by saying: what fits the concept 'true', or what the concept 'true' fits, is a proposition. So it is as if we had a concept of true and false, which we could use to ascertain what is, and what is not, a proposition. What *engages* with the concept of truth (as with a cog-wheel) is a proposition.
(*PI* §136)

'But this is a bad picture', Wittgenstein says of this conception of truth and falsity as 'fitting' or 'engaging' with propositions. It treats a grammatical remark as a metaphysical one. That is, it regards the concept of truth and the proposition as two distinct self-standing entities, which, as a matter of metaphysical fact, engage with one another in a particular way. 'It is as if one were to say "The chess king is *the* piece that one puts in check"', Wittgenstein adds. 'But this can mean no more than that in our game of chess only the king is put in check' (*PI* §136). Although we are not wrong to say that a proposition is whatever can be true or false, we risk confusion if we treat this claim as an explanation of the nature of propositions rather than a description of language-games.

That we say true and false things, according to Wittgenstein, is a feature of the language-games we play. In this respect, language-games have a similar place in Wittgenstein's treatment of truth as discoveredness does in Heidegger's. But Wittgenstein pointedly does not call the rules of language-games 'true' in some further ontological sense. On the contrary, he emphasizes that these rules are not themselves subject to evaluation in terms of correctness or incorrectness, truth or falsity. So, on one hand, Wittgenstein and Heidegger both want to situate our ordinary concepts of truth and falsity within the context—of forms of life or the disclosedness of Dasein—in which they have a use, but on the other hand, Heidegger but not Wittgenstein regards this context as the primordial ground of truth.

The difference between Wittgenstein and Heidegger here becomes clearer if we consider a second difference-in-similarity in relation to the flip side of Heidegger's claim that Dasein is in the truth: that Dasein is equiprimordially in untruth. Being in untruth, as I indicated above, means covering over the being of beings—as, for instance, Heidegger thinks the philosophical tradition does in treating beings of all kinds—notably Dasein and equipment—as being in the mode of presence-at-hand.

When Wittgenstein talks about this kind of misapprehension—a misapprehension not of fact but of grammar—he says the result is nonsense. In attempting to articulate how sensations might be private, Wittgenstein's interlocutor proposes: 'Well, only I can know whether I am really in pain; another person can only surmise it' (*PI* §246). Wittgenstein replies: 'In one way this is false, and in another nonsense'. The utterance is false if 'we are using the word "know" as it is normally used (and how else are we to use it?)': other people often can know when I am in pain. 'Yes, but all the same', Wittgenstein's interlocutor replies, 'not with the certainty with which I know it myself!' But the interlocutor's utterance is nonsensical rather than false if she wants to construe the difference between her experience of her own pain and her experience of the pain of others in terms of knowledge: 'It can't be said of me at all (except perhaps as a joke) that I *know* I'm in pain' (*PI* §246). Wittgenstein goes on to link the grammar of knowing to the grammar of learning: something I can *know* is something I can *come to know* through learning. It makes sense that someone else might come to know that I am in pain but there is no similar process of discovery on my own part. Coming to know can be conceived as bridging an epistemic gap, and there is no such gap between myself and my pain.

One source of the confusion in this case is that the interlocutor treats pain too much on the model of a physical object—as a *thing* about which I can have knowledge. The confusion in this case, then, is quite similar to the untruth Heidegger sees in a philosophical tradition that regards everything as present-at-hand. In both cases, our protagonists identify a pernicious tendency to assimilate diverse phenomena under a single category, thereby failing to appreciate sufficiently the distinctive kind of being of certain phenomena.

However, the diagnostic categories of untruth and nonsense are importantly different. If an inauthentic philosophy is complicit in untruth conceived as covering over, the authentic response is to uncover something, which involves the positive task of bringing the concealed truth into view. If an inauthentic philosophy is complicit in speaking nonsense, the authentic response is to uncover the nonsense with no additional positive task to undertake.[10] It might seem as if Wittgenstein is coming up short here: he goes half the distance Heidegger does but fails to articulate the positive vision his critical work makes possible. I will argue, on the contrary, that Wittgenstein's insight lies precisely in 'recognizing as the solution something that looks as if it were only a preliminary to it'. As he sees it, '[t]he difficulty here is: to stop' (*Z* §314). One way to appreciate

---

[10] In section 5.7, I noted this difference in Heidegger's and Wittgenstein's use of the language of discovering and uncovering (*entdecken*): Heidegger wants to discover beings in their being and Wittgenstein wants to discover nonsense. In section 8.1, I will return to the ways in which the differences in their vocabularies of criticism reveal differences in method.

Wittgenstein's admonition is to consider some of the difficulties Heidegger encounters in trying to articulate a positive vision.

7.6. Heidegger's Dependency Claim

Heidegger most directly tries to articulate his positive vision of reality and truth in *Being and Time* in §43(c) and §44(c) respectively. To begin with his treatment of truth, he returns to the claim that 'Dasein is essentially in the truth' (*BT* 226) and elaborates: '"There is" truth only insofar as Dasein is and as long as it is' (*BT* 226). If truth is primordially discoveredness, and if Dasein's disclosedness is the site of discovering, then truth depends on the being of Dasein. McManus (2012, 128 and 181–9) calls this Heidegger's 'Dependency Claim' about truth, and Heidegger presents it as his answer to the question of what kind of being truth possesses if not the being of *adaequatio intellectus et rei*.

This position leads Heidegger to the seemingly paradoxical claim that Newton's laws of motion have been true only since Newton formulated them: 'Before there was any Dasein, there was no truth; nor will there be any after Dasein is no more.... Before Newton's laws were discovered, they were not "true"' (*BT* 226). This claim may seem less paradoxical if we confine it to general scientific laws. Newton's Laws are not themselves particular truths, but rather provide a framework within which we can make sense of particular truths. We were only able to formulate truths about objects in motion in terms of force and momentum once Newton had provided the framework within which such formulations could be made. However, Heidegger applies this claim about truth generally. He focuses primarily on laws rather than empirical truths, but he does not draw any such distinction—and makes no use of scare quotes—when he writes: 'Newton's laws, the law of contradiction, **and any truth whatsoever**, are true only as long as Dasein *is*' (*BT* 226).

The worry is that Heidegger comes very close to sounding like an idealist here. And this worry arises from the assertoric form of Heidegger's pronouncements. They have the ring of a this-rather-than-that statement of a philosophical thesis, which naturally invites one to consider the 'that' to Heidegger's 'this'. Almost any interesting assertion is also contestable, and the contestability of an assertion implies that its negation is also plausible. Consider the negation of a sentence such as 'Before there was any Dasein, there was no truth': 'There was truth before there was

Dasein'. And now it seems like we have rival theses, the former idealist and the latter realist. Rather than transcending the debate between realists and idealists, Heidegger here sounds like he is advocating an idealist conception of truth as constituted by Dasein as against a realist position that considers truth to be independent of Dasein. Because Heidegger couches his account of truth in assertoric form, he risks recapitulating the problematic he sought to overcome.

One response to this puzzle is to kick Heidegger's idealism upstairs, so to speak. Although he rejects the subject–object dichotomy that gives rise to the dilemma of realism and idealism as it has traditionally been formulated, he nevertheless remains an *ontological* idealist. That is, he does not say that beings are in some way dependent on Dasein as a knowing subject, but he does say that the *being* of beings is dependent on Dasein as being-in-the-world.[11] Heidegger certainly says things at times that strongly support this reading, most strikingly at *BT* 212:[12]

> [O]nly as long as Dasein *is*, that is, as long as there is the ontic possibility of an understanding of being, 'is there' being. If Dasein does not exist, then there 'is' no 'independence' either, nor 'is' there an 'in itself'. Such matters are then neither comprehensible nor incomprehensible. If Dasein does not exist then inner-worldly beings, too, can neither be discovered, nor can they lie in concealment. *Then* it can neither be said that beings are, nor that they are not. It can *now* indeed be said that as long as there is an understanding of being and thus an understanding of presence-at-hand, that *then* beings will still continue to be.... [B]eing (not beings) is dependent upon the understanding of being.

Construed as an expression of ontological idealism, Heidegger here is providing an *explanation* for why the traditional problematic of realism and idealism cannot arise. Such an explanation is purportedly grounded in a fact, albeit a fact of a very particular kind. It is grounded in the *ontological* 'fact' that being is dependent on Dasein.

But, as I understand it, part of the confusion that Heidegger wants to overcome is precisely this idea that we can talk coherently about ontological 'facts'. The attempt to convey ontological facts is precisely the move that the Wittgenstein of the *Tractatus* wants to expose as a

---

[11] Blattner (1999) offers probably the most influential articulation of this position. We see a recent sophisticated formulation of this position in McDaniel (2016). Richardson (2012) goes further to defend a reading of Heidegger as holding a modified *ontic* idealism as well.

[12] This passage occurs in §43(c) of *Being and Time*, which I see twinned with §44(c), and whose difficulties seem to me to be closely entwined.

nonsensical gesture. I am therefore in sympathy with Carman, who proposes a deflationary account of Heidegger's most idealist-sounding passages. Carman reads Heidegger as an ontic realist, who 'is trying to point out the vacuity and futility of all efforts to stake out a distinct transcendental standpoint from which to engage such issues' (Carman 2003, 171).[13] Any standpoint we could take on the question of how the world is disclosed to Dasein would be a standpoint in which we would have to apprehend Dasein's relation to the world from sideways on.

The trouble is that it is very hard to construe some of Heidegger's claims about truth as *not* trying to apprehend our relation to truth from sideways on. Consider the claim Heidegger makes about Newton's Laws:

(1) Newton's Laws were not true before Newton discovered them.

Now consider two claims that seem fairly uncontroversial:

(2) Newton's Laws are disclosed as true to Dasein, and it is only Dasein that recognizes them as true, and
(3) Newton's Laws are disclosed to Dasein as *atemporally* true.

Some truths are disclosed as temporally indexed: the proposition 'Justin Trudeau is the Prime Minister of Canada' has been true *since 2015* and will not remain true indefinitely; the proposition 'A Canadian hockey team is the current Stanley Cup champion' *has been true* at various times before 1994 but has not, alas, been true since (at least not at the time of writing). Newton's Laws, by contrast, are not disclosed with any temporal indexing: the Second Law tells us that the rate of change of the momentum of a body is directly proportional to the force applied to it and makes no further claim about *when* this relation holds.[14]

---

[13] Cerbone (2005) offers a similar deflationary account, emphasizing that the passage from *BT* 212 cited above focuses on what can be *said* about beings rather than making an ontological claim about what is or is not. McManus (2012) can be read as providing a book-length attempt to work through Heidegger's treatment of the problematic of realism and idealism in a way that avoids the sideways perspective. See especially chaps. 6 and 7. McManus offers a compelling account of Heidegger founding our use of assertions in a mastery of descriptive practices, although he ultimately concludes there is no way of construing what he calls the 'Dependency Claim' of *BT* §44 that escapes all the difficulties it raises (see McManus 2012, 181–9).

[14] Note that there is a difference between a proposition being *atemporally* true and being *eternally* true. Eternal truths *are* time-indexed: something that is eternally true is true *at all times*. An atemporal truth, by contrast, is one that is not indexed to time. That three squared is nine is not true at all times: it is confused altogether to ask *when* three squared is nine.

To talk about the truth of Newton's Laws in terms of a temporal index—as not being true until they were discovered by Newton—is to try to talk about Newton's Laws from outside the horizon of their disclosure. Statement (2) above seems fairly uncontroversial but it does not entail (1). Furthermore, (3) conflicts with (1), and it too seems fairly uncontroversial. Statement (3) describes how Newton's Laws are disclosed to Dasein. But that means that, since we are Dasein, the truth of Newton's Laws is *not* disclosed to us as having a temporal index, which is what (1) requires. Asserting (1) manifests an attempt to apprehend Newton's Laws from some perspective outside the perspective from which we apprehend them. And the aspiration to take such a perspective is precisely what I have characterized as the attempt to apprehend our lives from sideways on.

The impulse driving Heidegger's Dependency Claim is one that would be sympathetic to an admirer of Wittgenstein. In claiming that Newton's Laws were not true before Newton, Heidegger does not claim to be discovering something new about the nature of truth, but to be drawing our attention to an important but neglected aspect of the concept of truth as we already know it—namely that our concept of truth is constituted by the kind of being that Dasein is. Wittgenstein also draws attention to the broader human context in which our concepts are embedded. In other words, we might want to argue, Wittgenstein is just as keenly attuned to the status of our concept of truth as constituted by us as Heidegger is.

But Wittgenstein applies pressure to the idea that any insight of this kind can find expression. We can insist that understanding the concept of truth means understanding how it is used within our forms of life, but this is true of any concept. Saying, 'The truth is constituted by us' amounts to saying, 'The concept of truth is a concept', and that says precisely nothing. That we need *reminding* that the concept of truth is a concept reveals something deep about the nature of philosophical confusion, but any attempt to *say* what it reveals will end up saying something else instead.

7.7. The Form of Formal Indication

I do not think this is simply a slip on Heidegger's part, a misstatement that could be corrected without much further ado. I think the slide toward a sideways perspective that is most manifest in §44(c) points to a more general problem in Heidegger's method. On one hand, Heidegger wants to strictly separate his ontological investigations from ontic investigations of empirical fact. But on the other hand, he still tries to couch the outcome of his ontological investigations in the form of assertions that have many of the characteristics of factual claims. To assert the dependency of being or truth on Dasein makes it sound as if Heidegger is staking out one metaphysical position as distinct from an alternative. But these alleged alternatives only seem like alternatives as long as we are under the illusion that we can occupy a position from outside ourselves from which to apprehend these alternatives. A central aim of an authentic philosophy, as I understand it, is precisely to wean us off this illusion.

In section 7.4, I explored the idea of formal indication as Heidegger's alternative to the sort of factual claims that are problematic at the ontological level. The thought is that he wants to convey not ontological 'facts' but rather to call our attention to our prior understanding of how beings are accessible to us. That understanding is founded not in our grasping truths but in our relating ourselves to a meaningful world. The difficulty Heidegger encounters, as I read him, is that the *form* he finds for his formal indications is insufficiently radical for the 'content' (or rather the lack thereof) that he wishes to convey. As long as they are couched in assertoric form, his formal indications invite us to consider their negations. And as long as their negations have a ring of plausibility, he can understandably be read as trafficking in the kind of theses that betray a conception of philosophy that is insufficiently mindful of the ontological difference.

Daniel Dahlstrom (2001) acknowledges the difficulty of style that Heidegger faces, but argues that it should not concern us overmuch. On Dahlstrom's reading, Heidegger holds a two-tiered conception of truth. On an empirical level, we have truths that could also have been falsehoods, which are expressed in bivalent propositions. On a transcendental level, we have the original disclosure that makes the empirical realm meaningful in the first place, and hence subject to judgments of truth and falsity. Heidegger's account of transcendental truth shows how the bivalence of empirical truth is possible: only given the primordial disclosure of being can beings be uncovered, as they are in themselves or otherwise. Heidegger's primordial-truth-as-disclosedness is not bivalent, but it provides the ground upon which bivalent propositions can be asserted.

7.7. THE FORM OF FORMAL INDICATION

Dahlstrom acknowledges that any assertion of the truth of disclosedness must take the form of a proposition, which 'must be considered prima facie bivalent' (Dahlstrom 2001, 421). Nevertheless, these assertions can serve as formal indications, he claims, which help us retrieve a conception of primordial truth. Language does not lend itself readily to expressing this primordial conception of truth, Dahlstrom claims, but we should not take this to be a disaster:

[T]here is no inherent reason why we should not be able to use true ... propositions to point to this truth that underlies every ... propositional truth. Since we succeed in speaking of things, including speech itself, there is every reason to suppose that we can speak about what, while not identical to speech, makes the connection between speech and what is spoken of—or, better, the disclosive event of discourse—possible at all.   (Dahlstrom 2001, 407)

I think Dahlstrom's own language here conveys the difficulty. If primordial disclosure were a 'thing', we would presumably be able to talk about it. But if the being of beings is not itself a being then we are committing a category mistake in talking about primordial disclosure as a 'thing'. Even Dahlstrom's 'what' conveys the idea that there is some*thing* that we can speak about.[15]

This notion of a two-tiered conception of truth comes under criticism in a different form at *PI* §402. Wittgenstein is considering a would-be solipsist objecting to the proposition 'He has pains': if pain is something that, by the solipsist's definition, only *I* have, then it is wrong to say of anyone else that he or she has pains. The problem with that objection, according to Wittgenstein, is that the would-be solipsist is mistaking a dispute about our forms of expression for a dispute about facts.

At the same time, we're tempted to say that our way of speaking does not describe the facts as they really are. As if, for example, the proposition 'he has pains' could be false in some other way than by that man's *not* having pains. As if the form of expression were saying something false, even when the proposition *faute de mieux* asserted something true.   (*PI* §402)

---

[15] I remarked earlier on some similarities between Heidegger's concern about assertions as a vehicle for ontological truth and Wittgenstein's concern about propositions as a vehicle for philosophical truth in the *Tractatus* so it is worth nothing a similar tension there regarding 'what' is being 'said'. In his discussion of solipsism, Wittgenstein writes: 'For what the solipsist *means* is quite correct; only it cannot be *said*, but makes itself manifest' (*TLP* 5.62). If what the solipsist allegedly 'means' cannot be said, it is unclear how there is nevertheless a 'what' that is unsayable—and how that 'what' can be 'meant' even if not said.

The idea of a two-tiered conception of truth seems to have a similar *'faute de mieux'* structure: Heidegger does not want to deny that momentum was directly proportional to force back when dinosaurs were kicking around boulders but wants to insist that *nevertheless* Newton's Laws were not *true* until Newton discovered them. As if the person who insists that Newton's Laws were true before Newton discovered them were saying something false even when the proposition asserts something true.

If the aim of formal indication is to lead us from an ontic to an ontological level of reflection, its very form is an impediment to that aim. These formal indications could serve as stepping stones toward an ontological investigation, of course, and further work could clarify the nature of the investigation that formal indication is meant to lead us toward. But that work would need to be done, and that work is precisely what Heidegger's stylistic innovations were supposed to do. I argued that Heidegger makes a number of stylistic innovations in order to overcome the formal difficulty of articulating an ontological understanding that he thinks is covered over in our ordinary forms of speech. But these stylistic innovations at best only partially extricate Heidegger from this difficulty. That is not to say that Heidegger *cannot* extricate himself from this difficulty, but the foregoing discussion hopefully at least illustrates why such extrication itself is difficult.

The difficulty, in short, is that an authentic philosophical method is one that renounces a sideways perspective on our practices, one that, in Carman's words, renounces all efforts to stake out a distinct transcendental standpoint. The fantasy of the sideways perspective is the fantasy of a privileged point of view from which we can see more clearly what others have missed. But if we do not have some privileged point of view, how are we able to see more clearly than those who are captivated by that fantasy? The problem I find with Heidegger's method of formal indication is that, in taking the form of assertions, Heidegger seems to be trying to speak from such a privileged position—one from which he can characterize Dasein's relation to being in a general way—and the attempt to do so leads him to make claims about the nature of reality and truth for which I struggle to find a felicitous interpretation.

To find a searching exploration of philosophical method that acknowledges the shortcomings of *Being and Time* while also trying to preserve what is great about that book, the obvious place to look is Heidegger's own later writings. My turn to consider Wittgenstein's method might seem abrupt by comparison. But besides the scholarly value of treating this comparison rather than the more well-worn question of the nature of Heidegger's turn, the comparison helps us to keep in view the theme of the ordinary or everyday that animates both *Being and Time* and Wittgenstein's later philosophy.

I find Wittgenstein's response to this challenge of an authentic philosophy elegant on two counts. First, I think he manages to address the fantasy of self-transcendence manifest in the temptation to take the sideways perspective without himself claiming a privileged perspective of his own. And second, he does this by finding a form of philosophical criticism that does not commit him to making positive philosophical claims. Rather than making assertions, Wittgenstein deploys points of telling contrast—what he calls pictures or objects of comparison—and the dialogue form to dismantle claims that purport to occupy a sideways perspective. Happily for our purposes, one of the sets of claims he considers is the problematic of realism and idealism. I will consider Wittgenstein's approach to that problematic in the next chapter, where I will explore his method in more detail.

8

Wittgenstein's Pursuit of Authenticity in Philosophy

8.1. Ordinary Language and Terms of Criticism

The previous chapter brought to the fore a problem of method that had been intermittently present in the first two parts of this book. In their pursuit of an authentic philosophy, Wittgenstein and Heidegger need to rethink radically what it means to do philosophy. And that in turn calls for a radical departure from the traditional forms of philosophical expression. In the previous chapter, I considered Heidegger's method of formal indication as a way of sidestepping some of the limitations he finds with assertions, and I questioned the ultimate effectiveness of this method. To the extent that Heidegger's tools for gesturing at a deeper ontological understanding have the same form as tools that often cover over that ontological understanding, his language strains against the problematic he seeks to overcome. Heidegger's language seems unsuited to his task, a fact that Heidegger himself acknowledges in his introduction:

> With regard to the awkwardness and 'inelegance' of expression in the following analyses, we may remark that it is one thing to report narratively about *beings* and another to grasp [*fassen*] beings in their *being*. For the latter task not only are most of the words lacking but above all the 'grammar'. (BT 38–9)

This acknowledgment is revelatory both in showing that Heidegger is mindful of the methodological challenge he faces and in illuminating Heidegger's understanding of that challenge. One way in which Heidegger would later move away from the project of *Being and Time* is precisely in this notion that the being of beings is something to be 'grasped'. This language of grasping is consonant with the assertoric form of his formal indications. Assertions point things out so that we can grasp them conceptually. In aspiring to 'grasp' beings in their being, Heidegger figures being on analogy with graspable ontic content. His frustration, then, is that the analogy is imperfect: the being of beings, as Heidegger is very well aware, is not the sort of thing that can be grasped the way that conceptual content can be.

The 'awkwardness and "inelegance"' of Heidegger's writing bespeaks a complicated relationship with ordinary language. On one hand, he thinks our ordinary forms of expression are often deeply revealing. He thinks he can recover an ontological understanding of phenomena like death, conscience, and guilt by digging *into* our ordinary uses of those words rather than by rejecting ordinary usage, and he remarks on the way that ordinary phrases reveal an ontological understanding if we learn to hear them right—for instance, when we remark at the passing of anxiety that 'it was really nothing' (*BT* 187). On the other hand, he also thinks we habitually hear these expressions as 'one' hears them and in such a way as to conceal their deeper ontological significance. This dual character of ordinary language as both revealing and concealing is evident in Heidegger's treatment of idle talk in §35 of *Being and Time*. He remarks that 'language harbours in itself an interpretedness of the understanding of Dasein' (*BT* 167) and adds: 'In the totality of its structured contexts of signification, expression preserves an understanding of the disclosed world and thus equiprimordially an understanding of the Dasein-with of others and of one's own being-in' (*BT* 168). But while discourse can bring us toward 'what is talked about' (*das Beredete*), it can also lull us into simply passing along what is 'said-in-the-talk' (*das Geredete*; *BT* 168, translation modified).

Although Wittgenstein is taken as a spokesman for what came to be known as 'ordinary language philosophy', he, too, shows some ambivalence about ordinary language. We see this tension clearly in two neighbouring passages. At *PI* §116, he famously announces his intention 'to brings words back from their metaphysical to their everyday use', but in the section immediately preceding he issues an equally famous warning about the way that language can ensnare us: 'A *picture* held us captive. And we couldn't get outside it, for it lay in our language, and language seemed only to repeat it to us inexorably' (*PI* §115).

Despite this ambivalence on both sides, Wittgenstein shows far greater confidence in the liberating potential of ordinary language. Where Heidegger feels ordinary language working against him, Wittgenstein, says Cavell, 'entrusts the health of the human spirit to ordinary language' more than any other modern philosopher (Cavell 1989, 33). Where Heidegger aspires to achieve authentic understanding by reaching beyond the constraints of ordinary language, Wittgenstein aspires to achieve authentic understanding from within ordinary language, and precisely by achieving an understanding of ordinary language that does not see it as constraining.

This difference is particularly apparent when we consider an important difference in the terms of criticism that Wittgenstein and Heidegger deploy. Heidegger's language of deficient, inauthentic, or levelled off forms of understanding differs markedly from Wittgenstein's confusions and temptations: Heidegger's criticisms are more condemnatory, the prospect of redemption seems more remote.[1] In section 5.7, I remarked on a particularly striking point of contrast: Heidegger talks about authentic modes of apprehension as 'covered up' (*verdeckt*) and sees his phenomenological method as a process of 'uncovering' or 'discovering' (*entdecken*) beings in their being, whereas Wittgenstein's discoveries (*Entdeckungen*) are consistently discoveries of nonsense rather than being.

As we will see shortly, Wittgenstein's treatment of the problematic of realism and idealism reaches the conclusion that there is *nothing* substantial to debate. In some respects, Heidegger's treatment echoes this form of criticism. For instance, he characterizes the debate between realism and idealism as empty rather than false: the '"problem of reality" ... turns out to be an impossible one ... because the very being which serves as its theme repudiates such a line of questioning, so to speak' (*BT* 206). Heidegger characterizes idealism as constructing an interpretation of reality 'in a vacuum' (*BT* 207),[2] and of realism he says that 'it cannot even be said that it is untenable, because it has not yet even pressed forward at all into the dimension of philosophical problems, the level

---

[1] I want to draw attention to differences in their terms of criticism, but I should also note that there are important similarities: both find forms of expression or understanding *empty* and frequently call attention to *misunderstandings*. Heidegger's critical talk of indeterminacy and undifferentiation is similar to Wittgenstein's emphasis on noticing differences between things that seem superficially the same.

[2] Macquarrie and Robinson have 'the Interpretation of Reality which idealism constructs is an empty one', which would support this line of argument even better. But the German reads '... baut er [der Idealismus] die Interpretation der Realität ins Leere', where what is empty is clearly not the interpretation of reality itself, but the space within which the idealist tries to construct an interpretation of reality.

8.1. ORDINARY LANGUAGE AND TERMS OF CRITICISM

where tenability and untenability are decidable' (*BPP* 167). He frequently charges the philosophical tradition with unclarity and indefiniteness in its formulations, suggesting that these formulations are guilty of lacking sense rather than stating something definite but false.

On the other hand, the language of Heidegger's criticism conveys the strong impression that the tradition is confused because there is *something* that it fails to apprehend: what is 'ontologically decisive' gets 'covered over' (*verdeckt*: *BT* 204), and Heidegger uses words like 'covered over' (*verdeckt*), 'concealed' (*verborgen*), and 'burying' (*begraben*) to describe Dasein's deficient (*defizient*) ontological understanding. Of this deficient understanding, Heidegger says that 'it **lacks something which it actually has** and would have to have as a world' (*HCT* 219). Heidegger aspires to 'discover' (*entdecken*) and 'disclose' (*erschliessen*) something more 'primordial' (*ursprünglich*), a 'basis' (*Boden*) or 'the fundamental constitution [*Grundverfassung*] of the "subject", of Dasein, as being-in-the-world' (*BT* 204). To the extent that the problematic of realism and idealism is fundamentally confused, the remedy lies in uncovering a more fundamental ontological understanding.

This language of uncovering what lies hidden shares many of the features that I identified in section 1.1 as characteristic of a certain cast of metaphysical thinking: Heidegger purports to be making a deep discovery and he claims that ordinary language is inadequate to convey this deep discovery—and is even complicit in covering it over. Heidegger is not a metaphysician of the kind I examined in Chapter 1, of course, because he does not claim that what he has discovered is factual in nature. On the contrary, he shares with Wittgenstein—if anything, he maintains even more vigorously than Wittgenstein—the conviction that treating philosophical discoveries as factual discoveries mistakes ontological investigations for ontic ones. But his understanding of the nature of ontological investigation commits him to a similar diagnosis as the metaphysician: ordinary language encodes assumptions in its grammar and vocabulary that impede philosophical progress.

Starting in section 8.3, I will explore Wittgenstein's treatment of the problematic of realism and idealism as a way of getting clearer on Wittgenstein's approach and how it contrasts with Heidegger's. But before I do that, I want to look more closely at these metaphors of hiddenness and discovery and ask what they can show us about Wittgenstein's and Heidegger's differing methodological self-understanding.

8.2. Hiddenness and the Hermeneutics of Suspicion

The metaphor of hiddenness is a central trope of hermeneutics generally. If nothing is hidden, after all, what need is there for the work of interpretation? In particular, literary studies for most of the past century has been dominated by a so-called 'hermeneutics of suspicion' that Paul Ricoeur (1970, 32–6) traces to Marx, Nietzsche, and Freud.[3] In different ways, all three offer a diagnosis of false consciousness: what we really mean is different from what we think we mean and hermeneutical work can dig out the 'hidden' meaning from beneath the surface of false consciousness. Through their influence, various strategies of reading have emerged—Marxist, feminist, deconstructionist, psychoanalytical, and so on—that take as their primary task the interpretation not of what a text *reveals* but of what it *conceals*, and, furthermore, to engage in a critique of the mechanism of concealment.

The metaphor of hiddenness lends itself to the metaphor of one thing covering over another: what we see on the surface covers over what is hidden underneath, and the task of interpretation is to look beneath the surface and bring what is covered into the light. Much of Heidegger's critical language supports this metaphor. In addition to the language of covering (*Deckung*), Heidegger frequently talks about phenomena being veiled (*verhüllt*).[4] He presents the aim of phenomenology as revealing 'the *being* of beings', which is 'what remains *concealed* [*verborgen*] in an exceptional sense, or what falls back and is *covered up* [*Verdeckung*] again, or shows itself only in a "*disguised*" [*verstellt*] way' (*BT* 35). The question of what covers what is a complicated one that I will return to, but the methodological significance of the metaphors is clear: what we seek is inaccessible because it is covered over and so our task is to remove the covering so that we can see what is underneath.

The metaphors of hiddenness and covering are meant to account for the fact that we are unable to see the thing we want to see. These metaphors seem so natural that we might forget that we can also fail to

---

[3] Ricoeur talks about a 'school of suspicion' but 'hermeneutics of suspicion' has become the more familiar expression.
[4] Derivations of the verb *verhüllen* occur at *BT* 30, 36, 59, 69, 74, 81, 103, 104, 135, 140, 158, 159, 166, 253, 258, and 262.

8.2. HIDDENNESS AND THE HERMENEUTICS OF SUSPICION

see things that are right before our eyes. Consider the contrast between games of perfect and imperfect information. Poker is a game of imperfect information: in most variants, players have information about their own cards that their opponents do not have and lack information about their opponents' cards that their opponents do have. In Texas hold 'em, two of each of my opponents' cards are hidden from me, and bets are placed at a time when some of the relevant cards are hidden from all players. By contrast, chess is a game of perfect information: both players have access to the positions and capabilities of all the pieces at all times in the game. In an informational sense, then, nothing is hidden in chess. Discovery in chess comes not in acquiring new information but in noticing patterns or combinations that had been open to view all along.

One way in which Wittgenstein's later philosophy departs from the *Tractatus* is in its diagnosis of our confusion. In the *Tractatus*, Wittgenstein tells us that the logic of language is 'disguised' by the 'clothing' of ordinary language (*TLP* 4.002) so that we have to learn how to see beneath the surface features of language to apprehend its underlying logical structure. Writing in a diagnostic spirit, and at least partly in self-criticism, Wittgenstein later writes of feeling 'as if we had to *see right into* phenomena' (*PI* §90). Wittgenstein gives voice to this aspiration in terms of uncovering something hidden, remarking that it is 'as if there were something hidden in [our usual forms of expression] that had to be brought to light' (*PI* §91). And shortly after that:

For it sees the essence of things not as something that already lies open to view, and that becomes *surveyable* through a process of ordering, but as something that lies *beneath* the surface. Something that lies within, which we perceive when we see *right into* the thing, and which an analysis is supposed to unearth.
'*The essence is hidden from us*': this is the form our problem now assumes.   (*PI* §92)

This last passage indicates the alternative of a 'surveyable representation' (*PI* §122) that is so central to Wittgenstein's later thought. Rather than figuring language in terms of a game of imperfect information, where we need to uncover something hidden, Wittgenstein figures it in terms of a game of perfect information, where we need to arrange what is already before us in a way that we can see patterns or connections that resolve the tension we are struggling with.

In contradistinction to a hermeneutics of suspicion, Wittgenstein's surveyable representations disavow the metaphorics of hiddenness.

'Since everything lies open to view, there is nothing to explain', Wittgenstein remarks: 'For whatever may be hidden is of no interest to us' (*PI* §126). Later, when responding to an interlocutor's befuddlement by telling her that 'nothing is hidden' (*PI* §435), Wittgenstein remarks that supposing otherwise gets us into a 'dead end in philosophizing' (*PI* §436). We get one picture of that dead end in Poe's 'Purloined Letter', in which the Prefect of the Police and his men turn the Minister's hotel room inside out looking for a hidden letter—and they fail to see the letter, hidden in plain sight, precisely because they assume at the outset that it must be concealed.[5] Likewise, the pursuit of the hidden essence of language leads us to look in the wrong places. In section 8.4, I discuss how misleading 'pictures' frame expectations that guide our investigations. The picture of the essence of language as hidden is one of the most pernicious such pictures according to Wittgenstein's diagnoses.

Toril Moi has recently invoked Wittgenstein as a model for what, if not suspicious critique, literary scholars should be engaging in: '[I]n Wittgenstein's vision of language there simply is no need to think of texts and language as hiding something' (Moi 2017, 178). Rather than try to uncover what texts conceal, Moi argues, careful readers work to render surveyable aspects of a text that were already visible but that we might otherwise have overlooked or seen differently. On Moi's account, a hermeneutics of suspicion mischaracterizes our need as readers in much the same way that Wittgenstein thinks the search for a hidden essence mischaracterizes our philosophical need.

Is Heidegger a suspicious hermeneut? As anyone who has struggled through §7 of *Being and Time* can attest, the answer is complicated. I have registered the pervasiveness of metaphors of hiddenness and coveredness in Heidegger's work. However, Heidegger is just as clear that the phenomenon of phenomenology is 'what shows itself, the self-showing, the manifest' (*BT* 28). He also stresses that what is hidden is not some additional *something* distinct from what covers it. 'The being of beings can least of all be something "behind which" something else stands, something that "does not appear"' (*BT* 35-6). Heidegger insists that phenomenology does not have its own proper domain of

---

[5] Moi (2017, 185) also draws the connection between Poe and Wittgenstein, and Cavell (1988) explores this connection as part of a rich investigation of uncanniness in Wittgenstein, Heidegger, Freud, and others.

investigation precisely because, unlike other sciences, it does not investigate a particular domain of beings: there are no distinctively phenomenological 'objects' that phenomenology discovers. Sounding very much like Wittgenstein, Heidegger characterizes phenomenology as a 'how' rather than a 'what' and calls his method essentially descriptive (*BT* 35). We could quite plausibly read Heidegger as taking a similar methodological stance as Wittgenstein, working to achieve clarity by helping us to see what is already open to view. In section 7.4, I argued that Heidegger's formal indications do not point to something *other than* the familiar phenomena of our everyday existence, but rather that they push us to apprehend these phenomena in the appropriate ontological light.

Moi remarks that the same could be said of self-professed practitioners of the hermeneutics of suspicion. She considers two 'poster-figures for the hermeneutics of suspicion' (Moi 2017, 178), Sherlock Holmes and Sigmund Freud, noting that the actual practice of both of these figures does not involve uncovering anything hidden even in a metaphorical sense but rather involves looking attentively at details that are in plain sight but that others have missed. If Moi is right, practitioners of a hermeneutics of suspicion are guilty of mischaracterizing their own practice.

I think some version of that criticism is warranted for Heidegger. Because he is taken in by his own metaphorics of hiddenness, he sees himself as trying to reach beyond what is open to view, and the problematic features of his practice that I identified in the previous chapter manifest this methodological self-understanding. On the surface, it might seem as if Newton's Laws were true before Newton formulated them, but, Heidegger indicates, if we uncover the ontological significance of the concept of truth, we will find ourselves saying the opposite. Because Heidegger thinks that something of significance has been covered over, he also thinks that there is something new to be said once we have done the uncovering. And it is precisely in those moments where Heidegger strains to *tell* us something that I think he gets himself into trouble.

By contrast, Wittgenstein does not see his work as uncovering anything and so his work does not result in pronouncements regarding the newly-visible-because-uncovered phenomena. Instead, he encourages us to look differently at what was already open to view. A closer look at how he does this, and what its effects are, will occupy the remainder of this chapter. And I will begin by returning to the problematic of realism and idealism, whose treatment by Heidegger I considered in the previous chapter.

8.3. Wittgenstein on the Problematic of Realism and Idealism

Wittgenstein remarks only briefly on the 'dispute' between realism and idealism at *PI* §402 as part of a discussion of solipsism and the self.[6] The thread that leads to this remark begins at *PI* §398, where Wittgenstein responds to the insistence of an interlocutor that she has a distinctive kind of ownership over her own imaginings. By pushing on this insistence, Wittgenstein reaches a point where purported theses of realism, idealism, and solipsism cannot clearly express a substantive difference from one another.

PI §398 begins with the interlocutor's insistence that 'when I imagine something, or even actually *see* objects, surely I have *got* something which my neighbour has not' (*PI* §398).[7] But, Wittgenstein claims, her words do not do the work she wants them to do: '[C]an't one add: "There is here no question of a 'seeing'—and therefore none of a 'having'—nor of a subject, nor therefore of the I either"?' (*PI* §398). To speak of 'having' a visual experience makes the connection between the self and the experience too weak. My relationship to my experience, unlike my relationship to my shoes, or even to my feet, is not one of having, since talk about having something suggests that I might also not have it. I can cease to have *this* visual experience—by turning my head, for instance. But when I turn my head, the visual experience does not then slip out of my possession as I might cease to have a coin if it fell out of my pocket.

---

[6] These topics receive more extended treatment in the *Blue Book*, but the discussion there strikes me as more limited. In the *Blue Book*, Wittgenstein focuses almost exclusively on the idea that realists, idealists, and solipsists insist on different forms of expression, and on the different uses of 'I' as subject and object. In *Philosophical Investigations*, Wittgenstein engages in a more nuanced and sympathetic dialectic with his interlocutor. This footnote is a good moment to commend Minar (1998), who offers a subtle reading of these passages, and a more detailed one than I provide here.

[7] At the end of section 7.1, I noted that Wittgenstein's engagement with the problematic of realism and idealism begins with an interlocutory impulse in the direction of idealism. I begin to register that impulse here.

The visual experience has no existence independent of my having it, and so the transitivity of the verb 'to have' is misleading.[8]

Similarly, to the extent that speaking of experience in terms of ownership is confused, so is it confused to speak of an *owner*. Conceiving of the visual experience of a room as the 'visual room', Wittgenstein writes: 'I can as little own it as I can walk about it, or look at it, or point at it' (*PI* §398). Wittgenstein's interlocutor gets muddled early on when she insists on having something 'which [her] **neighbour** has not'. I may stand next to my neighbour, but visual experiences do not have neighbours. I cannot pick out visual experiences the way I can pick out shoes, saying that *these* ones are *mine*, but *those* ones are not. The visual room is an entirely different kind of thing from the sorts of things—physical rooms, for instance—that can be pointed at or stand in an owner–owned relationship: 'One could also say: surely the owner of the visual room has to be of the same nature as it; but he isn't inside it, and there is no outside' (*PI* §399). Not only are talk of 'I' and 'having' confused, but the familiar dichotomy of inner and outer lacks clear sense when we deal with a neighbourless experience that has no 'outside'.

Then, responding to the idea that the visual room constitutes a discovery (*Entdeckung*), Wittgenstein struggles to find a more appropriate characterization, ultimately settling on 'conception' (*Auffassung*: *PI* §401). Wittgenstein frequently uses *Auffassung* and its derivations to talk about a way of conceiving of a matter where other options are available, and no absolute criteria for correctness compel a particular choice. For instance, in exploring the uses of 'simple' and 'composite' in relation to one another, Wittgenstein writes that we need not think of the smaller parts as simple and the larger as composite, but that 'we are sometimes even inclined to conceive [*wir . . . geneigt sind . . . aufzufassen*] the smaller as the result of a composition of greater parts, and the greater as the result of a division of the smaller' (*PI* §48).[9] His interlocutor's visual room is not a *something* that she has *got*, but rather constitutes an alternative way of speaking, which we can take or leave, but we should not confuse it for a discovery.

---

[8] Relatedly, Heidegger says that 'have' is too weak to express the relation between Dasein and its ownmost possibility (*BT* 42).

[9] For other uses of *Auffassung* and its derivations in this way, see *PI* §§2, 4, 20, 28, 29, 38, 58, 201, 520, 539, and 557.

Wittgenstein frequently insists that we distinguish moves in a language-game from the preparatory work of naming and stating rules that establish what language-game we are playing. The confusion here, as elsewhere, is that the interlocutor thinks that stating her 'discovery' of a visual room is a move in a language-game, an assertion about some feature of reality. To the extent that she is articulating a conception rather than a discovery, she is not making a move in an established language-game but rather recommending a different language-game from the familiar one: a language-game in which talk of visual rooms has a definite place.

Step by step, Wittgenstein works to dismantle the language with which his interlocutor struggles to give expression to her impulse. Revealingly, however, Wittgenstein does not try to shut down or refute his interlocutor, but actively encourages the dialectic: 'I understand you' is his initial response at *PI* §398. Note that Wittgenstein does not say, 'I understand *what you are saying*'. His interlocutor does not herself know what she is saying: what he understands is not the sense of a proposition, but an impulse that finds words in a confused manner.

> It's true I said that I knew deep down what you meant. But that meant that I knew how one thinks to conceive this object [*wie man diesen Gegenstand aufzufassen... meint*], to see it, to gesture at it, as it were, by looking and pointing. I know how one stares ahead and looks about one in this case—and the rest. (*PI* §398)

Rather than shut down the interlocutor's confused impulse, Wittgenstein teases it out. The endgame is not to make his interlocutor agree with him, but to help her see that they did not disagree about anything substantial in the first place.

This dialectic with the interlocutor drives the investigation forward. Wittgenstein's initial 'I understand you' precedes an attempt to give clearer expression to the interlocutor's insistence, and the block quotation in the previous paragraph leads Wittgenstein to the coinage of the 'visual room'. When, at *PI* §402, his interlocutor expresses dissatisfaction with the use of 'have' to characterize our visual experiences, Wittgenstein tries to rephrase this dissatisfaction, suggesting that his interlocutor misplaces the blame in finding something suspect about our ordinary way of speaking. In this way, Wittgenstein prods his interlocutor's initial impulse to the point where it moves from a sense of discovering new facts to a feeling of discomfort with our ordinary forms of speaking.

Only at this point does Wittgenstein bring in the isms of philosophical debate:

For *this* is what disputes between idealists, solipsists and realists look like. The one party attacks the normal form of expression as if they were attacking an assertion; the others defend it, as if they were stating facts recognized by every reasonable human being. (*PI* §402)

In contrast to the 'positions' in the problematic of realism and idealism that Heidegger's 'assertion' seeks to 'negate' (*BT* 207; translation modified), Wittgenstein identifies the impulse to speak of positions here as itself part of the problem. For Wittgenstein, the point at which confusion creeps in—the 'decisive movement in the conjuring trick' (*PI* §308)—is not in formulating theses of philosophical idealism, solipsism, or realism, but in the discomforts, inclinations, temptations, and pictures that accompany our ordinary use of language. His response is to work through these difficulties with his interlocutor to the point where the temptation to advance them as substantive philosophical theses subsides.

By reframing the temptation toward one or another philosophical thesis in terms of a dispute over forms of expression, Wittgenstein pushes us to see that, on any question of substance—on any question where actual moves in a language-game are at stake rather than disputes over the rules by which the language-game is played—realists and idealists do not disagree. He discusses this point at *Zettel* §§413–14:

One man is a convinced realist, another a convinced idealist and teaches his children accordingly. In such an important matter as the existence or non-existence of the external world they don't want to teach their children anything wrong.
[...]
But the idealist will teach his children the word 'chair' after all, for of course he wants to teach them to do this and that, e.g. to fetch a chair. Then where will be the difference between what the idealist-educated children say and the realist ones? Won't the difference only be one of battle cry?

In contrast to *PI* §§398–402, where Wittgenstein engages with an interlocutor struggling to give coherent expression to an impulse, the passage in *Zettel* imagines two antagonists who think they have full-blown philosophical positions to communicate. But in terms of what they actually *do*—and teach their children to do—they are no different. The difference between them boils down to empty sloganeering.

In both cases, Wittgenstein does not only not try to *refute* his interlocutors—which would be contrary to the spirit of his investigation, as it would admit that they had advanced positive theses that could be contradicted—but he actively encourages them, working with the interlocutor of *PI* §§398–402 toward some articulation of her view and imagining a life for the realist and idealist of *Zettel* §§413–14. This encouragement is central to Wittgenstein's method: he does not play the role of language police, telling people to stop saying the wrong things, but rather develops what they are saying to the point where it loses the force it initially appeared to have.

To see the significance of this approach more clearly, it might help to contrast Wittgenstein's approach with Carnap's ([1928] 2003), who also argues that realism and idealism fail to give expression to distinct theses. Carnap reaches this conclusion by laying out a meaning criterion, according to which all meaningful propositions express factual content. Then, in a spirit reminiscent of Wittgenstein's realist and idealist parents of *Z* §414, he imagines realist and idealist geographers agreeing on all the facts regarding the location of a mountain, and realist and idealist psychologists agreeing on all the facts regarding the psychological state of a subject, where the only differences between them amount to meaningless pseudo-statements that they try to append to the factual content on which they agree.[10]

The difference between Carnap's approach and that of the later Wittgenstein is that Carnap thinks he can establish a meaning criterion in advance of his investigation so that our task is then the mechanical one of testing claims against the criterion and judging them meaningful or meaningless accordingly. By contrast, Wittgenstein does not have a fixed criterion of meaning that he can place, like a yardstick, against any given claim.[11] Where Carnap's meaning criterion is an external requirement imposed on the investigation, Wittgenstein works from

---

[10] Carnap's argument here is even closer to Wittgenstein's claim at *TLP* 5.64 that 'solipsism, when its implications are followed out strictly, coincides with pure realism'.

[11] Moi (2017, 192) contrasts the practice of close reading with the methods of the natural and social sciences. A method, she claims, is 'a systematic protocol, a clearly defined series of steps to be taken in a specific order in order to reach a replicable result', and by that standard, the various theoretical approaches to reading do not qualify as methods. By the same standard, we might say the difference between Carnap and Wittgenstein is that Carnap has a method whereas the later Wittgenstein does not. Carnap, after all, aspires to a 'scientific' philosophy whereas Wittgenstein does not.

within, pushing his interlocutor to give voice to her discomfort with no established criteria for what would constitute success or failure. Ultimately, the standard for meaningfulness that Wittgenstein's interlocutor is unable to meet is her own.

One reason to tease out these philosophical impulses is that they often arise as responses to perfectly legitimate unease. Both Wittgenstein and Heidegger identify something positive in the impulse toward solipsism: the solipsist's privileging of first personal experience can be understood as a reaction against the view of the self as one being in the world among many, as one more piece of present-at-hand furniture in a denuded ontology. For Heidegger, solipsism is a manifestation of the individualization of Dasein in anxiety and so points toward the possibility of authentic disclosure (*BT* 188).[12] If we simply reject the solipsist, we are no better off than we were at the outset. By thinking with the solipsist, we can grasp what she is reacting against in a way that might free us of the temptation to get embroiled in the problematic.

The endgame for Wittgenstein is to reach a point where his interlocutor realizes that none of the words she is reaching for will get her any closer to the insight she thinks she has, but to reach that point in a way that honours the unease that prompted her to speak. Wittgenstein's particular insight is that what we need is not new words—hence the relative absence of jargon in his work—but the right perspective on the words we use. Wittgenstein's methods for effecting the appropriate shifts in perspective are various, but I will emphasize two in particular. The first is to place what we are inclined to say alongside something else—an object of comparison or a picture—where the contrast resolves our confusion. And the second is the dialogical form of the *Investigations*, which is mimetic and aporetic rather than diegetic and assertoric. I will consider the first of these features in sections 8.4–8.6 and the second in the remainder of this chapter.

---

[12] Heidegger here alludes to an 'existential "solipsism"' (*BT* 188), which bears a striking resemblance to the 'transcendental solipsism' that Williams (1981, 150) claims to find in the *Tractatus*. I will not dwell on the matter here, but the line of interpretation with regard to Wittgenstein developed by Williams and Lear (1982, 1984) holds interesting homologies to idealist readings of Heidegger.

8.4. Pictures and Objects of Comparison

In section 7.3 I registered a difficulty shared by Heidegger and the Wittgenstein of the *Tractatus*: if propositions or assertions are tools for pointing out aspects of the world, how can we use them to get behind intraworldly discourse to the essential features of the world? The Wittgenstein of *Philosophical Investigations* has similar concerns about relying philosophically on assertions. *Philosophical Investigations* opens with a discussion of 'a particular picture of the essence of human language' according to which 'the words in language name objects' and 'sentences are combinations of such names' (*PI* §1). Wittgenstein thinks that a conception of language that places primary or exclusive emphasis on assertion risks distracting us from the fact that there 'are *countless* kinds' of sentences (*PI* §23). Where Heidegger directs our attention to our original comportment with beings, Wittgenstein directs our attention to the use of our words (*PI* §43), and reminds us that 'the *speaking* of language is part of an activity, or a form of life' (*PI* §23). In a move that resembles Heidegger's formal indication, Wittgenstein resists the picture of words as names and of language as primarily assertoric by reminding us of the life that this language is a part of.

Wittgenstein's response to the challenge of how to work philosophically with the potentially misleading assertoric form is disarmingly straightforward: he does not rely very heavily on assertions. Much of what might pass for assertion in the *Investigations* is not a statement of ontological or grammatical truth but a description of a picture or object of comparison. Wittgenstein describes language-games as '*objects of comparison* which, through similarities and dissimilarities, are meant to throw light on features of our language' (*PI* §130). More generally, Wittgenstein frequently draws comparisons of various sorts. We do not find the same emphasis on language-games in *PI* §§398–402 as we find in the opening passages of the *Investigations*, but expressions of comparison occur throughout that discussion: Wittgenstein often proposes alternative forms of expression ('[o]ne could also say' at *PI* §399 and 'one could even say' at *PI* §400), frequently uses 'as if' to characterize the sorts of illusions his interlocutor is working with, and offers a contrast between rival pictures in speaking of 'a picture in our heads which conflicts with the picture of our ordinary way of speaking' (*PI* §402). The invocation of 'conceptions' (*Auffassungen*) that I discussed earlier falls into the same category of criticism.

These comparisons dislodge a confused way of thinking and speaking without replacing it with something else. Wittgenstein's criticism engages at the level at which confusions in our thinking give rise to philosophical problematics in the first place. He frequently speaks both of these confusions and of his method of dispelling them in terms of pictures, and his thinking on these matters is related to some of the things he says about literal pictures.[13]

Much of what Wittgenstein says about pictures is of a piece with what he says about rules. In particular, he emphasizes that pictures cannot dictate their own application. What sense we make of a picture depends in large part upon us, and upon the uses we make of pictures. Consider the second boxed remark between PI §139 and §140:

I see a picture; it represents an old man walking up a steep path leaning on a stick. — How? Might it not have looked just the same if he had been sliding downhill in that position? Perhaps a Martian would describe the picture so. I don't need to explain why *we* don't describe it so. (PI p. 60)

The picture on its own seems open to more than one interpretation, and Wittgenstein describes reading a picture in a particular way as an 'application' of the picture, or a 'method of projection'.[14] No further attempt to disambiguate the picture has any guarantee of succeeding since any expression of disambiguation is also open to more than one application. Suppose we were to draw an arrow pointing up the hill. Not only could we equally read that arrow as pointing back down the hill (cf. PI §85), but we need not read the arrow as signifying the direction of the man's movement at all. In cases of genuine doubt, instruction or interpretation can clarify the application of a picture, but they can no more remove the possibility of ambiguity in an absolute sense than can the picture itself—or indeed than can any form of explanation. The point here is not that the picture is inescapably ambiguous, but that neither the picture itself nor further instruction or interpretation can irresistibly dictate the picture's application. For the most part, we apply pictures

---

[13] Some of the material that follows was first published in Egan (2011), which examines Wittgenstein's use of pictures in more detail. That paper also distinguishes my reading of Wittgenstein on pictures from Gordon Baker's (see especially Baker 2004c).

[14] For talk of methods of projection, see PI §§139, 141, and 366.

similarly, but only because we share a sense of what pictures are, what they tend to depict, how people communicate with them, and so on.[15] The idea of climbing a mountain is familiar to us, as is using a stick to help in the climb, as is the practice of depicting such scenes from life. Sliding backwards down a hill while holding a stick is alien to us, and so it takes an effort to see the picture in this way. Wittgenstein's Martian might not apply the picture similarly because it might not share with us the forms of life that incline us toward a particular application of it.

What we see in the picture depends on how the picture relates to other activities, how we habitually apply pictures, and so on, and we draw on this background in specifying what a picture depicts. If we see a picture as ineluctably pointing to a particular application, we treat it as a 'super-picture' (*LRB* 67), and fail to consider the use we make of it.[16] Wittgenstein finds the same danger of misunderstanding lurking in our language:

> In the first place, our language describes a picture. What is to be done with the picture, how it is to be used, is still obscure. Quite clearly, however, it must be explored if we want to understand the sense of our words. But the picture seems to spare us this work: it already points to a particular use. This is how it takes us in.   (*PPF* vii §55)[17]

In talking about language as describing a picture, Wittgenstein draws our attention to the way in which our language and our habits in using language prejudice us at a deep level that comes before deliberate reflection. Pictures, in this distinctively Wittgensteinian sense of the word, are the basis for reflection rather than the result of reflection. They frequently escape critical notice because they lie so deep, and do not simply shape the answers we give to philosophical questions but are the source of the confusions that give rise to the questions in the first place.[18] The

---

[15] Wittgenstein imagines ways in which our practices with pictures could have been different: 'We could easily imagine people who did not have this attitude to such pictures [that a face in a photograph represents a person's face]. Who, for example, would be repelled by photographs, because a face without colour, and even perhaps a face reduced in scale, struck them as inhuman' (*PPF* xi §198). See also *PG* 42.

[16] Wittgenstein uses 'super-' as a prefix to denote the kind of superlative rigidity that we do not find in life but often seek in philosophy. See e.g. *PI* §§97, 192, 197, 389.

[17] Similarly, at *PI* §§422–7, Wittgenstein repeatedly urges us to consider the application of pictures that seem innocuous to us.

[18] Warren Goldfarb writes about Wittgenstein's engagement with 'protopictures' (Goldfarb 1983, 280) and the 'proto-philosophical level' (Goldfarb 1997, 78) as central to

'picture of the essence of human language' (*PI* §1) that Wittgenstein discusses at the beginning of the *Philosophical Investigations* does not *tell* us anything,[19] but it encourages us to ask certain questions in certain ways. If we picture words as names for things, we are inclined to investigate the relation between word and thing, and expect that that relation could then reveal the essence of language.

If confusion arises from treating pictures as super-pictures, whose application is somehow given in the picture itself, Wittgenstein's treatment of the confusion consists in situating our pictures within a different context. At *PPF* xi §125, Wittgenstein invites us to consider two pictures of the duck-rabbit, one surrounded by other pictures of rabbits, the other surrounded by other pictures of ducks. A person unfamiliar with the double aspect of the duck-rabbit may reflexively see the duck-rabbit in the former picture as a rabbit, and only notice the duck aspect when presented with the second picture. By providing the right contrast, Wittgenstein aims to change the way we look at a matter. This change is not a change from the wrong view to the right view, but rather a change from regarding a view as expressing a truth about the world—say, the discovery of 'a new object' or 'a quasi-physical phenomenon' (*PI* §401)—to regarding that view as simply one way of looking at things—say, a 'form of expression'. A change from seeing our investigation as concerned with facts to seeing it as concerned with grammar.

Wittgenstein's objects of comparison take a variety of forms—from reminders of familiar but easily overlooked facts (cf. *PI* p. 62) to mooted characterizations of what might be going on inside a person when he speaks or acts—but the most striking, and perhaps the most common, are the sorts of imaginary scenarios we find in language-games. According to Cerbone (1994), these imaginary scenarios are a way of getting a perspective on our practices without succumbing to the temptation to try

---

his method, describing this level as 'the way of looking at things that we tend to adopt at the start, without noticing that a step has been taken, which then functions to establish what questions are to be asked and answered by philosophical theorizing' (Goldfarb 1997, 78).

[19] Cavell emphasizes that Augustine's account of language acquisition could strike us as commonplace or astonishing depending on how we look at it (Cavell 1990, 98–9), and that the parable of the builders at *PI* §2 reads differently depending on the context in which we situate it (Cavell 1989, 60–4).

to adopt a sideways perspective on our practices.[20] We cannot look in on our lives from the outside, but illuminating objects of comparison can throw a cast of defamiliarization on our ordinary practices that helps us 'to *recover* our own familiar concepts *as* our own and to see the extent to which our (form of) life is inseparable from them' (Cerbone 1994, 178). There is no single way in which these scenarios operate—and even calling them 'imaginary' is contestable, since in some cases Wittgenstein applies pressure precisely to the question of whether we are imagining anything definite at all—but each serves, in some way or other, to mark an intervention in our habitual way of thinking so that we see what we took to be a familiar case in a new light.[21] In particular, these scenarios help us to recover a clearer view of the use concepts have within our forms of life. As Cerbone puts it, Wittgenstein's scenarios dissolve the notion that 'a concept is something (some *thing*) specifiable and available apart from the practices in which that concept is applied' (Cerbone 2000, 302).

8.5. Pictures and Aesthetic Criticism

One of Wittgenstein's most explicit statements of what he is up to with his objects of comparison comes at *PI* §144. In the previous section, he imagines a teacher instructing a pupil in writing out a series of numbers according to a particular formation rule. He considers the various ways the teacher might instruct the pupil as well as various ways the student could go wrong, ranging along a continuous spectrum from random to systematic mistakes. In each case, he explores the possibility that the pupil will simply not understand, that the teacher can do nothing that will bring the pupil to write out the series as the teacher intends. Wittgenstein investigates possible strategies by which the teacher might

---

[20] Cerbone does not explicitly invoke McDowell or the idea of a sideways perspective, but the idea is fairly clearly present in his treatment of Wittgenstein's imaginary scenarios. Cerbone (2000) also explores this theme.

[21] Cerbone (1994) presents three different case studies that show Wittgenstein's imaginary scenarios operating in different ways. The question of whether these scenarios are meant to be imaginable possibilities is a subject of considerable debate in the secondary literature. Although they disagree on many points, Lear (1982, 1984) and Stroud (1965, 1984) both argue that alternative forms of life are unintelligible, whereas Baker and Hacker (2009) argue forcefully for their intelligibility. Williams (1981) and Cassam (1986) occupy a middle ground, providing conflicting evidence on the matter.

wean the pupil from a systematic error, and then concludes, 'And here too, our pupil's ability to learn may come to an end' (*PI* §143).

Immediately afterwards, he questions this last remark:

What do I mean when I say 'the pupil's ability to learn *may* come to an end here'? Do I report this from my own experience? Of course not. (Even if I have had such experience.) Then what am I doing with that remark? After all, I'd like you to say: 'Yes, it's true, one could imagine that too, that might happen too!' — But was I trying to draw someone's attention to the fact that he is able to imagine that? — I wanted to put that picture before him, and his *acceptance* of the picture consists in his now being inclined to regard a given case differently: that is, to compare it with *this* sequence of pictures. I have changed his *way of looking at things*. (Indian mathematicians: 'Look at this!')[22] (*PI* §144)

Wittgenstein wants to weaken the grip of a certain picture of how rules work by giving us an alternative picture, one that helps us see the former in a different light. In the particular case of *PI* §143, he draws our attention to the scene of instruction between teacher and pupil so that we see rule following as a practice that we learn in particular contexts, and see that nothing guarantees this teaching will succeed. Presenting the establishment of rules in a medium as organic and fragile as human communication helps to weaken the notion of rules as rigid, mechanical, as 'rails invisibly laid to infinity' (*PI* §218).

Note, first of all, that Wittgenstein's teaching relies crucially on the '*acceptance* of the picture' by his interlocutor. Wittgenstein cannot dictate how his interlocutor will take up the pictures he presents, nor even that his interlocutor will take them up at all (he'd *like* his reader to say 'one could imagine that too', but he cannot compel this response). Second, the acceptance of a picture is crucially different from the acceptance of a proposition or a thesis. In accepting a picture, we do not accept an opinion that Wittgenstein wants us to adopt, but rather we accept a way of looking at a matter. To return to a contrast I drew in section 6.2, Wittgenstein is not explaining something to us but rather training us. As he once remarked to his pupil Rush Rhees: 'I don't try to make you *believe* something you *don't* believe, but to *do* something you won't do' (Rhees 1970a, 43).

Wittgenstein's pictures work on us in a way that is closer to the work traditionally assigned to literature than to philosophy. Where philosophy

---

[22] Cf. Z §461: 'I once read somewhere that a geometrical figure, with the words "Look at this", serves as a proof for certain Indian mathematicians. This looking too effects an alteration in one's way of seeing'.

presents arguments, makes a case, literature tells stories, and what we make of these stories is up to us. Literature nevertheless can have considerable impact: stories shape the way we look at things, and can reorient our perspective or draw out the salience of matters we had neglected. Wittgenstein aims not so much at refuting arguments as at interrupting patterns of thought. Responding to thesis *p* with *not-p* often retains the structure of the problematic that caused the problem in the first place. We cannot easily be argued into shifting the terms on which we approach a problem, but the right picture, the right object of comparison, can help us to see these terms in a different light, and open us up to the possibility of alternatives. Diamond (1991, 2000) sees the imaginative engagement called forth by literature as a crucial component of moral reasoning. A similar demand for imaginative engagement is present in Wittgenstein's use of pictures.

Indeed, what Wittgenstein says about his own method in philosophy sounds strikingly similar to things he says about explanations in aesthetics. In his *Lectures on Aesthetics*, Wittgenstein resists the idea that we can give any satisfactory causal or empirical explanation for aesthetic phenomena. What marks an aesthetic explanation as correct is not its agreement with experience, Wittgenstein claims, but that others accept it (*LA* 18). In saying this, Wittgenstein does not mean to reduce aesthetic explanation to a game of brute persuasion: he insists that aesthetic explanation is fundamentally concerned with reasons. However, these reasons, he says, are 'of the nature of further descriptions' (*MWL* 19). Moore recalls him saying:

> [Y]ou can make a person see what Brahms was driving at [in rejecting a suggestion by Joachim regarding the opening of his Fourth Symphony] by showing him lots of different pieces of Brahms, or by comparing him with a contemporary author; and all that Aesthetics does is 'to draw your attention to a thing', to 'place things side by side'. He said that if, by giving 'reasons' of this sort, you make another person see what you see but it still doesn't appeal to him, that is 'an end' of the discussion. (*MWL* 19)

Wittgenstein's conception of 'reasons' in aesthetics involves the use of objects of comparison.[23] Like Wittgenstein's own procedures in philosophy,

---

[23] *PI* §527 also talks about explaining one's understanding of music in terms of comparisons.

8.5. PICTURES AND AESTHETIC CRITICISM

we cannot compel agreement in aesthetics, but we can draw comparisons that encourage our interlocutor to see things in a certain way.

Aesthetic investigations, then, provide a helpful analogy for how Wittgenstein conceives of philosophical investigations. Stanley Cavell has proved particularly sensitive to this point.[24] Cavell considers the task of the Wittgensteinian philosopher to be similar to that of the artist:

> The philosopher appealing to everyday language turns to the reader not to convince him without proof but to get him to prove something, test something, against himself. He is saying: Look and find out whether you can see what I see, wish to say what I wish to say.... If we do not, then the philosopher's remarks are irrelevant to us. Of course he doesn't think they are irrelevant, but the implication is that philosophy, like art, is, and should be, powerless to *prove* its relevance; and that says something about the kind of relevance it wishes to have. All the philosopher, this kind of philosopher, can do is to express, as fully as he can, his world, and attract our undivided attention to our own.
>
> (Cavell 1976c, 95–6)

Wittgenstein's objects of comparison are part of an overall strategy that is more aesthetic than scientific. Like literary texts, they provide occasionally startling contrasts that cast our understanding of ourselves and our world in a different light. And like literary texts, their peculiar power lies not in proving anything to us but in shifting perspective, focusing attention, loosening prejudice, in ways that we could not perform unaided.[25]

Maintaining the analogy between Wittgenstein's pictures and literature gives us an insight into how a picture might be 'false', a term Wittgenstein applies to pictures on several occasions,[26] and which might seem to clash with my claim that Wittgenstein's use of pictures engages his reader at a deeper level than one of true or false assertions. Wittgenstein does not

---

[24] See especially Cavell (1976c) and (1996), although the aesthetic dimension of Wittgenstein's investigations is a ubiquitous theme in Cavell's writings on Wittgenstein.

[25] It is worth noting that the *fictional* status of Wittgenstein's imaginary scenarios is not essential. In the passage from *PI* §144 that I cited above, he remarks that his own experience is irrelevant to the point he is making, *even if he has had* such an experience. Likewise, the contrast between *PI* §415 and *PPF* xii §366 suggests that Wittgenstein is not too concerned whether his natural histories are true. The same could be said of literature, to some extent. Works of literary non-fiction may be answerable to the facts in a way that works of literary fiction are not, but, like literary fictions, they provide narratives that engage our imagination in particular ways. With regard to certain aesthetic aims at least, the fictionality or non-fictionality of a narrative is unimportant.

[26] See *PI* §604, *Z* §20 and §111, and *OC* §249.

mean pictures are false in the weak sense that the stories we find in the Book of Genesis are false; that, *pace* creationism, for instance, an anthropomorphic deity did not create the world in seven days in the not-so-distant past. This weak sense misapplies the stories of the Bible by misunderstanding the role they have in our lives, as if they would cease to have any power over us if they were historically inaccurate. Rather, Wittgenstein finds problematic pictures false in the strong sense that Nietzsche finds much of the New Testament false. 'Mythically false', as Cavell describes Wittgenstein's attitude to pictures that lodge particularly deep in our thinking: 'Not just untrue but destructive of truth' (Cavell 1979, 365).

How can pictures be 'destructive of truth'? Consider Z §111:

We are not at all *prepared* for the task of describing the use of e.g. the word 'to think' (And why should we be? What is such a description useful for?)
And the naïve idea that one forms of it does not correspond to reality at all. We expect a smooth contour and what we get to see is ragged. Here it might really be said that we have constructed a false picture.

The 'false picture' here is not the same as the 'naïve idea' one forms as a description of the use of the word 'to think'. The picture at issue at Z §111 is not a specific set of refutable ideas about how we use a certain word, but rather the expectation of what such ideas must look like. It is not simply that people caught in this picture want to grasp the concept 'to think' and expect that such a concept will have smooth contours, but rather they will not consider the concept grasped until they have found a satisfactory description that has smooth contours. The expectation of smoothness determines a *telos* for the investigation, such that abandoning this picture means abandoning the investigation.

'Concepts have smooth contours' might seem like a false proposition, but we have to consider its role in the investigation. It functions not as an assertion but as the demand that guides the investigation. In the sections leading up to the passage cited above, Wittgenstein explores a diverse range of examples where we might be prepared to talk about thinking, and concludes: '"Thinking", a widely ramified concept. A concept that comprises many manifestations of life. The *phenomena* of thinking are widely scattered' (Z §110). As long as we hold to the picture that leads us to expect smooth contours, we turn away from examining the details that show otherwise. The picture is not just false, but destructive of truth,

8.5. PICTURES AND AESTHETIC CRITICISM 217

because it makes us resist making the examinations we ought to make. In investigating and probing philosophical pictures, Wittgenstein is interested in 'what it is in philosophy that resists such an examination of details', something, he claims, 'we have yet to come to understand' (*PI* §52).

The comparison between Wittgenstein's pictures and works of literary fiction makes room for one further point, which is that, despite his disavowal of disputable theses, Wittgenstein's work is nevertheless disputable. Obviously, works of literary fiction *can* be disputed in some sense. Their being fictional does not place them beyond reproach. The apparatus of criticism for literary fiction is different from the apparatus of criticism for philosophical arguments—we are more likely to criticize a story for being insipid, unimaginative, or flat in its characterizations and we are more likely to criticize an argument for being invalid, muddled, or unconvincing—but disputation is a prominent feature of our engagement with literature. We can reject a work of literature just as we can reject an argument. The author of a work, like Wittgenstein's Indian mathematician, says 'Look at this!' and the critic turns away in disgust, saying 'No!'

Likewise, even if Wittgenstein does not push disputable claims on us, we can still dispute the objects of comparison he presents us with. Not only may we choose not to accept a picture, but we may have principled reasons for our resistance. Wittgenstein's imaginary scenarios must be carefully chosen if they are going to have the appropriate effect on us. Wrongly chosen pictures might have no effect on us, or a deleterious one. A wrongly chosen object of comparison might reinforce unhelpful prejudices or deepen our confusion—consider his response to the picture of a proposition engaging like a cog-wheel with the concept of truth at *PI* §136. Wittgenstein endeavours to change our way of looking at things, but if that change can be for the better then it can also be for the worse. The same can be said for literature: it can help us see things with greater honesty, precision, or sensitivity, but it can also prompt a more hateful, more selfish, or uglier way of seeing. I am inclined to see Wittgenstein as closer to Shakespeare than to Ayn Rand in this regard, but I do not want to proclaim Wittgenstein to be immune from criticism on account of his method. Legitimate criticism is still possible, but this criticism, if it responds sensitively to Wittgenstein's method, will need to find terms other than those normally directed at philosophical arguments.

8.6. Truth and Untruth in Wittgenstein's Pictures

Wittgenstein's characterization of some pictures as 'false' invites the objection that Wittgenstein is closer than I admitted to sharing Heidegger's two-tiered conception of truth, which I criticized in the previous chapter. As I have presented it, Wittgenstein allows not only that the things we say can be true or false, but that, in addition, there is a further domain of pictures, which can also be true or false in some respect. A false picture does not assert a demonstrable falsehood but rather frames a matter in such a way that we are liable to fall into confusion. Wittgenstein never talks about 'true' pictures, but he does characterize some pictures as better than others—for instance: 'The human body is the best picture of the human soul' (*PPF* iv §25)—and these pictures are presumably better because they help us to see things more clearly, or to steer clear of confusion. How far are we, then, from Heidegger's characterization of Dasein as being equiprimordially in the truth and in untruth? In section 7.5, I compared Heidegger's claims about truth and untruth to Wittgenstein's talk about expressions as having a use or as being nonsensical, and argued that Wittgenstein avoids characterizing language-games themselves as true or untrue. But now it seems that Wittgenstein does make room to characterize as false something more primordial than factual claims made within established language-games.

If it holds, this objection presents me with a dilemma. In the previous chapter, I argued that Heidegger gets himself into trouble precisely because he tries to talk about truth at a transcendental level. If Wittgenstein's treatment of pictures is similar enough in the relevant ways to Heidegger's treatment of truth, I will have to admit either that Wittgenstein gets himself into the same sort of trouble as Heidegger or that Heidegger's treatment of truth is less problematic than I claimed it was. If I want to claim Wittgenstein's method offers advantages over Heidegger's, I had better be able to show some difference between them.

Fortunately, I think I can. And again, I think the crucial difference lies in the different ways that the metaphor of hiddenness features in Wittgenstein's and Heidegger's work. For Wittgenstein, a 'bad' or 'false' picture makes us think that what is essential is hidden and a 'good' picture does the opposite. Many of the pictures that Wittgenstein considers problematic—for instance the Augustinian picture of language at the opening of the *Investigations* or the picture of thought as a concept with smooth contours that we encountered in the previous section—are pictures that create an expectation of uniformity. In the opening sections of the *Investigations*, the interlocutor is captivated by the idea that there must be some general account of the meaning of a word. Granted, different kinds of words are used differently, but, the interlocutor reasons, there must be *something* common in all cases such that we can say of all words that they have a meaning or signification. Because that uniformity is not evident on the surface, we face the temptation to find some hidden, underlying uniformity, to look beyond what is said to apprehend what a given expression 'really means' (*PI* §19). The picture of an underlying uniformity then feeds the impulse to suppose that '[t]he essence is hidden from us' (*PI* §92).

Consider, by contrast, the human body as the picture of the human soul from *PPF* iv §25. Wittgenstein is responding to a picture of the human soul as concealed within us, such that the question whether a person is a human being or an automaton is essentially unknowable. On this picture, the human body *conceals* the human soul, such that our selves are essentially—and tragically—inaccessible to one another. In responding to this picture by asserting that the human body is the best picture of the human soul, Wittgenstein pushes us to see the human body not as essentially *concealing* the self but as essentially *expressive* of the self.[27] In doing so, he is not advancing an alternative metaphysics of the self—one, say, that identifies the self with the body—but rather indicating where we ought to look. My failure to know how it is with another person is not due to a metaphysical incapacity to see what cannot be seen but rather due to a failure or unwillingness on my part to make clear sense of what can be seen.[28] If I construe my failure as a metaphysical incapacity, that lets me off the hook: if the essential thing cannot be known, there is no point in looking more closely, or differently, and reflecting carefully. The human body is a 'good' picture of the

---

[27] This idea, along with the complex ways in which we might acknowledge, deny, or avoid our openness to others, and theirs to us, is the central concern of Part IV of Cavell's *The Claim of Reason*.

[28] Cf. Cavell (1979, 368): 'The block to my vision of the other is not the other's body but my incapacity or unwillingness to interpret or to judge it accurately, to draw the right connection. The suggestion is: I suffer a kind of blindness, but I avoid the issue by projecting this darkness upon the other'.

human soul because it confronts us with our responsibility for the expressiveness of our bodies and our responsiveness to others.

I think Wittgenstein's characterization of some pictures as 'good' or 'bad' does bear a resemblance to Heidegger's characterization of Dasein as being equiprimordially in truth and untruth. Both authors think that local questions about whether the things we say are true or false are themselves framed in ways that can foster or hinder understanding. But where Heidegger deploys a metaphorics of hiddenness to suggest our complicity in concealing the essence of the matter from ourselves, Wittgenstein avers that what confuses us is precisely the metaphor of hiddenness itself. These differing diagnoses in turn lead to different treatments. If the essential thing is hidden, unconcealing it means showing us something we had not seen before—for instance, that there is truth only as long as there is Dasein. But if the essential thing is already open to view, then our failure to see it can be rectified by inducing us to see the same old things, but under a different aspect.

In exploring Heidegger's and Wittgenstein's methodological innovations, I have emphasized the challenge posed by assertion conceived as a kind of pointing out. Heidegger presents his formal indications as an alternative: they *indicate* rather than *point*, and what they indicate is formal rather than having a definite content. One difficulty with this approach, I argued in the previous chapter, is that formal indication is not sufficiently different from assertion. One advantage of Wittgenstein's objects of comparison is that they seem to offer a solution to this problem of pointing: instead of trying to indicate the phenomenon you wish to uncover, point at something else. 'Point at a piece of paper', Wittgenstein writes. 'And now point at its shape—now at its colour—now at its number (that sounds odd)' (*PI* §33). We feel a certain strain in trying to 'mean' the same act of pointing in different ways.[29] But, as Cavell (1979, 74–5) observes, pointing to the colour of an object normally does not involve pointing at that object in some sort of special way, but rather pointing to another object that can serve as a sample of that colour. The analogy is imperfect in a number of ways, but I sense a similar strain with Heidegger's formal indication. What is the difference between indicating

---

[29] Cf. *RPP* II §296, where Wittgenstein figures the strain of trying to mean different things with the same ostensive act as trying to pick out one thing 'with a particularly refined pair of mental tweezers, without catching hold of anything else'.

'death' as a biological phenomenon and indicating it as 'the possibility of the absolute impossibility of Dasein' (*BT* 250)? There is a sense of strain as Heidegger attempts to use familiar—and sometimes unfamiliar—words to point behind the ways they are normally taken up. By contrast, Wittgenstein does not try to point to a 'more primordial' understanding of a given word; instead, he finds illuminating contrasts that allow us to drop confused ways of thinking about that word without the strain.

That said, I think we can find a neighbour strategy to Wittgenstein's objects of comparison in Heidegger's destruction of the history of ontology, which he discusses explicitly at *BT* 22–7 and employs throughout *Being and Time*, and in a modified and more extensive form in his later writings. Heidegger thinks the pictures that hold us captive are historically rooted and a rigorous excavation of the genealogy of ontological concepts can liberate us from the sense of necessity that attaches to certain ways of framing them. Heidegger pursues such a strategy in §44(a) of *Being and Time*, for instance, where he uncovers the ontological foundations of the traditional concept of truth. By helping us see the conception of truth as '*adaequatio intellectus et rei*' as historically conditioned, Heidegger dislodges the sense of necessity that clings to that conception. That Heidegger thinks the pertinent objects of comparison are historically situated while Wittgenstein draws on actual or fictitious natural histories—Heidegger's approach is diachronic while Wittgenstein's is synchronic—marks an important difference in approach, but the overall strategy—of dislodging the sense of necessity that attaches to a way of framing a matter so that a fresh investigation becomes possible—is similar.

The important difference on my reading is that, at least in *Being and Time*, Heidegger treats this destructive strategy as a preliminary to offering positive claims of his own. The destruction of the traditional conception of truth in §44(a) yields in §44(c) to a general claim about the being of truth. Where Wittgenstein dislodges prejudices that allow us to see more clearly, Heidegger also tries to tell us what there is to see. And, as I argued in section 7.6, trying to do this leads Heidegger to make assertions that are difficult to situate within the horizon of Dasein's disclosedness. Both Wittgenstein and Heidegger have strategies for working within the horizon of Dasein's disclosedness to address conceptual confusion and prejudice, but Heidegger also tries to step beyond the limits of that horizon.

8.7. Thought Experiments and Questions

In the previous section, I confronted the objection that Wittgenstein's objects of comparison are not so different from a Heideggerian strategy I had criticized. Another more obvious objection is that Wittgenstein is doing nothing at all unusual in challenging our presuppositions by presenting us with imaginary scenarios. Philosophers use imaginary scenarios all the time—they call them thought experiments. Thought experiments are normally part of an argumentative apparatus that involves the kinds of theses expressed in assertoric form that Wittgenstein wants to avoid. So if Wittgenstein's objects of comparison are to be understood as not contributing disputable claims to a theoretical discourse, they must be doing something different than what thought experiments are doing.

What work thought experiments *are* doing in philosophy is itself a matter of some controversy.[30] But what makes an imaginary scenario a thought experiment is not the scenario on its own but rather its situation within an argumentative apparatus. In particular, philosophers often press thought experiments into service as a way of addressing a given philosophical problem by analogy: they provide a scenario that affords a fairly clear answer to a problem that is analogous to a less tractable problem they wish to address. For instance, Putnam thinks the question of whether an Earthling and a Twin Earthling refer to the same thing when they say 'water' admits of a fairly clear answer, and wants to bring that clarity to the muddier issue of semantic externalism. Thomson thinks the question of whether we are permitted to unplug ourselves from an unconscious violinist to whom we have been unwittingly attached admits of a fairly clear answer, and wants to bring that clarity to the muddier issue of abortion. Jackson thinks—or at least at one time thought—the question of whether Mary learns something new when she leaves her black-and-white room admits of a fairly clear answer, and wants to bring that clarity to the muddier issue of the epistemic and metaphysical status of phenomenal experience.

---

[30] John D. Norton and James Robert Brown represent far ends of a spectrum of views on thought experiments. Norton's empiricism sees thought experiments as nothing more than ordinary arguments, 'disguised in a vivid pictorial or narrative form' (Norton 2004, 45; see also Norton 1996), whereas Brown's Platonism maintains that thought experiments are an autonomous source of a priori knowledge (see especially Brown [1991] 2011).

8.7. THOUGHT EXPERIMENTS AND QUESTIONS

Wittgenstein's imaginary scenarios resemble typical philosophical thought experiments in this respect. As he begins to explore the language of the builders that he introduces at *PI* §2, he writes: 'It disperses the fog if we study the phenomena of language in primitive kinds of use in which one can clearly survey the purpose and functioning of the words' (*PI* §5). In other words, Wittgenstein's imaginary scenarios also aim to provide clarity by exploring cases that are less resistant to clear thinking. And, superficially at least, we can see in his presentation of these scenarios something like the structure of a thought experiment. He opens the *Investigations* by citing a passage from Augustine's *Confessions*, in which he claims to find 'a particular picture of the essence of human language' (*PI* §1). Soon afterward, he introduces his story of the builders by writing: 'Let us imagine a language for which the description given by Augustine is right' (*PI* §2). He then describes a pair of builders with a four-word language that they use on a building site. At the end of his story, he comments: 'Augustine, we might say, does describe a system of communication; only not everything that we call language is this system' (*PI* §3). All of this fits one standard form of using thought experiments in philosophical arguments: Wittgenstein, as we might be inclined to read him, uses a thought experiment to show that the kind of people for whom Augustine's characterization is correct have a much more rudimentary language than our own—in particular, all the words in their language have the same use. Since the words of our own language have a diversity of uses, we need a richer theory of language than the one Augustine provides. Ergo, Augustine's 'picture of the essence of human language' is wrong.

However, we should be suspicious of this kind of reading. For one thing, it has Wittgenstein attacking a straw man: any philosopher whose theory of language cannot account for anything more sophisticated than the builders' four-word language is not worth taking seriously.[31] On this reading, Wittgenstein's imaginary scenario is not disputable only because it is uninteresting. It makes an argument, all right, but this argument achieves very little. Furthermore, Wittgenstein's imaginary

---

[31] If Wittgenstein is targeting influential views about language, Frege would be one of his likeliest targets. And yet, where Wittgenstein remarks that 'Augustine does not mention any difference between kinds of word' (*PI* §1), Frege insists that we must 'never lose sight of the distinction' between concept-words and object-words (Frege [1884] 1980, x).

scenario remains disputable on this reading for another reason. Recall that he introduces the builders by inviting us to 'imagine a language for which the description given by Augustine is right'. Part of the 'picture' he extracts from Augustine's words at *PI* §1 is 'the words in language name objects'. Are the words in the builders' language names for objects? It is far from clear that this is true. If these four words are the only words in their language, and they issue them as commands, what reason do we have for calling them names? One of the issues Wittgenstein explores in subsequent sections is precisely this question of what it means to say that a word is a name for an object, or for a word to signify something. And one thought that emerges from that exploration is that it starts to make sense to describe certain words as names when we can see them in contrast with other words that have different uses. If all the words in the builders' language have the same use, it is not clear what justifies Wittgenstein in saying that they are used as names.[32]

At pain of trivializing Wittgenstein, we should not read his story of the builders as providing a step in an argument that provides a solution to a problem. And here we see a crucial difference between Wittgenstein's imaginary scenarios and thought experiments: philosophers put thought experiments to use as a way of providing clear answers to questions. Wittgenstein's later philosophy is not short on questions—over one thousand in the 693 sections that make up *Philosophical Investigations*—but almost none of them are questions to which Wittgenstein thinks we can give a coherent and non-trivial (and hence disputable) answer.[33]

Consider the following classification of the main types of questions that occur in the *Investigations*. This classification should be read as suggestive rather than definitive. I suspect it would be impossible to provide a definitive classification of the types of questions in the *Investigations*, since the type of question, and the type of answer we should provide, is often unclear, and part of the point of the investigation is precisely to get clearer on what kind of question we are dealing with.

---

[32] Many of the ideas in this paragraph come from Goldfarb (1983), and by extension Cavell (1995), to which Goldfarb acknowledges a debt.
[33] Malcolm ([1958] 2001, 28) recalls Wittgenstein telling him that 'a philosophical treatise might contain nothing but questions (without answers)'.

(1) Confused questions from Wittgenstein's interlocutors. These sorts of questions tend to predominate early in a given stretch of text, where the investigation takes a new turn. These interlocutory questions tend to represent a temptation to push toward a solution prematurely, before we have a clear handle on what we are dealing with. Wittgenstein's response tends to be a variation on his exhortation, 'Take your time!' (*CV* 91). He responds either by encouraging his interlocutor to stick with the description at hand and not to try to jump to further questions just yet (he responds in this way to the interlocutory questions to his first imagined scenario at *PI* §1), or by telling his interlocutor that the answer to the question does not matter (e.g. 'it is as you please' at *PI* §16): you are mistaken if you think that answering *this* question will get you closer to resolving your confusion. He often begins to answer the question with 'well' (*nun* in the German), as if to signal with a kind of sigh that the interlocutor is asking the wrong question. In each case, Wittgenstein resists giving an answer to the question and instead endeavours through further exploration to show why the question was confused.

(2) Rhetorical questions: questions that admit of one obvious answer. When Wittgenstein's interlocutor struggles to give meaning to the expression '*All* tools serve to modify something' by suggesting that a rule modifies our knowledge of a thing's length, a glue-pot the temperature of the glue, and nails the solidity of a box, Wittgenstein replies, 'Would anything be gained by this assimilation of expressions?' where the implied answer is a firm 'no' (*PI* §14). Wittgenstein's rhetorical questions could admit of dispute—he might be wrong to think they have such obvious answers—but he certainly regards them as not admitting of dispute.

(3) Aporetic questions: questions that admit of no coherent answer. Wittgenstein uses these questions to draw out confusions in our thinking. Either (i) the question itself clearly admits of no answer and so brings a line of questioning to a standstill, or (ii) it prompts an investigation that leads to aporia.

  (i) In addressing the question of whether a language is 'complete' if it consists only of orders, Wittgenstein asks, 'And how many houses or streets does it take before a town begins to be a town?' (*PI* §18). The question does not admit of a coherent answer, but it also helps us see the hopelessness of specifying how many kinds of words a language needs to have before we consider it to be complete.

(ii) Some of these questions do not so obviously resist coherent answers, and Wittgenstein needs to ask further questions to bring about aporia. We find such a case at *PI* §19, where Wittgenstein asks: 'But why shouldn't I conversely have called the sentence "Bring me a slab" a *lengthening* of the sentence "Slab!"?' Instead of accepting that her line of thinking is confused, however, Wittgenstein's interlocutor answers: 'Because anyone who calls out "Slab!" really means "Bring me a slab"'. This answer then prompts further discussion of what it means to 'really mean' one thing while saying another, a discussion even denser in questions than normal, and which finds no satisfactory conclusion.

(4) Investigative questions: questions that admit of no definite answer. When Wittgenstein asks, 'But how many kinds of sentence are there?' (*PI* §21), the answer is (a) more than you suppose, and (b) it depends on how you choose to classify them. His point in asking the question is to prompt a kind of brainstorming that helps us to see diversity where we might have been inclined to see unity. At *PI* §23 he gives us a partial list to help us see the diversity.

The overriding theme here is that the ubiquitous questions in *Philosophical Investigations* do not simply fail to allow for clear answers but that they rather point out fundamental confusions. Wittgenstein does not want to tell us that we are answering questions wrong, but rather wants to show us that we are asking the wrong questions.

Although they do not lead to clear answers, Wittgenstein's questions do not simply shut down the investigation. When Wittgenstein gives expression to a confused interlocutory question, poses a rhetorical question, or leads us toward aporia, he wants us to ask why we might have been drawn to this impasse in the first place. By leading us from 'unobvious nonsense to obvious nonsense' (*PI* §464), Wittgenstein wants us to ask, for instance, and returning to the rhetorical question of *PI* §14, why we were inclined to try to assimilate these expressions in the first place.

8.8. The Dialogical Form of Wittgenstein's Investigations

The dialogical form is essential to this kind of investigation. *Philosophical Investigations* does not begin in Wittgenstein's own voice; he is initially called to speak by a passage in Saint Augustine's *Confessions*. From that point forward, the investigation proceeds in dialogue: one voice calls another to respond, and even the moments of aporia do not bring the investigation to a halt but rather give rise to alternative investigative paths. As I noted above, Wittgenstein's response to his interlocutory voices is primarily encouraging. He uses his interlocutors as indispensable participants in a dialogue that fumbles toward clarity.

Who are Wittgenstein's interlocutors? One answer is that these voices are all Wittgenstein's in some respect. Cavell (1976b, 70–2) develops this point: he characterizes the form of the *Investigations* as a confession, and links the confessional form to the dialogue. Even leaving aside passages where Wittgenstein is clearly engaging with the author of the *Tractatus*, we find him frequently giving voice to temptations and inclinations that indicate that he is not free of the confusions he wishes to overcome. Wittgenstein presents his later philosophy as a continuous discipline: 'Problems are solved (difficulties eliminated), not a *single* problem' (*PI* §133). Wittgenstein refers to his method as therapeutic (*PI* p. 57), and one way of understanding the dialogical form of the *Investigations* is as a kind of self-therapy: in confessional mode, Wittgenstein is actively working at the purification of his own mind.

Or we could reply that we are Wittgenstein's interlocutors. This answer need not stand in conflict with the answer that Wittgenstein's interlocutor is himself: Wittgenstein's frequent use of the first person plural suggests a merging of the author with his readers. When Wittgenstein gives voice to interlocutory doubts or objections, he gives voice to concerns he thinks we might have, or should have. All writers address themselves to their readers in some form, of course, but Wittgenstein calls for an engagement from his readers that is far more direct and active than most philosophers. In addition to his pervasive use of the interrogative mood, we also find frequent imperatives: we are instructed to imagine things, compare things, describe things, and so on. Again, Wittgenstein does not want us to *believe* something but to *do* something.

The pervasiveness of interrogative and imperative moods suggests a close kinship between Wittgenstein's use of objects of comparison and the dialogical form of the *Investigations*. In presenting us with objects of comparison, Wittgenstein tell us to *do* something—namely to compare a given case 'with *this* sequence of pictures' (*PI* §144)—and asks us questions about what happens when we do this. The outcome of such an investigation is not a new set of propositions but a new '*way of looking at things*' (*PI* §144). By contrast, the monologic and the indicative are natural kin. When only one voice is speaking, the natural register for that voice is to make statements. Heidegger finds the form of the assertion problematic but he also presents his work in a style that makes the frequent use of assertion almost inevitable.

Both Wittgenstein and Heidegger take description to be central to their method,[34] but their mode of descriptive practice differs. Heidegger's is almost entirely *diegetic* whereas Wittgenstein's is to a considerable extent *mimetic*. That is, where Heidegger straightforwardly describes phenomena, Wittgenstein does not just describe but also steps inside and enacts the phenomena he describes—and invites his readers to do the same.

Consider the differing ways in which anxiety features in Heidegger's and Wittgenstein's texts. Heidegger offers a careful and insightful *description* of the mood of anxiety and its ontological significance. The word 'anxiety', by contrast, does not occur once in *Philosophical Investigations*,[35] but we see in the passages where the sceptical voice is most pronounced stylistic features that signal a kind of unease or disturbance. Consider *PI* §209, where Wittgenstein grapples with the sense that *something else* must be at work in my grasp of a rule beyond the training I have received:

'But then doesn't our understanding reach beyond all examples?' — A very curious expression, and a quite natural one! —

---

[34] Wittgenstein: 'All *explanation* must disappear, and description alone must take its place' (*PI* §109). In characterizing his method as phenomenological, Heidegger says the phrase 'descriptive phenomenology' is a 'basically tautological expression' (*BT* 35).

[35] Admittedly, Wittgenstein uses the German word *Angst* at *PI* §303, but even if we go against the natural choice to translate this word as 'fear', it is clear from the context that Wittgenstein has in mind something other than what Heidegger calls a fundamental mood.

8.8. DIALOGICAL FORM IN WITTGENSTEIN 229

But is that *all*? Isn't there a deeper explanation; or at least, mustn't the *understanding* of the explanation be deeper? — Well, have I myself a deeper understanding? Have I *got* more than I give in the explanation? — But then, whence the feeling that I have more?
Is it like the case where I interpret what is not limited as a length that reaches beyond every length?

Exploring these issues seems to agitate Wittgenstein's interlocutor. The italicization in 'is that *all*?' suggests a kind of astonished disbelief, and the italicized '*understanding*' that follows it seems to be reaching for a word that both is and is not the word the interlocutor wants. On one hand, 'understanding' is the right word: the interlocutor wants to say that, somehow, I have within me something more than just what the outward training has given me. But on the other hand, this 'somehow' reveals the difficulty: for the moment, 'understanding' is nothing but a placeholder for a kind of mechanism that might extend beyond the training, but the nature of this mechanism—the very conceivability of such a mechanism—is still in doubt. 'Understanding' is the word the interlocutor wants, but it also does not seem able to do the work she wants it to do.

This kind of verbal agitation is symptomatic of a particular kind of philosophical difficulty. The interlocutor's words are failing her: she feels dissatisfied with the way the situation has been put before her but she cannot find the words to express this dissatisfaction. In other words, she is having an experience that might be characterized as a loss of meaning. And she is losing grip on her words in the face of a more generalized sense of meaninglessness. With apparently nothing to establish the correctness of her language-games and rule-following practices, the fact that she, say, follows the rule 'Add 2' after 1000 with 1002 instead of 1004 seems arbitrary. The significant world of her practices and forms of life recedes into irrelevance. This verbal agitation suggests something considerably closer to Heideggerian anxiety than to traditional framings of philosophical scepticism.

The anxiety in this passage is not something Wittgenstein *describes* but is rather something he *performs*. Consider the following stylistic features—all present in *PI* §209 but also in *Philosophical Investigations* more generally—which exhibit a mood of anxiety:

(1) Frequent interjections from his interlocutor(s), often abrupt. Rather than a smooth flow of thought, Wittgenstein gives us a

train of thought that is jagged, taking abrupt turns, unable to find confident footing.

(2) The use of dashes. Sometimes these dashes signal a change in voice between Wittgenstein and his interlocutor, but not always. They heighten the sense, mentioned above, that the flow of thought is taking sharp turns.

(3) The use of italics. The impression created is often one of strain, as if the ordinary use of a given word, with its ordinary emphasis, cannot convey what the speaker wishes to convey. Words are failing her.

(4) The use of question marks, a feature I have commented on already. The questioning, both in Wittgenstein's own voice and in the interlocutory voice, suggest something unsettled, open to doubt, or uncertain.

(5) The use of exclamation marks. These marks frequently suggest a sudden interjection or an expression of exasperation or surprise.

All of these stylistic features are ubiquitous in Wittgenstein's later philosophy. Although he says nothing explicitly about anxiety, he represents this mood mimetically in discussions that—as I argued in Chapters 4 and 5—have close parallels to Heidegger's diegetic account of anxiety.

The mimetic quality of Wittgenstein's work is not unidirectional. He engages with us less as a performer on a stage might engage with a passive audience, and more as an improviser might with fellow improvisers. He does not record the results of his reasoning, but rather invites his reader to think with him, and to play with him—a point I discussed in Chapter 6. Beth Savickey (2017) explores the importance of improvisation exercises and acts of imagination in Wittgenstein's investigations, arguing that Wittgenstein invites active engagement in these exercises. We can imagine and act out the shopping expedition of *PI* §1 or the builders of *PI* §2 in a number of different ways, and imagining this diversity is crucial to following Wittgenstein's investigations. Wittgenstein wants to consider the life and language that emerge in our engagement with one another, and enacting such engagement is an essential part of his considerations. Both the form and content of the *Investigations* highlight the interpersonal play that lies at the heart of our attunement.

8.8. DIALOGICAL FORM IN WITTGENSTEIN

Savickey shows that play is not simply something that we can draw from Wittgenstein's writings, but also something we must bring to them in order to understand their richness. Wittgenstein does not expect his words to dictate their own projection, but rather invites his readers to project his words into a variety of imagined scenarios and explore for themselves the consequences of these projections. In this respect, there is no single answer to what we should make of, say, the wood sellers of *RFM* I §149. Instead, we should improvise with this scenario, imagine various alternatives for what kinds of people these wood sellers might be and how interactions between them, and with foreigners, might unfold. Savickey remarks that the secondary literature on the builders of *PI* §2 normally imagines them as mechanical or animal-like, but that a playwright like John Mighton (1988) has the imaginative capacity to project a number of more lively possibilities on to this scenario. The readers of Wittgenstein with whom I feel the greatest affinity—Cavell, Diamond, and Mulhall most prominently—all engage in this kind of imaginative reading, not simply remarking on what Wittgenstein says, but exploring how these words might be expanded and projected.

The performative aspect of Wittgenstein's later philosophy is more than just a vivid way of presenting thoughts he could have presented by other means. It is rather a central feature of a distinctive response to the challenge of doing philosophy authentically. I have presented authenticity as a matter of recognizing our selves and our world as inextricably coupled, the one responsive to the other, and an authentic philosophy is one that brings us to this recognition by helping us to apprehend our existence from within.

In particular, the mimetic quality to Wittgenstein's work is connected to the emphasis that he places on play, which I discussed in Chapter 6. Wittgenstein's style reflects this conception of play as central to our self-understanding. As I remarked there, Heidegger does not exactly deny or reject this conception of play, but he gives it a far less prominent place. That lesser prominence is most manifest in his method, where he seems to struggle against himself to *tell* his reader things that, by his own methodological conviction, are not the sorts of things to be told. Wittgenstein, by contrast, develops a way of inducing his readers to play their own way into an authentic self-understanding.

Conclusion

Both Wittgenstein and Heidegger have been associated with the idea of an 'end of philosophy': their work is sometimes read as representing a fundamental rupture in the philosophical tradition, such that the discipline formerly known as 'philosophy' can no longer continue as before in the wake of their intervention—and this is a reading they sometimes encourage.[1] The idea of a rupture certainly warrants investigation, and the question of whether we should call post-Wittgensteinian or post-Heideggerian thought 'philosophy' would require a more rigorous analysis than I will provide here of what distinction exactly we wish to mark and what is at stake in marking it. But I do want to conclude by rejecting a certain conception of what an 'end of philosophy' might look like, one particularly associated with certain readings of the *Tractatus*, but certainly open to readers of either Wittgenstein or Heidegger, early or late. That conception is that the aim of Wittgenstein's and Heidegger's philosophy is to bring philosophy to a stop, to bring us to a point where the questioning that once occupied us under the heading of 'philosophy' will cease to occupy us, now and—thanks to the intervention of our protagonists—forevermore.

I hinted at the problem with such a reading in my introduction. That reading represents an aspiration to a kind of philosophical apotheosis, and what I find remarkable about Wittgenstein and Heidegger is their resolute rejection of that aspiration. In bringing us back to the everyday, they do not want to resolve our confusions definitively but, quite the

---

[1] Rorty (1979) represents a particularly famous expression of this reading. To see Wittgenstein as encouraging such a reading of his work, consider *BB* 28: 'One might say that the subject we are dealing with is one of the heirs of the subject which used to be called "philosophy"'. Later in his career, Heidegger talks about 'thinking' and 'poetry' as successors of a kind to the 'metaphysics' or 'philosophy' he takes himself to have moved beyond.

contrary, to wean us off the hope that such resolution is available to us. Our impulse to think philosophically is not a monstrous aberration grafted on to an otherwise healthy human spirit but rather one inalienable feature of what it means to be human. As long as we take thought and use language, we will be subject to the confusions and the self-bafflement that Wittgenstein and Heidegger attempt to treat. The densest stretch of methodological reflection in *Philosophical Investigations* ends not with a promise of a definitive end to our problems, but with the promise that we will be better armed when problems arise: 'Problems are solved (difficulties eliminated), not a single problem' (*PI* §133).

The desire to transcend the human—to end the heartache and the thousand natural shocks that flesh is heir to—is deeply human. In their different ways, Wittgenstein and Heidegger teach us to recognize our inclination to self-bafflement precisely in the desire to eliminate the possibility of that self-bafflement. What we need, they show us, is not to transcend the everyday but to inhabit it honestly and without rebuff. In overcoming our aversion to our everyday existence, we accept it as authentically our own.

Wittgenstein and Heidegger do not want to provide the last word on anything, and neither does this book. I have kept my focus deliberately narrow, considering the problematic of authenticity as it arises in *Being and Time* and hearing echoes of that problematic in Wittgenstein's later philosophy. This strategy leaves at least two broad avenues for further investigation. First, how does the account of Wittgenstein and Heidegger that I give in this book fit into the broader history of the philosophy of authenticity? And second, what different echoes might we hear if we sounded Wittgenstein's later philosophy off the later writings of Heidegger? Is the later Heidegger's disavowal of the ideal of authenticity a problem for Wittgenstein? Or do Heidegger's *Holzwege* and his emphasis on releasement (*Gelassenheit*) provide more salient parallels than does *Being and Time* to the criss-cross philosophy of the *Investigations* and its call for improvisatory responsiveness?

Another question this book leaves open is what these two authors should mean to us nearly a century after the publication of *Being and Time* and Wittgenstein's post-*Tractatus* return to philosophy. In intertwining the problematic of authenticity with questions of philosophical method, I hope to have made salient a concern that animates both of these authors, and which I touched on at the end of the introduction: that how we do philosophy is intimately entwined with how we are in the world. And the emphasis on the everyday from which the problematic of authenticity arises suggests that the 'we' that does philosophy is all of us. Insofar as we exist as Dasein, the question of the meaning of our being is a matter of concern for us. Wittgenstein and Heidegger take seriously the idea that philosophy is not the preserve of an academic elite but an inescapable responsibility for human beings generally.

Wittgenstein and Heidegger do not then leave us with nothing to do. They leave us armed with a new understanding of the work that we as philosophers are confronted with, and a new appreciation of the difficulty of that task. Above all, they leave us not with a doctrine to be believed but with a series of techniques for noticing when and how we have become lost to ourselves and for bringing ourselves back to ourselves. Although the final two chapters of this book deal most explicitly with the question of method, the book as a whole is a book about philosophical method: Wittgenstein's and Heidegger's teaching is a teaching of *how to do* something.

The performative aspects of Wittgenstein's later philosophy have a particular salience in this regard. Wittgenstein wants to train his readers to be vigilant against certain habitual patterns of thinking, and to show them the way out of the muddles they will inevitably find themselves in. He teaches us to be improvisers, to understand ourselves—as I put it in section 6.4—more as players than as agents. The frequent return to scenes of instruction in *Philosophical Investigations* is itself a kind of instruction, training us to return with his strange tribes and recalcitrant pupils to the games in which our shared lives take shape.

This approach allows us to see an alternative moral to the parable of the wayward pupil of *PI* §185. Perhaps the wayward pupil is not confused, or alien, as the teacher supposes. Perhaps the wayward pupil is the one doing the teaching. The pupil works to induce in the teacher the recognition that the unshakeable nature of our mathematical procedures itself relies on the unshakeability with which we go on in the same way. If we imagine the pupil as a child, we can imagine that this pupil is teaching the teacher one of the things adults continually forget and of which children remind them: that we are, at heart and at our best, creatures that play.

Bibliography

Alter, Robert. (1996). *Genesis*. New York, NY: Norton.
Aristotle. (2014). *Nicomachean Ethics*. Roger Crisp, Trans. Cambridge: Cambridge University Press.
Saint Augustine. (1992). *Confessions*. Henry Chadwick, Trans. Oxford: Oxford University Press.
Austin, J. L. (1962). *Sense and Sensibilia*. G. J. Warnock, Ed. Oxford: Oxford University Press.
Austin, J. L. (1979). *Philosophical Papers* (3rd ed.). J. O. Urmson and G. J. Warnock, Eds. Oxford: Oxford University Press.
Austin, J. L. (1979a). The Meaning of a Word. In Austin (1979), 55–75.
Austin, J. L. (1979b). Other Minds. In Austin (1979), 76–116.
Austin, J. L. (1979c). A Plea for Excuses. In Austin (1979), 175–204.
Baker, Gordon. (2004). *Wittgenstein's Method: Neglected Aspects*. Katherine Morris, Ed. Oxford: Blackwell.
Baker, Gordon. (2004a). Wittgenstein on Metaphysical/Everyday Use. In Baker (2004), 92–107.
Baker, Gordon. (2004b). Italics in Wittgenstein. In Baker (2004), 224–59.
Baker, Gordon. (2004c). Wittgenstein: Concepts or Conceptions? In Baker (2004), 260–78.
Baker, G. P., and P. M. S. Hacker. (2005). The Language-Game Method. In *Wittgenstein: Understanding and Meaning: Part I – Essays* (2nd ed.). Oxford: Blackwell, 45–64.
Baker, G. P., and P. M. S. Hacker. (2009). Grammar and Necessity. In *Wittgenstein: Rules, Grammar and Necessity* (2nd ed.). Oxford: Wiley-Blackwell, 241–370.
Blattner, William D. (1994). The Concept of Death in *Being and Time*. *Man and World*, 27: 49–70.
Blattner, William D. (1995). Decontextualization, Standardization, and Deweyan Science. *Man and World*, 28: 321–39.
Blattner, William D. (1999). *Heidegger's Temporal Idealism*. Cambridge: Cambridge University Press.
Blattner, William D. (2013). Authenticity and Resoluteness. In Wrathall (2013), 320–37.
Blattner, William D. (2015). Essential Guilt and Transcendental Conscience. In McManus (2015), 116–34.
Brandom, Robert B. (1994). *Making It Explicit: Reasoning, Representing, and Discursive Commitment*. Cambridge, MA: Harvard University Press.

Brandom, Robert B. (2002). *Tales of the Mighty Dead: Historical Essays in the Metaphysics of Intentionality*. Cambridge, MA: Harvard University Press.

Braver, Lee. (2007). *A Thing of this World: A History of Continental Anti-Realism*. Evanston, IL: Northwestern University Press.

Braver, Lee. (2012). *Groundless Grounds: A Study of Wittgenstein and Heidegger*. Cambridge, MA: MIT Press.

Brown, James Robert. ([1991] 2011). *The Laboratory of the Mind: Thought Experiments in the Natural Sciences*. New York, NY: Routledge.

Burch, Matthew. (2010). Death and Deliberation: Overcoming the Decisionism Critique of Heidegger's Practical Philosophy. *Inquiry*, 53 (3): 211–34.

Burnyeat, M. F. (1987). Wittgenstein and Augustine De Magistro. *Proceedings of the Aristotelian Society, Supplementary Volume*, 61: 1–24.

Caillois, Roger. ([1958] 2001). *Man, Play, and Games*. Meyer Barash, Trans. Urbana, IL: University of Illinois Press.

Carman, Taylor. (1994). On Being Social: A Reply to Olafson. *Inquiry*, 37 (2): 203–23.

Carman, Taylor. (2003). *Heidegger's Analytic: Interpretation, Discourse, and Authenticity in Being and Time*. Cambridge: Cambridge University Press.

Carnap, Rudolf. ([1931] 1959). The Elimination of Metaphysics through Logical Analysis of Language. Arthur Pap, Trans. In A. J. Ayer (Ed.), *Logical Positivism*. New York, NY: The Free Press, 60–81.

Carnap, Rudolf. ([1928] 2003). Pseudoproblems in Philosophy. In *The Logical Structure of the Word; and, Pseudoproblems in Philosophy*. Rolf A. George, Trans. Peru, IL: Open Court, 301–43.

Cassam, Quassim. (1986). Necessity and Externality. *Mind*, 95 (380): 446–64.

Cavell, Stanley. (1976). *Must We Mean What We Say? A Book of Essays*. Cambridge: Cambridge University Press.

Cavell, Stanley. (1976a). Must We Mean What We Say? In Cavell (1976), 1–43.

Cavell, Stanley. (1976b). The Availability of Wittgenstein's Later Philosophy. In Cavell (1976), 44–72.

Cavell, Stanley. (1976c). Aesthetic Problems in Modern Philosophy. In Cavell (1976), 73–96.

Cavell, Stanley. (1976d). Knowing and Acknowledging. In Cavell (1976), 238–66.

Cavell, Stanley. (1979). *The Claim of Reason: Wittgenstein, Skepticism, Morality, and Tragedy*. Oxford: Oxford University Press.

Cavell, Stanley. (1988). The Uncanniness of the Ordinary. In *In Quest of the Ordinary: Lines of Skepticism and Romanticism*. Chicago, IL: University of Chicago Press, 153–80.

Cavell, Stanley. (1989). Declining Decline. In *This New Yet Unapproachable America: Lectures after Emerson after Wittgenstein*. Albuquerque, NM: Living Batch Press, 29–76.

Cavell, Stanley. (1990). The Argument of the Ordinary: Scenes of Instruction in Wittgenstein and in Kripke. In *Conditions Handsome and Unhandsome: The Constitution of Emersonian Perfectionism*. Chicago, IL: University of Chicago Press, 64–100.

Cavell, Stanley. (1994). *A Pitch of Philosophy: Autobiographical Exercises*. Cambridge, MA: Harvard University Press.

Cavell, Stanley. (1995). Notes and Afterthoughts on the Opening of Wittgenstein's *Investigations*. In *Philosophical Passages: Wittgenstein, Emerson, Austin, Derrida*. Oxford: Blackwell, 125–86.

Cavell, Stanley. (1996). Epilogue: The *Investigations*' Everyday Aesthetics of Itself. In Stephen Mulhall (Ed.), *The Cavell Reader*. Oxford: Blackwell, 369–89.

Cavell, Stanley. (2005). The Wittgensteinian Event. In *Philosophy the Day After Tomorrow*. Cambridge, MA: Harvard University Press, 192–212.

Cerbone, David R. (1994). Don't Look But Think: Imaginary Scenarios in Wittgenstein's Later Philosophy. *Inquiry*, 37 (2): 159–83.

Cerbone, David R. (2000). How To Do Things With Wood: Wittgenstein, Frege, and the Problem of Illogical Thought. In Crary and Read (2000), 293–314.

Cerbone, David R. (2005). Realism and Truth. In Hubert L. Dreyfus and Mark. A Wrathall (Eds.), *A Companion to Heidegger*. Oxford: Blackwell, 248–64.

Conant, James. (1992). The Search for Logically Alien Thought: Descartes, Kant, Frege, and the *Tractatus*. *Philosophical Topics*, 20 (1): 115–80.

Conant, James. (2000). Elucidation and Nonsense in Frege and Early Wittgenstein. In Crary and Read (2000), 174–217.

Conant, James. (2002). The Method of the *Tractatus*. In Erich H. Reck (Ed.), *From Frege to Wittgenstein: Perspectives on Early Analytic Philosophy*. Oxford: Oxford University Press, 374–462.

Conant, James. (2004). Varieties of Scepticism. In Denis McManus (Ed.), *Wittgenstein and Scepticism*. London: Routledge, 97–136.

Conant, James. (2011). Wittgenstein's Methods. In Oskari Kuusela and Marie McGinn (Eds.), *The Oxford Handbook of Wittgenstein*. Oxford: Oxford University Press, 620–45.

Conant, James. (2012). Two Varieties of Skepticism. In Günter Abel and James Conant (Eds.), *Rethinking Epistemology, Volume 2*. Berlin: Walter de Gruyter, 1–73.

Coyne, Ryan. (2016). *Heidegger's Confessions: The Remains of Saint Augustine in Being and Time and Beyond*. Chicago, IL: University of Chicago Press.

Crary, Alice, and Rupert Read (Eds.). (2000). *The New Wittgenstein*. London: Routledge.

Dahlstrom, Daniel O. (1994). Heidegger's Method: Philosophical Concepts as Formal Indications. *The Review of Metaphysics*, 47 (4): 775–95.

Dahlstrom, Daniel O. (2001). *Heidegger's Concept of Truth*. Cambridge: Cambridge University Press.

Dahlstrom, Daniel O. (2013). *The Heidegger Dictionary*. London: Bloomsbury.
Derrida, Jacques. ([1967] 1976). *Of Grammatology*. Gayatri Chakravorty Spivak, Trans. Baltimore, MD: Johns Hopkins University Press.
Derrida, Jacques. ([1966] 1978). Structure, Sign, and Play in the Discourse of the Human Sciences. In *Writing and Difference*. Alan Bass, Trans. Chicago, IL: University of Chicago Press, 278–94.
Diamond, Cora. (1989). Rules: Looking in the Right Place. In D. Z. Phillips and Peter Winch (Eds.), *Attention to Particulars: Essays in Honour of Rush Rhees (1905–1989)*. London: Macmillan, 12–34.
Diamond, Cora. (1991). Anything but Argument? In *The Realistic Spirit: Wittgenstein, Philosophy, and the Mind*. Cambridge, MA: MIT Press, 291–308.
Diamond, Cora. (2000). Ethics, Imagination and the Method of Wittgenstein's Tractatus. In Crary and Read (2000), 149–73.
Diamond, Cora. (2004). Criss-Cross Philosophy. In Erich Ammereller and Eugen Fischer (Eds.), *Wittgenstein at Work: Method in the Philosophical Investigations*. London: Routledge, 201–20.
Dreyfus, Hubert L. (1991). *Being-in-the-World: A Commentary on Heidegger's Being and Time, Division I*. Cambridge, MA: MIT Press.
Dreyfus, Hubert L. (1995). Interpreting Heidegger on *Das Man*. *Inquiry*, 38 (4): 423–30.
Dreyfus, Hubert L., and Jane Rubin. (1991). Appendix: Kierkegaard, Division II, and Later Heidegger. In Dreyfus (1991), 283–340.
Drury, Maurice O'Connor. (1984). Some Notes on Conversations with Wittgenstein. In Rush Rhees (Ed.), *Recollections of Wittgenstein*. Oxford: Oxford University Press, 76–96.
Dummett, Michael. (1959). Wittgenstein's Philosophy of Mathematics. *The Philosophical Review*, 68: 324–48.
Dummett, Michael. (1978). *Truth and Other Enigmas*. Cambridge, MA: Harvard University Press.
Egan, David. (2011). Pictures in Wittgenstein's Later Philosophy. *Philosophical Investigations*, 34 (1): 55–76.
Egan, David. (2012). *Das Man* and Distantiality in *Being and Time*. *Inquiry*, 55 (3): 289–306.
Egan, David. (2018). Rehabilitating Austin, Reassessing Grice: The Case of Cancellability. *Archiv für die Geschichte der Philosophie* 100 (4): 470–91.
Egan, David, Stephen Reynolds, and Aaron James Wendland (Eds.). (2013). *Wittgenstein and Heidegger*. New York, NY: Routledge.
Faraday, Michael. ([1861] 2011). *The Chemical History of a Candle*. Frank A. J. L. James, Ed. Oxford: Oxford University Press.
Fell, Joseph P. (1992). The Familiar and the Strange: On the Limits of Praxis in the Early Heidegger. In Hubert L. Dreyfus and Harrison Hall (Eds.), *Heidegger: A Critical Reader*. Oxford: Blackwell, 65–80.

Fink, Eugen. ([1960] 2016). *Play as Symbol of the World and Other Writings*. Ian Alexander Moore and Christopher Turner, Trans. Bloomington, IN: Indiana University Press.
Frankfurt, Harry. (2005). *On Bullshit*. Princeton, NJ: Princeton University Press.
Frege, Gottlob. ([1884] 1980). *The Foundations of Arithmetic*. J. L. Austin, Trans. Evanston, IL: Northwestern University Press.
Frege, Gottlob. ([1892] 1997). On Concept and Object. In Michael Beaney (Ed.), *The Frege Reader*. Oxford: Blackwell, 181–93.
Freud, Sigmund. ([1919] 2003). The Uncanny. In *The Uncanny*. David McLintock, Trans. London: Penguin, 212–62.
Friedman, Michael. (2000). *A Parting of the Ways: Carnap, Cassirer, and Heidegger*. Peru, IL: Open Court.
Gadamer, Hans-Georg. (1976). The Phenomenological Movement. In *Philosophical Hermeneutics*. David E. Linge, Ed. and Trans. Berkeley, CA: University of California Press, 130–81.
Gadamer, Hans-Georg. ([1960] 1989). *Truth and Method* (2nd ed.). Joel Weinsheimer and Donald G. Marshall, Trans. London: Sheed & Ward.
Glendinning, Simon. (2007). *In the Name of Phenomenology*. Abingdon: Routledge.
Goldfarb, Warren D. (1983). I Want You To Bring Me A Slab: Remarks on the Opening Sections of the *Philosophical Investigations*. *Synthese*, 56: 265–82.
Goldfarb, Warren D. (1985). Kripke on Wittgenstein on Rules. *The Journal of Philosophy*, 82 (9): 471–88.
Goldfarb, Warren D. (1997). Wittgenstein on Fixity of Meaning. In William W. Tait (Ed.), *Early Analytic Philosophy: Frege, Russell, Wittgenstein: Essays in Honor of Leonard Linsky*. Chicago, IL: Open Court, 75–89.
Guignon, Charles B. (1983). *Heidegger and the Problem of Knowledge*. Indianapolis, IN: Hackett.
Guignon, Charles B. (1990). Philosophy after Wittgenstein and Heidegger. *Philosophy and Phenomenological Research*, 50 (4): 649–72.
Hacker, P. M. S. (1990). *Wittgenstein: Meaning and Mind: Volume 3 of an Analytical Commentary on the Philosophical Investigations*. Oxford: Blackwell.
Harris, Roy (1988). *Language, Saussure and Wittgenstein: How to Play Games with Words*. London: Routledge.
Haugeland, John. (1982). Heidegger on Being a Person. *Noûs*, 16: 15–26.
Haugeland, John. (2000). Truth and Finitude: Heidegger's Transcendental Existentialism. In Mark A. Wrathall and Jeff Malpas (Eds.), *Heidegger, Authenticity, and Modernity: Essays in Honor of Hubert L. Dreyfus, Vol. 1*. Cambridge, MA: MIT Press, 43–78.
Heidegger, Martin. (1977). What is Metaphysics? In *Basic Writings*. David Farrell Krell, Ed. New York, NY: HarperCollins, 89–110. Referred to as *WM*.

Heidegger, Martin. (1985). *History of the Concept of Time: Prolegomena*. Theodore Kisiel, Trans. Bloomington, IN: Indiana University Press. Referred to as *HCT*.

Heidegger, Martin. (1988). *Basic Problems of Phenomenology* (Revised ed.). Albert Hofstadter, Trans. Bloomington, IN: Indiana University Press. Referred to as *BPP*.

Heidegger, Martin. (1995). *The Fundamental Concepts of Metaphysics: World, Finitude, Solitude*. William McNeill and Nicholas Walker, Trans. Bloomington, IN: Indiana University Press. Referred to as *FCM*.

Heidegger, Martin. (2000). *Introduction to Metaphysics*. Gregory Fried and Richard Polt, Trans. New Haven, CT: Yale University Press. Referred to as *IM*.

Heidegger, Martin. (2003). Seminar in Le Thor 1969. In *Four Seminars*. Andrew Mitchell and François Raffoul, Trans. Bloomington, IN: Indiana University Press, 35–63. Referred to as *SLT*.

Heidegger, Martin. (2008). *Phenomenological Interpretations of Aristotle: Initiation into Phenomenological Research*. Richard Rojcewicz, Trans. Bloomington, IN: Indiana University Press. Referred to as *PIA*.

Heidegger, Martin. (2010). *Being and Time: A Translation of Sein und Zeit*. Joan Stambaugh and Dennis J. Schmidt, Trans. Albany, NY: State University of New York Press. Referred to as *BT*.

Heidegger, Martin, and Eugen Fink. (1993). *Heraclitus Seminar*. Charles H. Seibert, Trans. Evanston, IL: Northwestern University Press. Referred to as *HS*.

Heller-Roazen, Daniel. (2005). *Echolalias: On the Forgetting of Language*. New York, NY: Zone Books.

Huizinga, Johan. ([1938] 1995). *Homo Ludens: A Study of the Play-Element in Culture*. Boston, MA: Beacon Press.

Hume, David. (1978). *A Treatise of Human Nature* (2nd ed.). L. A. Selby-Bigge and P. H. Nidditch, Eds. Oxford: Oxford University Press.

Hurka, Thomas. (2014). Introduction. In Suits (2014), ix–xxiii.

Jagodowski, T. J., David Pasquesi, and Pam Victor. (2015). *Improvisation at the Speed of Life: The TJ & Dave Book*. Chicago, IL: Solo Roma.

Kant, Immanuel. ([1781] 1997). *Critique of Pure Reason*. Paul Guyer and Allen W. Wood, Eds. and Trans. Cambridge: Cambridge University Press.

Keller, Pierre, and David Weberman. (1998). Heidegger and the Source(s) of Intelligibility. *Continental Philosophy Review*, 31 (4): 369–86.

Kenny, Anthony. (2006). *Wittgenstein* (Revised ed.). Oxford: Blackwell.

Kisiel, Theodore. (1993). *The Genesis of Heidegger's* Being and Time. Berkeley, CA: University of California Press.

Kripke, Saul A. (1982). *Wittgenstein on Rules and Private Language*. Cambridge, MA: Harvard University Press.

Kuusela, Oskari. (2008). *The Struggle against Dogmatism: Wittgenstein and the Concept of Philosophy*. Cambridge, MA: Harvard University Press.

Kuusela, Oskari. (2018). Heidegger and Wittgenstein: The Notion of a Fundamental Question and the Possibility of a Genuinely Philosophical Logic. In Oskari Kuusela, Mihai Ometiță, and Timur Uçan (Eds.), *Wittgenstein and Phenomenology*. New York, NY: Routledge, 93–115.

Lear, Jonathan. (1982). Leaving the World Alone. *The Journal of Philosophy*, 79 (9): 382–403.

Lear, Jonathan. (1984). The Disappearing 'We'. *Proceedings of the Aristotelian Society, Supplementary Volume*, 58: 219–42.

Lewis, David K. (1969). *Convention: A Philosophical Study*. Cambridge, MA: Harvard University Press.

McDaniel, Kris. (2013). Heidegger's Metaphysics of Material Beings. *Philosophy and Phenomenological Research*, 87 (2): 332–57.

McDaniel, Kris. (2016). Heidegger and the 'There Is' of Being. *Philosophy and Phenomenological Research*, 93 (2): 306–20.

McDowell, John. (1981). Non-Cognitivism and Rule-Following. In Steven Holtzman and Christopher M. Leich (Eds.), *Wittgenstein: To Follow A Rule*. London: Routledge, 141–72.

McDowell, John. (1984). Wittgenstein on Following a Rule. *Synthese*, 58: 325–63.

McManus, Denis. (2012). *Heidegger and the Measure of Truth: Themes from his Early Philosophy*. Oxford: Oxford University Press.

McManus, Denis. (Ed.). (2015). *Heidegger, Authenticity, and the Self: Themes from Division Two of Being and Time*. Abingdon: Routledge.

McManus, Denis. (2015a). Anxiety, Choice, and Responsibility in Heidegger's Account of Authenticity. In McManus (2015), 163–85.

Malcolm, Norman. ([1958] 2001). *Ludwig Wittgenstein: A Memoir*. Oxford: Oxford University Press.

Mighton, John. (1988). *Possible Worlds* (2nd ed.). Toronto, ON: Playwrights Canada Press.

Minar, Edward H. (1998). Wittgenstein on the Metaphysics of the Self: The Dialectic of Solipsism in *Philosophical Investigations*. *Pacific Philosophical Quarterly*, 79: 329–54.

Moi, Toril. (2017). 'Nothing Is Hidden': Beyond the Hermeneutics of Suspicion. In *Revolution of the Ordinary: Literary Studies after Wittgenstein, Austin, and Cavell*. Chicago, IL: University of Chicago Press, 175–95.

Moore, A. W. (1985). Transcendental Idealism in Wittgenstein, and Theories of Meaning. *The Philosophical Quarterly*, 35 (139): 134–55.

Moore, A. W. (2007). Wittgenstein and Transcendental Idealism. In Guy Kahane, Edward Kanterian, and Oskari Kuusela (Eds.), *Wittgenstein and his Interpreters: Essays in Memory of Gordon Baker*. Oxford: Blackwell, 174–99.

Moore, G. E. (1955). Wittgenstein's Lectures in 1930–33. *Mind*, 64 (253): 1–27. Referred to as *MWL*.

Mulhall, Stephen. (1994). Wittgenstein and Heidegger: Orientations to the Ordinary. *European Journal of Philosophy*, 2 (2): 143-64.

Mulhall, Stephen. (2001). *Inheritance and Originality: Wittgenstein, Heidegger, Kierkegaard*. Oxford: Oxford University Press.

Mulhall, Stephen. (2005a). *Philosophical Myths of the Fall*. Princeton, NJ: Princeton University Press.

Mulhall, Stephen. (2005b). *Routledge Philosophy Guidebook to Heidegger and Being and Time* (2nd ed.). Abingdon: Routledge.

Mulhall, Stephen. (2007a). *Wittgenstein's Private Language: Grammar, Nonsense, and Imagination in* Philosophical Investigations, *§§243-315*. Oxford: Oxford University Press.

Mulhall, Stephen. (2007b). *The Conversation of Humanity*. Charlottesville, VA: University of Virginia Press.

Mulhall, Stephen. (2008). 'Hopelessly Strange': Bernard Williams' Portrait of Wittgenstein as a Transcendental Idealist. *European Journal of Philosophy*, 17 (3): 386-404.

Mulhall, Stephen. (2013). The Meaning of Being and the Possibility of Discourse: Heidegger and Wittgenstein Converse. In Egan, Reynolds, and Wendland (2013), 19-33.

Nietzsche, Friedrich. ([1887] 1998). *On the Genealogy of Morality*. Maudmarie Clark and Alan Swensen, Trans. Indianapolis, IN: Hackett.

Norton, John D. (1996). Are Thought Experiments Just What You Thought? *Canadian Journal of Philosophy*, 26 (3): 333-66.

Norton, John D. (2004). Why Thought Experiments Do Not Transcend Empiricism. In Christopher Hitchcock (Ed.), *Contemporary Debates in Philosophy of Science*. Oxford: Blackwell, 44-66.

Philipse, Herman. (1998). *Heidegger's Philosophy of Being*. Princeton, NJ: Princeton University Press.

Plato. (1992). *Republic* (2nd ed.). G. M. A. Grube and C. D. C. Reeve, Trans. Indianapolis, IN: Hackett.

Plato. (1997). *Cratylus*. Trans. C. D. C. Reeve. In *Complete Works*. John Cooper and D. H. Hutchinson, Eds. Indianapolis, IN: Hackett, 101-56.

Polt, Richard. (1999). *Heidegger: An Introduction*. Ithaca, NY: Cornell University Press.

Priest, Graham. (2002). *Beyond the Limits of Thought*. Oxford: Oxford University Press.

Putnam, Hilary. (1981). *Reason, Truth, and History*. Cambridge: Cambridge University Press.

Putnam, Hilary. (1994). Sense, Nonsense, and the Senses: An Inquiry into the Powers of the Human Mind. *Journal of Philosophy*, 91 (9): 445-517.

Rhees, Rush. (1970). *Discussions of Wittgenstein*. London: Routledge & Kegan Paul.

Rhees, Rush. (1970a). 'The Philosophy of Wittgenstein'. In Rhees (1970), 37–54.
Rhees, Rush. (1970b). Wittgenstein's Builders. In Rhees (1970), 71–84.
Rhees, Rush. (2006). *Wittgenstein and the Possibility of Discourse* (2nd ed.). D. Z. Phillips, Ed. Oxford: Blackwell.
Richardson, John. (2012). *Heidegger*. Abingdon: Routledge.
Ricketts, Thomas. (1996). Pictures, Logic, and the Limits of Sense in Wittgenstein's *Tractatus*. In Hans Sluga and David G. Stern (Eds.), *The Cambridge Companion to Wittgenstein*. Cambridge: University of Cambridge Press, 59–99.
Ricoeur, Paul. (1970). *Freud and Philosophy: An Essay on Interpretation*. Denis Savage, Trans. New Haven, CT: Yale University Press.
Rorty, Richard. (1979). *Philosophy and the Mirror of Nature*. Princeton, NJ: Princeton University Press.
Rorty, Richard. (1993). Wittgenstein, Heidegger, and the Reification of Language. In Charles Guignon (Ed.), *The Cambridge Companion to Heidegger* (1st Ed.). Cambridge: Cambridge University Press, 33–57.
Rouse, Joseph. (1985). Science and the Theoretical 'Discovery' of the Present-at-Hand. In Don Ihde and Hugh J. Silverman (Eds.), *Descriptions*. Albany, NY: State University of New York Press, 200–10.
Saussure, Ferdinand de. ([1916] 2011). *Course in General Linguistics*. Perry Meisel and Haun Saussy, Eds., Wade Baskin, Trans. London: Columbia University Press.
Savickey, Beth. (2017). Improvisation and Imagination in Wittgenstein's *Investigations*. In Garry Hagberg (Ed.), *Wittgenstein on Aesthetic Understanding*. Cham: Palgrave Macmillan, 31–60.
Schatzki, Theodore R. (1993). Wittgenstein + Heidegger on the Stream of Life. *Inquiry*, 36 (3): 307–28.
Schatzki, Theodore R. (2013). Human Activity as Indeterminate Social Event. In Egan, Reynolds, and Wendland (2013), 179–94.
Scott, Charles E. (1988). The Middle Voice in Being and Time. In John C. Sallis, Giuseppina Moneta, and Jacques Taminiaux (Eds.), *The Collegium Phaenomenologicum: The First Ten Years*. Dordrecht: Kluwer, 159–73.
Staten, Henry. (1984). *Wittgenstein and Derrida*. Lincoln, NE: University of Nebraska Press.
Stern, David G. (1991). Heraclitus' and Wittgenstein's River Images: Stepping Twice into the Same River. *The Monist*, 74 (4): 579–604.
Stone, Martin. (2000). Wittgenstein on Deconstruction. In Crary and Read (2000), 83–117.
Streeter, Ryan. (1997). Heidegger's Formal Indication: A Question of Method in *Being and Time*. *Man and World*, 30: 413–30.
Stroud, Barry. (1965). Wittgenstein and Logical Necessity. *The Philosophical Review*, 74 (4): 504–18.

Stroud, Barry. (1984). The Allure of Idealism. *Proceedings of the Aristotelian Society, Supplementary Volume*, 58: 243–58.

Suits, Bernard. ([1978] 2014). *The Grasshopper: Games, Life, and Utopia* (3rd Ed.). Peterborough, ON: Broadview Press.

Tasioulas, John. (2006). Games and the Good. *Proceedings of the Aristotelian Society, Supplementary Volume*, 80: 237–64.

Taylor, Charles. (1985). Theories of Meaning. In *Human Agency and Language: Philosophical Papers*, Vol. 1. Cambridge: Cambridge University Press, 248–92.

Taylor, Charles. (1995). Heidegger, Language, and Ecology. In *Philosophical Arguments*. Cambridge, MA: Harvard University Press, 100–26.

Thomson, Iain. (2013). Death and Demise in *Being and Time*. In Wrathall (2013), 260–90.

Tolstoy, Leo. ([1886] 2009). *The Death of Ivan Ilyich*. Richard Pevear and Larissa Volokhonsky, Trans. New York, NY: Vintage.

van Buren, John. (1994). *The Young Heidegger: Rumor of the Hidden King*. Bloomington, IN: Indiana University Press.

von Wright, G. H. ([1958] 2001). A Biographical Sketch. In Malcolm (2001), 1–20.

Waismann, Friedrich. (1979). *Wittgenstein and the Vienna Circle*. Brian McGuinness, Ed., Joachim Schulte and Brian McGuinness, Trans. Oxford: Blackwell. Referred to as *WVC*.

White, Carol J. (2005). *Time and Death: Heidegger's Analysis of Finitude*. Mark Ralkowski, Ed. Aldershot: Ashgate.

Williams, Bernard. (1981). Wittgenstein and Idealism. In *Moral Luck: Philosophical Papers 1973–1980*. Cambridge: Cambridge University Press, 144–63.

Withy, Katherine. (2015). *Heidegger on Being Uncanny*. Cambridge, MA: Harvard University Press.

Wittgenstein, Ludwig. (1966). *Lectures and Conversations on Aesthetics, Psychology, and Religious Belief*. Cyril Barrett, Ed. Oxford: Blackwell.

Wittgenstein, Ludwig. (1966a). Lectures on Aesthetics. In Wittgenstein (1966), 1–40. Referred to as *LA*.

Wittgenstein, Ludwig. (1966b). Lectures on Religious Belief. In Wittgenstein (1966), 53–72. Referred to as *LRB*.

Wittgenstein, Ludwig. (1967). *Zettel*. G. E. M. Anscombe and G. H. von Wright, Eds., G. E. M. Anscombe, Trans. Oxford: Blackwell. Referred to as *Z*.

Wittgenstein, Ludwig. (1969). *Preliminary Studies for the 'Philosophical Investigations': Generally known as the Blue and Brown Books* (2nd ed.). Oxford: Blackwell. Referred to as *BB*.

Wittgenstein, Ludwig. (1974). *Tractatus Logico-Philosophicus*. D. F. Pears and B. F. McGuinness, Trans. London: Routledge. Referred to as *TLP*.

Wittgenstein, Ludwig. (1975a). *On Certainty*. G. E. M. Anscombe and G. H. von Wright, Eds., G. E. M. Anscombe, G. H. von Wright, and Denis Paul, Trans. Oxford: Blackwell. Referred to as *OC*.

Wittgenstein, Ludwig. (1975b). *Philosophical Remarks*. Rush Rhees, Ed., Raymond Hargreaves and Roger White, Trans. Oxford: Blackwell. Referred to as *PR*.

Wittgenstein, Ludwig. (1976). *Wittgenstein's Lectures on the Foundations of Mathematics: Cambridge, 1939*. Cora Diamond, Ed. Chicago, IL: University of Chicago Press. Referred to as *LFM*.

Wittgenstein, Ludwig. (1978). *Remarks on the Foundations of Mathematics* (3rd ed.). G. H. von Wright, Rush Rhees, and G. E. M. Anscombe, Eds., G. E. M. Anscombe, Trans. Oxford: Blackwell. Referred to as *RFM*.

Wittgenstein, Ludwig. (1979a). *Notebooks 1914–1916* (2nd ed.). G. H. von Wright and G. E. M. Anscombe, Eds., G. E. M. Anscombe, Trans. Chicago, IL: University of Chicago Press. Referred to as *NB*.

Wittgenstein, Ludwig. (1979b). *Wittgenstein's Lectures, Cambridge 1932–35, from the Notes of Alice Ambrose and Margaret MacDonald*. Alice Ambrose, Ed. Oxford: Blackwell. Referred to as *AWL*.

Wittgenstein, Ludwig. (1980a). *Philosophical Grammar*. Rush Rhees, Ed., Anthony Kenny, Trans. Oxford: Blackwell. Referred to as *PG*.

Wittgenstein, Ludwig. (1980b). *Remarks on the Philosophy of Psychology, Volume 1*. G. E. M. Anscombe and G. H. von Wright, Eds., G. E. M. Anscombe, Trans. Oxford: Blackwell. Referred to as *RPP I*.

Wittgenstein, Ludwig. (1980c). *Remarks on the Philosophy of Psychology, Volume 2*. G. H. von Wright and Hekki Nyman, Eds., C. G. Luckhardt and Maximilian A. E. Aue, Trans. Oxford: Blackwell. Referred to as *RPP II*.

Wittgenstein, Ludwig. (1998). *Culture and Value* (2nd ed.). G. H. von Wright, Hekki Nyman, and Alois Pichler, Eds., Peter Winch, Trans. Oxford: Blackwell. Referred to as *CV*.

Wittgenstein, Ludwig. (2005). *Big Typescript: TS 213*. C. Grant Luckhardt and Maximilian A. E. Aue, Eds. and Trans. Oxford: Blackwell. Referred to as *BTS*.

Wittgenstein, Ludwig. (2009a). *Philosophical Investigations* (4th ed.). P. M. S. Hacker and Joachim Schulte, Eds., G. E. M. Anscombe, P. M. S. Hacker, and Joachim Schulte, Trans. Oxford: Wiley-Blackwell. Referred to as *PI*.

Wittgenstein, Ludwig. (2009b). Philosophy of Psychology – A Fragment. In Wittgenstein (2009a), 182–243. Referred to as *PPF*.

Wittgenstein, Ludwig, and Rush Rhees. (2015). Wittgenstein's Philosophical Conversations with Rush Rhees (1939–1950): From the Notes of Rush Rhees. Gabriel Citron, Ed. *Mind*, 124 (493): 1–71. Referred to as *CRR*.

Wittgenstein, Ludwig, and Friedrich Waismann. (2003). *The Voices of Wittgenstein: The Vienna Circle*. Gordon Baker, Ed., Gordon Baker, Michael Mackert, John Connolly, and Vasilis Politis, Trans. London: Routledge. Referred to as *VW*.

Wrathall, Mark A. (Ed.). (2013). *The Cambridge Companion to Heidegger's Being and Time*. Cambridge: Cambridge University Press.

Wrathall, Mark A. (2015). 'Demanding Authenticity of Ourselves': Heidegger on Authenticity as an Extra-Moral Ideal. In Hans Pedersen and Megan Altman (Eds.), *Horizons of Authenticity in Phenomenology, Existentialism, and Moral Psychology: Essays in Honor of Charles Guignon*. Dordrecht: Springer, 347–68.

Wright, Crispin. (1980). *Wittgenstein on the Foundations of Mathematics*. Cambridge, MA: Harvard University Press.

Index

Acknowledgment 109n.26, 219n.27
Aesthetics 214–15, 215nn.24–5
Agreement *see* Attunement
Aletheia see Discoveredness
Ambiguity 90–1
Anti-realism 171, 171n.1, 172
Anxiety 4–6, 10–12, 43–4, 48–9, 65n.2,
 89, 90n.2, 94–7, 95n.9, 99, 103–9,
 106n.24, 107n.25, 110–11, 115–20,
 122, 124–6, 128–30, 132–3, 135,
 138, 153–4, 159, 172–3, 195, 207,
 228, 228n.35, 229–30
Aporia 207, 225–7
Aristotle 93, 93n.6
Assertion 16, 22, 24n.17, 27–9, 47–8,
 47n.12, 54–5, 127, 165, 170–1,
 175–9, 179n.6, 180, 182–3, 182n.9,
 186–7, 189–91, 191n.15, 192–5,
 204–5, 207–9, 215–18, 220–2, 228
 Assertion conditions 54–7, 68, 112
Attunement 9–10, 63–9, 69n.6, 70,
 72–3, 76–8, 124–6, 128–30, 135–8,
 141–2, 146–51, 154, 230
Augustine, Saint 5–6, 110, 142n.6,
 144–5, 151, 211n.19, 218–19,
 223–4, 223n.31, 227
 Confessions 5–6, 5n.7, 223, 227
Austin, J. L. 34n.26, 48–51, 50n.16, 58,
 58n.26, 59, 75, 108
Authenticity (*see also* Inauthenticity) 5–6,
 8–12, 21n.14, 36, 62–3, 72–3, 77,
 78n.22, 85, 89–93, 92n.5, 93nn.6–7,
 94–9, 109, 113, 115–19, 122–4,
 126–32, 131nn.17–18, 133–8,
 135n.23, 145, 152–6, 160–1, 161n.27,
 163–6, 170–1, 173, 179–80, 185–6,
 192, 196, 207, 231, 233–4
 In philosophy *see* Philosophy
Average *see* Everyday

Babel 1–5, 7–8, 125–6
Baker, Gordon 21n.14, 28n.20, 58n.24,
 141–2, 151n.14, 209n.13, 212n.21
Bedrock 124–7, 129–30, 146, 169

Being (*das Sein*) 4–5, 30–2, 33n.24,
 37–40, 38n.3, 62, 74, 82–3, 91–4,
 96, 97n.15, 98–9, 106–7, 107n.25,
 118–23, 131, 152, 161–2, 171,
 173–4, 179, 181–5, 185n.10, 186–7,
 189–92, 194–6, 198, 200–1
 Of beings 32, 62, 179, 181, 184, 187,
 194–5, 198, 200–1
 Question of (the meaning of) 4–5,
 30–2, 34–40, 46, 56, 106–7, 118–19,
 165, 173, 233–4
 Possibilities of 37–8, 41, 44–5, 62
Beings (*das Seiende*) 30–2, 37–8, 38n.3,
 39, 42–5, 45n.9, 47, 47n.12, 48–9,
 62, 74, 91–6, 98–9, 106–8, 118–19,
 121–4, 127–8, 161–3, 173–6,
 178–80, 179n.6, 181–4, 185n.10,
 187, 188n.13, 189–91, 194–8,
 200–1, 207–8
Being-in 162, 172–3, 195
Being-in-the-world 10, 39–42, 44–5,
 47n.12, 56, 90–1, 93–8, 98n.17,
 106–8, 118–19, 122–3, 128–9, 131,
 138, 162, 164, 172–5, 187, 197
Being-with/Being-with-one-another 10,
 62, 72–6, 78, 83–5, 89, 94, 116,
 123–4, 127–9, 172–3, 195
Blattner, William 48, 107n.25, 131n.18,
 161n.27, 187n.11
Brahmavihara 171
Brahms, Johannes 214
Brandom, Robert 47–8, 47n.12, 75,
 76n.18, 79
Braver, Lee 49n.14, 171n.1
Brown, James Robert 222n.30
Burch, Matthew 117n.9
Burnyeat, Myles 5n.7

Caillois, Roger 141n.3, 158
Care 78–9, 84–5, 119–20, 172–3, 177n.3
Carman, Taylor 47n.11, 75–6, 75n.15,
 76nn.16, 18, 84, 84n.26, 187–8, 192
Carnap, Rudolf 9n.12, 28–31, 97n.15,
 206–7, 206nn.10–11

248 INDEX

Cassam, Quassim 212n.21
Cavell, Stanley 3n.6, 21n.14, 49–52, 49n.15, 58–60, 62, 64–6, 72, 76n.17, 104–5, 106n.24, 108–9, 109n.26, 110–11, 110n.1, 113n.6, 115, 126–7, 131–2, 136n.24, 142–3, 142n.6, 148–9, 174, 195–6, 200n.5, 211n.19, 215–16, 219nn.27–8, 220–1, 224n.32, 227, 231
  The Claim of Reason 50, 59, 219n.27
Cerbone, David 170, 188n.13, 211–12, 212nn.20–1
Cheats 157–8, 158n.24, 159
Circumspection 43–6, 73–4, 74n.13, 177
Citron, Gabriel 9n.12
Clearing 5, 39, 92–3, 107–8, 119–20, 162, 179–80
Comportment *see* Relation
Conant, James 7n.9, 23n.15, 28n.20, 35n.28, 104–6, 104n.21, 105n.22, 106nn.23–4, 111n.4, 133n.20, 174
Concept 8–9, 20–1, 25–8, 49, 51–8, 60–3, 67–8, 7–20, 70n.10, 74, 101, 110, 113–15, 130, 141–2, 144, 149–55, 161, 175, 177–8, 182–4, 189, 201, 211–12, 216–19, 223n.31
  Conceptual investigation (*see also* grammatical investigation) 19–20, 26–7, 30–3, 49–50, 54–5, 68–9
  Fundamental 31–2
Conception (*Auffassung*) 182–7, 190–2, 203–4, 203n.9, 208–9, 218, 220–1
Concern 43–6, 73–4, 90–1, 118–19, 123, 177–8, 180, 233–4
Confusion 20–2, 27–9, 28n.20, 30–1, 52, 72, 108, 114, 134, 146, 149, 169, 184–5, 187–8, 188n.14, 196–7, 199, 203–5, 207, 209–11, 217–18, 220–1, 225–7, 232–4
  Metaphysical 7, 9–10, 19n.8, 20–1, 30
  Philosophical 21–2, 27, 53, 171–2, 189, 210–11
Conscience 119–23, 132, 162, 164, 177n.3, 195
  Call of 119–21, 120n.11, 122–4, 132, 162–4, 179–80
Considerateness (*Rücksicht*) 74, 74n.13
Conventionalism 68–70, 70n.10, 71–2, 111n.4, 117
Correctness 25–6, 28–9, 49–50, 68, 75, 79, 105, 107, 111–12, 114–15, 129–30, 145, 149–50, 152, 170, 184, 203, 214, 223, 229

Covering over 16, 28–9, 98n.17, 133–4, 164–5, 175–9, 183–6, 192, 194, 196–201
Coyne, Ryan 5n.7
Criteria 28–9, 49–51, 49n.15, 56–9, 69, 139–40, 148–9, 160, 203, 206–7
Criticism, terms of 11–12, 53, 133n.20, 185n.10, 196–7, 196n.1, 208–9, 217
Curiosity 90–1

Dahlstrom, Daniel 95n.10, 179n.5, 190–1
Dasein 6, 37–40, 39n.4, 40–5, 47–8, 47n.12, 49, 55–6, 62, 66n.4, 73–9, 78n.22, 81–5, 89–91, 90nn.2, 4, 91–3, 93n.7, 94–9, 94n.8, 97nn.14–15, 98n.17, 99, 103–7, 107n.25, 108–9, 116–24, 127–36, 152–5, 161–5, 169, 172–5, 177n.3, 178–80, 182–4, 186–90, 192, 195, 197, 203n.8, 207, 218, 220–1, 233–4
Das Man 72–83, 75n.15, 78n.22, 83n.25, 84–5, 89–91, 94–9, 103–4, 116–17, 120, 123–5, 127–31, 131n.17, 132, 135, 153–4, 172–3, 178, 195
  One-self 77, 78n.22, 85, 94, 116–17, 124, 127–9, 131–2, 131n.17, 135, 153
Death 107n.25, 124, 177n.3, 179–81, 181n.7, 195, 220–1
Derrida, Jacques 108, 151n.15
Descartes, René 100, 104n.21, 106, 108, 174–5
  Cartesian scepticism *see* Scepticism
  Meditations 100
Description 10, 23, 27, 33–4, 34n.25, 34n.26, 44–5, 57–8, 66–8, 71–2, 76, 89, 121–2, 139, 184, 200–1, 208–11, 214, 216, 223–5, 227–8, 228n.34
Dialogue 11–12, 21–2, 21n.14, 193, 204, 207, 227–8
Diamond, Cora 21n.14, 52n.17, 54–6, 113n.6, 115, 150n.12, 213–14, 231
Diegesis 207, 228, 230
Disclosedness 92–3, 93n.7, 95n.9, 118–19, 121, 162, 182–4, 186, 190–1, 221
Disclosure 11–12, 44–5, 47–9, 74, 116, 118–22, 129–30, 138, 152, 162–4, 179–80, 181n.8, 182–3, 187–91, 195, 197, 207
Discoveredness (*aletheia*) 182–4, 186

Discovery/Uncovering (*entdecken*)
  11–12, 16–18, 21–2, 67, 69, 132–4,
  133n.20, 181n.8, 182–6, 185n.10,
  187–90, 192, 196–204, 220–1
  See also Covering over
Distantiality 83–5, 84n.26, 90
Dogmatism 16, 21, 58n.24, 67, 160
Dreyfus, Hubert 39n.4, 75n.15, 76n.18,
  77–8, 82–4, 90n.2, 95n.10, 117,
  178n.4
Drury, Maurice O'Connor 5n.7
Duck-rabbit 211
Dummett, Michael 55, 55n.21, 57, 68,
  117, 171n.1

Eden 2–3, 2n.3, 3n.4
Ellis, William Webb 159, 159n.26
Elucidation 179n.6
Emerson, Ralph Waldo 108
Empirical 6–8, 16–17, 22, 56–7, 67–71,
  186, 190
  Investigation 10, 19–20, 32–4, 144
  Proposition 20–1, 30–1
  Verifiability 29, 70–1
  See also Fact
Equipment 10, 39n.5, 41–6, 42n.6, 47–9,
  55–6, 62–3, 73–6, 79, 154–5, 161,
  170, 177, 182–4
Essence 6–8, 15, 17–18, 23–4, 56–8,
  58nn.24–5, 60–2, 93–5, 144–5,
  171–2, 176, 179n.6, 199–200,
  218–20
  Of language *see* Language
Everyday/ordinary 5–6, 9–11, 34, 36,
  39–40, 44–5, 48–9, 49n.15, 62, 73–4,
  89, 101–4, 110n.1, 111, 115, 118–19,
  124, 128–31, 131n.18, 132–3,
  135–6, 138, 169, 179, 192–3, 232–4
  Authentic 89, 131
  Average 34–6, 39–40, 48, 73–9, 89,
    94n.8, 109, 131–2, 131n.17, 135–6,
    172–3, 177n.3
  Everyday existence/Dasein 5, 9–10,
    36, 73–4, 77, 82, 89, 98, 131n.17,
    173, 200–1, 233
  Everyday language/forms of
    expression 3–4, 7, 15–16, 18–19,
    21–2, 25–9, 28n.20, 34–5, 49, 65–7,
    70, 110–11, 124, 130–2, 134–5, 179,
    184, 191–2, 195–7, 199, 204–5, 215
  Everydayness 10–11, 89, 98–9,
    98n.17, 124, 130–1, 130n.15,
    131n.17

Practices/activities 28–9, 34–5, 74,
  90–1, 110–12, 124, 130, 132–3, 179,
  211–12
  See also Use
Exactness 53–4
Existence 10–11, 37–8, 38n.3, 39–41, 43,
  47–9, 72–6, 78, 83, 85, 89–91, 90n.4,
  92–3, 93n.7, 94, 96–8, 105–7,
  107n.25, 108–9, 117–19, 121–4,
  126–31, 131n.17, 152, 163–4,
  173–5, 179–81, 187, 231
  See also Everyday existence
Existential 38, 74–6, 78, 78n.22, 83,
  83n.25, 84–5, 90–1, 90n.2, 92–5, 98,
  107–8, 128, 163–4
Existentiell 78n.22, 90n.2, 178
Explanation 10–11, 27, 33–4, 34n.26,
  53–4, 57–8, 65–7, 70, 99–105, 107,
  113–14, 124–7, 134–5, 142–4,
  146–8, 170–1, 174, 184, 187,
  199–200, 213–14, 214n.23,
  228n.34, 229

Fact 7–8, 16–17, 18n.4, 19–21, 25, 27,
  44–5, 62, 66–70, 70n.10, 72–3, 102,
  111–12, 114–15, 115n.7, 118–22,
  169–72, 180–1, 181n.8, 184–5,
  187–8, 191, 197, 204–6, 211–12,
  215n.25
  Empirical 22, 68–9, 169–72, 189–90
  Factual claim 16, 20–1, 189–90,
    197, 218
  Factual investigation (*see also*
    empirical investigation) 19–20,
    30–3, 68–9, 144, 169, 211
  Metaphysical 20–2, 25, 28, 68,
    169, 184
  Transcendental 69
Faraday, Michael 19–20
Falling 10–11, 78, 84–5, 90–1, 90n.2,
  94–5, 98–9, 103–4, 120, 164–5, 183
Family resemblance 138–9, 157n.22
Fell, Joseph 48, 95n.10, 97n.13
Fink, Eugen 161n.27
Flight 77, 90n.2, 94–5, 98–9, 103–4,
  116–17, 129, 130n.15, 135
Formal Indication 11–12, 18n.6,
  179–80, 179n.5, 181, 181n.8,
  190–2, 194–5, 200–1, 208, 220–1
Form of life 10, 20–1, 54–6, 55n.23, 60,
  63–7, 69, 71–2, 77, 89, 99, 107–8,
  113–14, 129–30, 134, 138–9, 141–7,
  149–51, 184, 189, 208–12, 229

250 INDEX

For-the-sake-of-which 41, 55–6
Frankfurt, Harry 158n.23
Frege, Gottlob 23n.15, 32n.22, 176n.2, 223n.31
Freud, Sigmund 98nn.16–17, 198, 200n.5, 201
Friedman, Michael 117

Gadamer, Hans-Georg 157, 161n.27
Games 52–3, 61, 138–42, 141n.3, 145, 147–9, 151, 153n.16, 155–9, 157n.22, 158n.25, 159n.26, 160–1, 184, 198–9, 234
  See also Language
Glendinning, Simon 34n.26
Goldfarb, Warren 69n.6, 113n.6, 210n.18, 224n.32
Grammar 21, 57–8, 58nn.24–5, 60–1, 61n.27, 62, 67–8, 70n.10, 139–41, 144, 169, 184–5, 194, 197, 208–9, 211
  Arbitrariness 61–2, 61n.27
  Grammatical criteria 51
  Grammatical investigation 10, 19–20, 32–4, 52, 56–7, 61, 68, 70, 107–9, 144, 169, 171–2, 211
  Grammatical proposition/rule 19–22, 20n.13, 21n.14, 56–7, 60–1, 184
Ground 6–8, 65–6, 68–9, 69n.6, 72–3, 96–7, 103–4, 107, 117–18, 120–5, 128–9, 132, 134–6, 146, 153, 182–4, 187, 190
  Common 64, 125–6, 142–3, 147
  Groundlessness 103–4, 117–18, 122–5, 127–8, 132–3, 153
  Rough 6–9
Guignon, Charles 49n.14, 76n.18
Guilt 119, 121–3, 122n.12, 177n.3, 180, 195

Habermas, Jürgen 117n.9
Hacker, P. M. S. 21n.14, 57, 58n.25, 70n.10, 141–2, 144n.8, 151n.14, 212n.21
Hamlet 97n.14
Harris, Roy 140–1, 151n.15, 153–4
Haugeland, John 76n.18, 107n.25
Heaney, Seamus 37–8
Heidegger, Martin 3–6, 8–12, 9n.12, 18n.6, 28–36, 35n.28, 37–49, 38n.3, 39nn.4–5, 43n.7, 46n.10, 47n.12, 48n.13, 49n.14, 55–6, 61–3, 65n.2, 66n.4, 72–9, 74n.13, 75n.15, 76nn.16–18, 78n.22, 81–5, 89–99, 90nn.2, 4, 93n.6, 94n.8, 95n.9, 97nn.14–15, 98nn.16–17, 103–6, 106n.24, 107–9, 107n.25, 110–11, 115–25, 117n.9, 123n.13, 124n.14, 127–34, 130n.15, 131n.17, 135–6, 138, 152–7, 156n.21, 157–8, 160–6, 161n.27, 162n.29, 163n.30, 169–74, 171n.1, 174–83, 177n.3, 178n.4, 179nn.5–6, 181nn.7–8, 182n.9, 184–8, 185n.10, 187n.11, 188n.13, 189–91, 191n.15, 192–7, 196n.1, 198, 200–1, 200n.5, 201–2, 203n.8, 205, 207, 207n.12, 208, 218–22, 228, 228nn.34–5, 229–34, 232n.1
  Being and Time 28–9, 31–2, 36, 39n.4, 43–4, 43n.7, 48n.13, 73, 78, 78n.22, 82–3, 85, 91, 93, 95n.9, 106, 106n.24, 109, 117–19, 124, 124n.14, 129–31, 136, 156, 156n.21, 161–2, 164, 169, 172–3, 175, 177–8, 177n.3, 179, 179nn.5–6, 182–3, 186–7, 187n.12, 188n.13, 192–5, 200–1, 221, 233–4
  Fundamental Concepts of Metaphysics 94n.8, 95n.9
  Introduction to Metaphysics 95n.9, 119–20
  'What Is Metaphysics?' 9n.12, 28–30, 95n.9, 97n.15, 133–4
Heller-Roazen, Daniel 3n.5
Heraclitus 15–17, 15n.1, 18–19, 18nn.6–7, 21–3, 25, 27–9, 60–1, 66–7, 134–5, 160, 181n.8
Hermeneutics 39n.5, 93–4, 135, 177n.3, 198
  Hermeneutical priority 47–8, 73, 91
  Hermeneutic circle 9n.12, 39n.4
  Of suspicion 198–201
Hiddenness 33n.24, 197–201, 218–20
Holmes, Sherlock 201
Home 15, 98, 98n.16, 130, 136–7, 150
Huizinga, Johan 147, 157–9
Hume, David 108, 112, 112n.5
  Humean scepticism *see* Scepticism
  Treatise of Human Nature 112n.5
Hurka, Thomas 157n.22

Ideal 6–8, 53–4, 114, 125–6
Idealism 45, 162, 162n.29, 171–5, 182, 186–8, 188n.13, 193, 196–7, 196n.2, 197, 201–2, 202nn.6–7, 205–6, 207n.12
  Ontic 187n.11
  Ontological 187
  Transcendental 62, 69–70, 69n.8, 70n.10
Idle talk 90–1, 128, 156–8, 195
Imaginary scenario 111n.2, 129–30, 144–5, 211–12, 212nn.20–1, 215n.25, 217, 222–5, 227, 231
Improvisation 136–8, 151, 151n.14, 153–5, 153n.16, 154nn.17–18, 160–1, 163–4, 230–1, 233–4
Inauthenticity 5, 10–11, 34–5, 62, 72–3, 77–8, 78n.22, 85, 89–95, 99, 103–4, 111, 116–17, 119, 121–5, 127–8, 130–1, 133–5, 135n.23, 152–4, 163, 169–71, 183, 185–6, 196
Intelligibility 31–2, 47–8, 64, 74–7, 79, 83, 83n.25, 91, 135, 150, 182–3, 212n.21
Interpretation 31–2, 38–9, 48, 91–4, 101, 102n.19, 103–4, 113–15, 146, 152, 195, 198, 209–10, 219n.28, 229
  Self-interpretation 91–4, 97–8, 122, 127–8, 152

Jackson, Frank 222
Jagodowski, T. J. 154n.17
Joachim, Joseph 214
Justification 65–7, 65n.3, 70–1, 99, 104, 111–12, 115–17, 124–7, 129, 134–5, 142, 144, 223–4

Kant, Immanuel 7n.9, 23n.15, 104n.21, 150
  Kantian scepticism see Scepticism
Keller, Pierre 83n.25
Kenny, Anthony 141–2
Kisiel, Theodore 5n.7, 84n.26, 93n.6, 179n.5
Klinger, Florian 164n.31
Knowledge 18, 25–6, 31–3, 37, 46–7, 51–2, 60, 104–6, 111, 111n.4, 125, 148–9, 165–6, 170, 174–7, 184–5, 219–20, 222n.30
  Theory of 31–2, 32n.21

Kripke, Saul 10–11, 55n.21, 68, 69n.6, 111–13, 111nn.3–4, 114–17, 124–7, 134–5, 150–1, 171n.1
Kripkendegger 116–18, 122–3, 127–8
Kripkenstein 111n.3, 114–15, 118, 128
Kuusela, Oskari 28n.20, 35n.28, 58n.25, 70n.10

Language 1–4, 5n.7, 6–7, 10, 20–1, 23, 25–8, 32, 47–8, 55–8, 61–5, 68, 76, 79, 81, 89, 107–8, 126–7, 130, 133–4, 138–45, 151–2, 155–8, 161–2, 164–6, 175–8, 180–1, 191, 194–5, 199–200, 206, 208–11, 211n.19, 218–19, 223–4, 223n.31, 225–6, 230, 232–3
  Essence of 8, 144–5, 199–200, 208, 210–11, 223
  Everyday/ordinary see Everyday
  Language-game 9–12, 20–1, 20n.10, 23–4, 26, 34n.25, 49, 56, 64, 65n.3, 66–7, 89, 99–100, 114–15, 129–30, 138–42, 144–7, 149–51, 150n.13, 151nn.14–15, 152, 154–6, 158–61, 183–4, 204–5, 208–9, 211–12, 218, 229
  Metaphysical see Metaphysics
  Misuse 23–4, 49–50
Larkin, Philip 90n.2
Lear, Jonathan 69, 207n.12, 212n.21
Learning 58–60, 139–45, 142n.6, 146–52, 151n.14, 155–6, 184–5, 211n.19, 212–13, 234
Levinas, Emmanuel 117n.9
Lewis, David 80n.23
Literature 77–8, 81, 121–2, 213–16, 215n.25, 217
Logic 18n.5, 23n.15, 31–2, 32n.21, 71–2, 144–5, 176–7, 176n.2, 199
Lostness 4–5, 33, 76–8, 85, 94, 131–2, 234
Löwith, Karl 117n.9

Malcolm, Norman 5n.7, 224n.33
Marx, Karl 198
McDaniel, Kris 45n.9, 46n.10, 187n.11
McDowell, John 25–6, 71–2, 106n.24, 113n.6, 115, 130n.16, 212n.20
McManus, Denis 38n.2, 44n.8, 47n.11, 48, 96, 107n.25, 117–18, 121–2, 153, 186, 188n.13

INDEX

Meaning 33n.24, 38, 40–3, 54–7, 68, 72, 91–3, 96, 104–8, 107n.25, 111–14, 115n.7, 117–19, 122, 126–7, 134, 139, 144, 149, 152, 173–4, 178, 180–1, 183, 190, 191n.15, 198, 204, 206–7, 218–21, 220n.29, 223–6, 229
Mechanism 52–4
Metaphysics 15–18, 18nn.4, 6, 19–21, 19n.8, 22–5, 27–31, 34–5, 46, 46n.10, 56–7, 60–1, 66–7, 70–2, 108–9, 132–5, 138, 169–71, 181n.8, 184, 189–90, 197, 219–20, 232n.1
  Metaphysical confusion *see* Confusion
  Metaphysical language 3–4, 7, 15–16, 27–9, 28n.20
Method 11–12, 32–6, 62, 166, 172, 185n.10, 192–4, 197, 206n.11, 233–4
  Heidegger's 163–4, 166, 172, 185n.10, 189–90, 192–5, 197–8, 200–1, 218, 220–1, 228, 228n.34, 231
  Scientific 19n.8, 169, 206n.11
  Wittgenstein's 21n.14, 34n.25, 136–7, 166, 172, 185n.10, 192–3, 197, 206, 206n.11, 207, 210n.18, 214–15, 217–18, 220–1, 227–8, 232–3
Mighton, John 231
Minar, Edward 202n.6
Mimesis 207, 228–31
Mineness 118–19, 135n.23
Moi, Toril 200–1, 200n.5, 206n.11
Moment (*Augenblick*) 130–1, 163–4
Moore, A. W. 69n.8
Moore, G. E. 79, 214
Mulhall, Stephen 3n.6, 8, 20n.12, 32n.23, 39n.4, 69n.9, 106n.24, 108–9, 130n.15, 131, 131n.17, 153n.16, 156n.21, 164n.32, 177n.3, 231

Natural history 55, 55n.23, 215n.25
Nature 19n.9
Necessity 57, 58n.25, 67–72, 70n.10
Necker cube 46, 49, 65–6, 66n.4
Nelson, Priya 154n.18
Newton, Isaac 186–7, 189, 192, 201
  Newton's Laws 186, 188–9, 192, 201
Nietzsche, Friedrich 69n.7, 108, 198, 215–16
Nonsense 11–12, 21–2, 21n.14, 26, 28–30, 49–50, 133–4, 151n.14, 165, 176–7, 184–6, 185n.10, 187–8, 196, 218, 226

Norm/Normative 44–5, 75–6, 75n.15, 77, 79–85, 90, 126–7, 129–30, 148, 154
Norton, John D. 222n.30
Nothing 28–31, 97n.15, 119–20, 120n.11, 133–4

Objects of comparison 11–12, 27, 34n.25, 55n.23, 138–9, 138n.1, 163–4, 193, 207–9, 211–15, 214n.23, 215, 217, 220–2, 228
One-self *see Das Man*
Ontic 33n.24, 38, 39n.5, 40, 89, 90n.4, 119–20, 170–1, 178–9, 181–3, 187, 192, 194–5, 197
  Idealism *see* Idealism
  Investigation 10, 30–4, 169, 189–90
  Realism *see* Realism
  Science 31–2, 37, 44–7, 47n.12, 48
  Understanding *see* Understanding
  Truth 182–3
Ontology/ontological 11–12, 28–9, 33n.24, 38–40, 44–7, 76, 84, 89, 92–3, 98, 119–20, 174–6, 178–80, 182–4, 188n.13, 190, 191n.15, 192, 195, 197, 200–1, 207–9, 221, 228
  Fundamental 30–2, 37–9, 177
  Ontological difference 32, 34, 89, 169, 190, 197
  Ontological idealism *see* Idealism
  Ontological investigation 10, 30–4, 45, 169, 171–2, 189–90
  Ontological understanding *see* Understanding
  Pre-ontological understanding *see* Understanding
  Regional 31–2
Ordinary language *see* Everyday language

Pain 22, 184–5, 191
Pasquesi, David 154n.17
Phenomenology 31–4, 34n.26, 44–7, 92–3, 95–6, 133–4, 161–4, 169, 172–3, 177–8, 177n.3, 179, 181n.8, 196, 198, 200–1, 228n.34
Philipse, Herman 95n.10
Philosophy 27, 156n.21, 157–8, 164–6, 169, 182–6, 190, 194, 196–7, 199–200, 205, 206n.11, 209, 210n.16, 213–14, 216–17, 222, 229, 232–3, 232n.1, 233–4

As a cognitive discipline 10, 18
As an activity 17–18
Authentic 11–12, 36, 72–3, 166, 171, 185–6, 189–90, 192–4, 231
End of 232
Inauthentic 185–6
Philosophical confusion *see* Confusion
Philosophical criticism 21–2
Philosophical method *see* Method
Philosophical thesis 33–4, 34n.26, 57, 63–4, 186–7, 190, 191n.15, 202, 205–6, 213, 217, 222
Problems of 8–9, 17–18, 35, 53, 165–6, 173, 196–7
Picture 100, 113, 125, 140, 144–5, 149, 184, 193, 195, 199–200, 207–11, 209n.13, 210nn.15, 17–18, 213–21, 223–4, 228
Plato 15n.1, 108, 156–7, 156n.21, 172–3
Cratylus 15n.1
Gorgias 172–3
Phaedo 172–3
Phaedrus 172–3
Republic 156–7, 172–3
Sophist 156n.21
Platonism *see* Rules
Play 9–11, 21n.14, 136–41, 141n.3, 146–52, 151nn.14–15, 153–9, 157n.22, 160–1, 161n.27, 163–4, 166, 230–1, 234
Poe, Edgar Allen 199–200, 200n.5
'The Purloined Letter' 199–200
Polt, Richard 43n.7
Practice 10–11, 25–6, 34, 54, 60–2, 65–9, 71–3, 89, 102–4, 115–16, 118, 124, 126, 129–30, 132, 134–5, 142–5, 154, 192, 210n.15, 211–13, 229
Everyday *see* Everyday
Presence-at-hand 42n.6, 44–9, 45n.9, 46n.10, 73–5, 90n.4, 91, 93, 95, 95n.10, 99, 106–7, 121–2, 162, 171, 174–6, 178, 180, 184–5, 187, 207
Prica, Aleksandra 37n.1
Priest, Graham 32n.22
Privacy 20–1, 20n.12, 116, 149, 184–5
Project 4–5, 38, 90–1, 92n.5, 95–7, 97n.14, 99, 103–4, 106–8, 116–18, 120–2, 153, 163–4
Projection 148–51, 154–5, 160–1, 231
Method of 149

Proposition 61–4, 70–2, 79, 140, 176–8, 183–4, 188, 188n.14, 190–2, 191n.15, 204, 206, 208, 213, 216–17, 228
General form of 18n.4
Putnam, Hilary 106, 171n.1, 222

Questions 224–6, 224n.33, 228, 230

Rand, Ayn 217
Readiness-to-hand 10, 39n.5, 41–3, 42n.6, 44–9, 45n.9, 46n.10, 62, 73–5, 79, 89, 91, 95–6, 95n.10, 99, 123, 154–5, 170, 175–7, 182–3
Realism (*see also* Anti-realism) 45, 162, 162n.29, 170–2, 171n.1, 173–5, 182, 186–7, 188n.13, 193, 196–7, 201–2, 202nn.6–7, 205–6, 206n.10
Ontic 187–8
Reality 16, 18, 20–2, 25, 30, 66, 72, 152, 170, 173–4, 186, 192, 196–7, 196n.2, 204, 216
Of Language 155–7, 156n.20, 157–60
Problem of 173–5, 196–7
Referential totality 43–4
Relation/Comportment (*Verhalten*) 38–44, 62–3, 74, 161–2, 180, 190, 192, 208, 210
Releasement (*Gelassenheit*) 233
Relevance 55–6, 95–6, 99, 104, 106–8, 116–17, 163–4, 175–6, 229
Reminder 27, 33–4, 34n.25, 72–3, 165, 181n.8, 189, 211–12, 234
Representation 20n.13, 60–1, 170
Mode/form of 19–20, 67–8, 169
Surveyable 199–200
Resoluteness 10–11, 99, 117–19, 122–3, 127, 136–8, 152–3, 163–4, 177n.3
Responsiveness 9–11, 73, 92–3, 130, 141–2, 150–5, 153n.16, 160–2, 161n.27, 163–4, 170, 219–20, 231, 233
Reynolds, Stephen 179n.5
Rhees, Rush 32n.21, 56, 155–6, 155n.19, 156nn.20–1, 157–8, 160, 213
Richardson, John 92n.5, 187n.11
Ricketts, Thomas 176n.2
Ricoeur, Paul 117n.9, 198, 198n.3
Rorty, Richard 76n.18, 232n.1
Rouse, Joseph 48
Rubin, Jane 117

Rules 9, 20–1, 24, 49–50, 61, 67–8, 69n.6, 80, 103–4, 112–15, 129, 139–42, 141n.3, 143–51, 151n.14, 152, 153n.16, 155–8, 157n.22, 158n.25, 159–61, 184, 209, 212–13, 228–9
  Grammatical *see* Grammar
  Of a language-game 20–2, 184, 204–5
  Platonism 103–4, 111–13, 115, 134–5, 134n.22
  Rule following 10–11, 67–9, 69n.6, 70–1, 99, 102–5, 106n.24, 107–8, 111–16, 111n.4, 124, 129, 132–5, 134n.22, 135–6, 141–2, 145–6, 153–5, 213, 229
  Rule following scepticism *see* Scepticism
Russell, Bertrand 18n.5, 176–7, 176n.2
Ryle, Gilbert 34n.26

Saussure, Ferdinand de 151n.15
Savickey, Beth 230–1
Scene of instruction 142–52, 151n.14, 213, 234
Scepticism 10–11, 45, 99–100, 103–7, 104n.21, 105n.22, 106n.24, 108–14, 112n.5, 114–18, 125–6, 128–9, 134–6, 134n.22, 138, 153–4, 159, 171–2, 174, 228–9
  Cartesian 104–5, 104n.21, 106, 106n.24, 108–9, 111n.4
  External world 106, 173–5
  Humean 112
  Kantian 104–7, 104n.21, 105n.22, 106nn.23–4
  Other minds 73–4, 108–9
  Rule following 10–11, 99, 103–8, 106n.24, 111–15, 125–6, 132–4, 134n.22
Schatzki, Theodore 76n.18
Science 10, 18n.5, 19n.8, 30–1, 33, 44–5, 44n.8, 48–9, 169, 176–7, 200–1, 206n.11, 215
  See also Ontic
Scott, Charles 161n.28
Sensation 20–1, 20n.12, 24
Sense 21–2, 24n.17, 29, 128–9, 176–7, 204, 210
Shakespeare, William 217

Sideways perspective 25–6, 34, 34n.26, 60–1, 65–6, 71–2, 126, 130, 160, 187–8, 188n.13, 189–90, 192–3, 211–12, 212n.20
Significance 28–9, 40, 55–6, 61–3, 73–6, 92–3, 95–7, 107–8, 116–20, 126–9, 154–6, 159, 163, 170, 173–4, 195, 201, 228–9
Situation 163–4
Socrates 108, 156–7
Solicitude 74, 123
Solipsism 22, 191, 191n.15, 202, 202n.6, 205, 206n.10, 207, 207n.12
Sophistry 156–8, 156n.21, 159–60
Spoilsport 157–9, 158n.24, 160
Staten, Henry 151n.15
Stern, David G. 18n.7
Stone, Martin 113n.6, 115n.7, 134n.22
Streeter, Ryan 179n.5
Stroud, Barry 212n.21
Suits, Bernard 157–8, 157n.22, 158n.25
Surveyable representation *see* Representation

Tasioulas, John 157n.22
Taylor, Charles 76n.18
Teaching 102–3, 125–7, 138–9, 141–7, 142n.6, 148–52, 151n.14, 205, 209–10, 212–13, 234
Theory 26–7, 132
Therapy 35, 134, 136–8, 227
Thesis *see* Philosophy
Thomson, Iain 96n.11, 107n.25
Thomson, Judith Jarvis 222
Thoreau, Henry David 108
Thought/Thinking 25–6, 32, 76, 135–6, 140, 144–5, 169–70, 176–7, 216–19, 232–3, 232n.1
Thought experiments 222–3, 222n.30, 224
Thrasymachus 156–7, 159
Tolstoy, Leo 181n.7
  The Death of Ivan Ilyich 181n.7
Tools 42–4, 48–9, 56, 96, 152
Training 102–3, 143–7, 213, 228–9, 234
Transcendental *see* Idealism
Triflers 157–8
Truth 6, 16, 18–19, 30, 70–2, 93n.7, 132, 158n.23, 173, 176–7, 182–4, 182n.9, 185–92, 188n.14, 191n.15, 192, 201, 208–9, 211, 215–18, 220–1

Ontic *see* Ontic
Truth-claims 30–3
Truth-conditions 30, 54–5, 112
Untruth 183–6, 218, 220
See also Discoveredness
Tugendhat, Ernst 117n.9

Uncanniness 10–11, 89, 98–9, 98nn.16–17, 108–11, 110n.1, 129–30, 132, 134–8, 153, 159, 161n.27, 200n.5
Uncovering *see* Discovery
Understanding 2–3, 8–11, 16, 34–41, 39n.4, 47, 49, 52–4, 56, 60, 63, 91–3, 96–8, 100–5, 107, 107n.25, 113, 118–26, 133–4, 142–4, 146–9, 151n.14, 152, 154–8, 158n.24, 161–2, 164, 171–2, 175–8, 180–1, 181n.8, 189–90, 195–6, 196n.1, 204, 210, 212–13, 214n.23, 215–17, 220–1, 228–9, 234
  Authentic 10–11, 36, 115, 164–5, 173, 195–6, 231
  Average everyday 94n.8, 109
  Inauthentic 169–70
  Of being 37–40, 39n.4, 41, 120, 187
  Ontic 178
  Ontological 179–81, 192, 194–5, 197
  Pre-ontological/pre-theoretical 38–40, 178
  Primordial 133–4, 177–8, 181n.8
  Self-understanding 34, 36, 38–42, 44n.8, 91–4, 92n.5, 98–9, 118–19, 121–3, 128–9, 132–3, 152, 231
Use 3–4, 7–9, 15, 23–4, 26–7, 28n.20, 29, 32, 40–1, 43–5, 49–50, 52–63, 65, 68–9, 71–2, 89, 96, 113–14, 130, 140–1, 143–5, 148–52, 151n.14, 154–5, 161, 174–5, 180–1, 184, 202n.6, 204, 207–12, 216, 218–19, 223–4, 232–3
  Everyday/Ordinary 3–4, 7–8, 15, 28n.20, 65, 132, 195, 205, 230
  Metaphysical 3–4, 7, 15, 28n.20, 132, 195
  Misuse 23–4, 28n.20

Van Buren, John 5n.7
Victor, Pam 154n.17
Von Wright, Georg Henrik 5n.7

Wayward pupil 70–1, 102–3, 129–30, 146–7, 234
Weberman, David 83n.25
Wendland, Aaron James 78n.22
White, Carol 107n.25
Williams, Bernard 69, 69n.9, 207n.12, 212n.21
Withy, Katherine 98n.17, 161n.27
Wittgenstein, Ludwig 3–12, 9n.12, 15–24, 18nn.4–5, 7, 20nn.10, 13, 24nn.16–17, 26–8, 28n.20, 29–35, 32n.21, 34nn.25–6, 35nn.27–8, 36, 40, 49–58, 49n.14, 52n.17, 55nn.22–3, 58n.25, 61, 61n.27, 62–73, 65n.2, 66n.4, 69nn.6, 8–9, 70n.10, 76–7, 76n.18, 79, 85, 89, 99–104, 102n.19, 105–9, 106n.24, 110–17, 111nn.2–4, 118, 124–37, 130n.15, 136n.24, 138–47, 149–50, 149n.11, 150n.13, 151–3, 151nn.14–15, 154–6, 157n.22, 160–1, 161n.27, 163–6, 169, 171–2, 171n.1, 176–8, 176n.2, 179n.6, 183–6, 185n.10, 187–9, 191, 191n.15, 192–7, 196n.1, 197, 199–200, 200n.5, 201–5, 202nn.6–7, 206nn.10–11, 207n.12, 209n.13, 210nn.15–18, 212nn.20–1, 215–22, 215nn.24–5, 220n.29, 223–31, 223n.31, 224n.33, 228nn.34–5, 232–4, 232n.1
  Blue Book 202n.6
  Brown Book 145n.10
  Lectures on Aesthetics 214
  Notebooks 1914–1916 35n.27
  On Certainty 79, 140
  'On Heidegger' 9n.12
  Philosophical Investigations 5n.7, 21–2, 21n.14, 32n.21, 35, 52, 63–4, 66–7, 99–100, 107–8, 110–11, 110n.1, 113–14, 126–7, 136, 138–40, 142, 142n.6, 144–7, 150n.13, 164, 183, 191, 202–3, 202n.6, 204–13, 215n.25, 217–19, 223–4, 226–34
  Philosophy of Psychology – A Fragment 211, 215n.25, 219–20
  Remarks on the Foundations of Mathematics 231
  Tractatus Logico-Philosophicus 9n.12, 11–12, 28–9, 32n.21, 35, 54–5, 133–4, 133n.20, 176–8, 177n.3, 179n.6, 187–8, 191n.15, 199, 206n.10, 207n.12, 208, 227, 232–4

Wittgenstein, Ludwig (*cont.*)
  Voices of Wittgenstein 9n.12
  Zettel 141–2, 144, 149–50,
    205–6, 216
World 9–10, 23, 34–6, 38–49, 55–8,
  58n.26, 60–3, 66n.4, 73–4, 77, 84,
  90–1, 90n.4, 92–4, 94n.8, 95–9,
  106–8, 111, 116–25, 128–9, 135–6,
  147, 154–5, 158, 161–2, 164–5,
  169–80, 178n.4, 179n.6, 180–2,
  187–8, 190, 195, 197, 205, 207–8,
  211, 215, 229, 233–4
With-world 116, 119, 128–9
Worldliness 10, 43–4, 46–7, 56, 62, 73,
  89–91, 90n.4, 120, 120n.11, 172–5
Wrathall, Mark 93n.6
Wright, Crispin 55n.21, 68, 111n.4,
  171n.1